Education and Psychology of the Gifted Series

James H. Borland, Editor

*Planning and Implementing
Programs for the Gifted*

James H. Borland

*Patterns of Influence on Gifted Learners:
The Home, the Self, and the School*

Joyce L. VanTassel-Baska and Paula Olszewski-Kubilius, Editors

Patterns of Influence on Gifted Learners

The Home, the Self, and the School

EDITED BY

Joyce L. VanTassel-Baska

AND

Paula Olszewski-Kubilius

TEACHERS
COLLEGE
PRESS

Teachers College, Columbia University
New York and London

Published by Teachers College Press, 1234 Amsterdam Avenue,
New York, NY 10027

Copyright © 1989 by Teachers College, Columbia University

Library of Congress Cataloging-in-Publication Data

Patterns of influence on gifted learners : the home, the self, and the school / edited by
  Joyce L. VanTassel-Baska and Paula Olszewski-Kubilius.
    p.   cm. —(Education and psychology of the gifted series)
  Includes bibliographies and index.
  ISBN 0-8077-2938-8.   ISBN 0-8077-2937-X (pbk.)
  1. Gifted children—Education—United States.   2. Gifted children—United States—
Family relationships.   3. Gifted children—United States—Psychology.   I. VanTassel-
Baska, Joyce.   II. Olszewski-Kubilius, Paula.   III. Series.
LC3993.9.P38   1989   88-29486
371.95′0973—dc19   CIP

ISBN 0-8077-2938-8
ISBN 0-80777-2937-X (pbk.)

Manufactured in the United States of America
94 93 92 91 90 89   1 2 3 4 5 6

To my mother, Eleanor,
from whom I have inherited my drive and persistence,
to my husband, Lee,
from whom I have received indispensable support,
and to my daughter, Ariel,
who has taught me unconditional love

                                        J. VT.-B.

To my parents, Rita and Walter, and my husband, Christian,
for their faith and support

                                        P. O.-K.

Contents

PART III INFLUENCE OF THE SCHOOL   163

Foreword

It is with considerable pleasure and pride that I introduce *Patterns of Influence on Gifted Learners: The Home, the Self, and the School*, edited by Joyce VanTassel-Baska and Paula Olszewski-Kubilius, the second volume in the new series of books and monographs from Teachers College Press dealing with the psychology and education of the gifted. This book itself needs little by way of introduction. The names of most of the authors whose writings are collected herein will be familiar to anyone who has even the slightest knowledge of the field of the Education of the Gifted, and the prospect of new contributions to the literature by Gallagher, Passow, Roedell, Silverman, Stanley, et al. should be sufficient to whet the appetite of even the most jaded reader. For the most part, I will leave it to the deservedly high reputations and accumulated good works of these worthies to serve as their own best recommendation and use this space to discuss the rationale and intent of this new book series.

There is certainly no paucity of recent publications dealing with the nature and nurture of gifted children, as a casual skimming of any recent volume of *Books in Print* will demonstrate. Morris Stein, in his recent summary volume, *Gifted, Talented and Creative Young People* (New York: Garland, 1986), refers to "the information explosion in the literature on the gifted" (p. xi), and this is not mere hyperbole. Yet, it is pertinent to ask, as did T. S. Eliot in his poem, "The Rock," "where is the knowledge we have lost in information?" It is not my intention in editing this series simply to add to the accretion and recycling of printed information about the gifted. Rather, it is my goal, and the goal of Teachers College Press, to provide a forum for new voices, new perspectives, new ideas from within and without this often chaotic but always intriguing field of educational practice and theory. In short, we are seeking to encourage the generation of knowledge, not merely the proliferation of information.

I have long suspected that collectively we have grown too comfortable with unchallenged orthodoxies and unexamined received truths, that we have become too insular as a field, and that we spend too much time talking among ourselves about the same issues, repeating the same things to the same receptive audience. This intellectual parochialism is perhaps an inevitable consequence of our historical need to raise a unanimous voice in advocacy of the educational rights of gifted children, a voice that too often was either unheard or ignored. I hesitate to conclude that the need for advocacy is past, but I do believe that at this point in our history we can afford, and desperately need, an injection of new, discrepant, even contentious voices within the field. Intellectual give-and-take is the lifeblood of any vigorous discipline, and there is reason to fear that we have become somewhat anemic in this respect.

This is not to suggest that we should abjure the contributions, past and future, of those leaders within the field who have brought us to this point in our development. The list of contributors to this volume should disabuse anyone of the notion that this series will serve only as a forum for the musings of the sansculottes within the field, as valuable as they might be. The statement, attributed perhaps apocryphally to Newton, that one can see farther when one stands on the shoulders of giants comes to mind in this context. Thus, the reader who follows the progress of this series can be assured that he or she will encounter authors whose names and previous writings are quite familiar.

Nonetheless, there will be an emphasis on the fresh and the original, on encouraging antitheses to the entrenched theses, on dialectic in the service of greater dialogue. Let me illustrate this and clarify the raison d'être of the series by returning to the contents of this volume. The reader or browser with some knowledge of this field who has skimmed the table of contents of this book will probably have recognized the names of most of the contributors save, perhaps, that of the author of the book's concluding chapter, Richard Ronvik. It is apposite that this is the case, for Ronvik's chapter is the perfect example of the type and quality of thinking and writing, emanating from new sources and fresh perspectives, that the series was created to encourage.

Even among the estimable pieces found in this work, Ronvik's "An Essay on Gifted Education" stands out in my mind for its contribution to our discussion of what we as a field are, and should be, about. Ronvik's essay is radical in the original and best sense of the word: relating to the origin, going to the root of the issue. He forces us to examine one of our most cherished assumptions by asserting that "most programs for gifted children have almost no chance of positive long range educational effect because . . . many of the theoreticians who have designed models . . . and many of the practitioners who have developed and implemented local programs . . . have a less than clear notion about why they are doing what they do."

Ronvik goes on to decry the "plethora of theoretical cubes, triads and circles, taxonomic bars, and hierarchical charts" that serve as the basis or pretext for programs that are in too many cases "part-time, suitable for students other than gifted, occasionally superficial, largely separated from the standard curriculum of the school, and often resented by nonparticipating students and their parents and nonparticipating teachers." Further, because our discipline has "no common field theory, it . . . invites the abuse it sometimes receives" and provides a fertile breeding ground for "many of the popular proponents of gifted education" who "encourage definitions of giftedness that are so general as to compromise the credibility of the category and which have contributed greatly to the general trivialization of gifted education, . . . to say nothing of the hundreds of circuit lecturers and entertainers with their 'fun and games for the gifted' approach."

This is strong stuff indeed, the kind of stinging criticism those of us in the field of the Education of the Gifted occasionally hear from our critics outside the field, although rarely in such a cogent form, and to which we have become fairly well inured. And therein lies part of the problem. Because we have been subjected to so many attacks from those who view special education for the gifted as ineffective, unnecessary, or undemocratic, we have of necessity developed thick skins, the better to deflect the barbs of our more benighted adversaries. However, Ronvik is writing from the point of view of a longtime administrator of programs for the gifted; he is one of us. He does more than merely carp and criticize; he offers alternatives to the cant and superficiality that sometimes pass for "gifted education." It is clear that he cares about the education of gifted children and that he has something important to say. His voice should be heard. It is the goal of this series to provide opportunities for theorists and practitioners within the field of the Education of the Gifted and within the larger field of general education, as well as interested laypersons, to hear such voices.

I am excited by the prospect of encouraging not only the Gallaghers and the Passows but the Ronviks and others to tell us what we are doing that is right and what we are doing that is wrong, to challenge us to question our deeply rooted assumptions, to suggest new approaches to old problems, to pose new problems for our consideration, to develop new practices, and generally to infuse some new life into a field that, while far from moribund, could use a bit of the "shock of the new." And I am grateful to Joyce Van-Tassel-Baska and Paula Olszewski-Kubilius for compiling a selection of papers of high quality and far-ranging content to serve as a worthy addition to such an ambitious undertaking.

James H. Borland, editor
Education and Psychology of the
Gifted Series

Patterns of Influence on Gifted Learners

The Home, the Self, and the School

CHAPTER 1

Introduction

This book has been compiled to examine the nature of various patterns that influence the development of talent in children and young adults. The selections focus on the role of the home, the self, and the schooling process and on the extent to which each informs the talent development process. Neither prospective nor retrospective studies of giftedness account fully for the complex path to high-level talent development and adult eminence. Consequently, we need to ask the following types of questions in order to understand the talent development process in new ways:

1. How do institutions like the family and the school act as agents of the talent development process?
2. Within these institutions, are there key individuals whose influence is crucial in the life of a gifted learner? How might such influence be characterized?
3. What personal characteristics are most critical for students to possess in the talent development process?
4. How do these factors interrelate to produce successful patterns of talent development and at what developmental stages?

These questions are addressed in various ways by the chapters in this volume. Our intent has been to organize the book around the three areas of greatest potential influence on an evolving gifted individual—the home, the self, and the school.

How, then, might we begin to explore these three patterns of influence on talent development? Joyce VanTassel-Baska, Paula Olszewski-Kubilius, and Marilynn Kulieke have developed a heuristic model that synthesizes the existing literature in these areas (see Figure 1.1). The far-left column shows the influences of institutions and systems, as represented in the work of Bloom (1985) and Clark (1984). Their research has focused on the importance of the home in developing achievement patterns and attitudes conducive to talent development.

1

Figure 1.1   A Heuristic Model of Influences on Talent Development

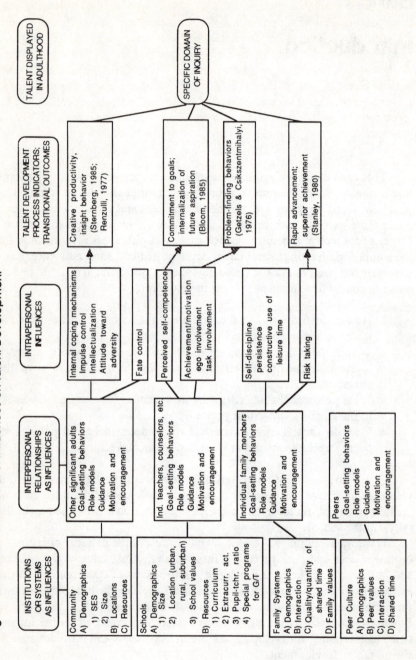

In some studies, including Bloom's (1985) and Clark's (1984), the role of schools in talent development has been shown to be relatively insignificant. Yet current work in talent development (VanTassel-Baska, 1988) suggests that creating access to appropriate educational experiences at a critical stage of development can have a positive impact on students. The longitudinal work of Benbow and Stanley (1983) suggests that students who participate in special advanced academic programs for gifted learners generally tend to become more in charge of their own learning. Thus, schooling may have a significant influence for some students who are intellectually talented.

The role of the peer culture may be particularly important to study, as it has been shown to have more impact on economically disadvantaged and/or minority group children (Harnischfeger & Wiley, 1981). Kulieke (1985) found that behaviors of black children in black suburban environments were more highly related to their peers' behavior than were the behaviors of black children living in white middle-class suburbs.

There is strong evidence for including individuals as an important sphere of influence for talent development (see Figure 1.1, second column from the left). Goertzel and Goertzel (1962) found that the mother was often the most important influence on the child's involvement in the pursuit of a talent area. In a recent study of the MacArthur Fellows, researchers Cox, Daniel, and Boston (1985) found many instances where an adult had a profound impact on a child's talent development. Bloom (1985) found that the right teacher at the right stage of development in the talent area was an important aspect of growth in that area. Rubin (1980) cited parental modeling of goal-setting behaviors as important for the future success of students.

There is also evidence that personal characteristics of the individual play a major role in the talent development process (see the middle column of Figure 1.1). Snarey and Vaillant (1985) found that internal coping mechanisms such as intellectual rationalizing and impulse control differentiated low socioeconomic males who entered the professions from those who did not. Rowe (1984) viewed fate control as an important contributor to success and suggested that inner-city youth must be able to see themselves as capable of taking control of their lives, in order to move out of adverse circumstances. Low levels of perceived self-competence have been cited as a factor accounting for negative learning patterns and underachievement (Whitmore, 1980). Nicholls (1983) stressed the importance of achievement motivation as a contributor to individual development. Finally, a recent study of adolescence (Csikszentmihalyi & Larson, 1985) has found that differences between high- and low-achieving students of equal ability lie in their use of leisure time, with high-achieving students spending significantly more time on homework, working on projects, and pursuing specific interests.

Recent research on the talent development process itself has been predominantly retrospective in nature, focusing on key elements from an eminent individual's childhood as markers of developing talent. In the model, the second column from the right contains a list of transitional outcome variables for characterizing the process of talent development. Bloom's work (1985), for example, cited a commitment to the talent area and internalization of standards for excellence and future aspirations. The Oden (1968) study of life satisfaction and career success among males in the Terman longitudinal group suggested that higher educational aspirations differentiated the high and low achievers.

Another marker of adult success appears to be problem-finding behaviors. A study of adult artists found that the major difference between those individuals who were successful in the pursuit of an art career and those who were not was that the former were able to find or create problems, rather than simply solve problems; that is, they had a facility for asking important questions that lead to advances in the field and are therefore not restricted to merely working on existing questions for which an algorithmic response can be formulated (Getzels & Csikszentmihalyi, 1976). Benbow and Stanley's work (1983) has demonstrated another factor: Many highly able students who accelerate their academic progress and exhibit superior achievement at early ages continue to accrue educational advantage and enter prestigious colleges and careers. Sternberg's recent work on intelligence (1985) suggests that insight and synthetic thinking are powerful intellectual skills that contribute to the success of intelligent people. And Renzulli (1977) suggests that a student's capacity to engage in creative production is evidence of talent at work.

The talent development process indicators, then, might be viewed as transitional outcomes for students being studied during the secondary school years, students who show academic promise but who have not reached a high level of adult creative productivity in a talent domain. These indicators provide a way of characterizing several different dimensions that are reflective of what we currently know about the talent development process during adolescence.

The far-right column represents the activation of talent in a given field of inquiry; that is, it signifies the talented individual having reached a level of adult competence that will open up another level of talent development, the path toward adult productivity and perhaps eminence. At this second level, a new pattern of influence begins that becomes important in the productivity of adulthood.

Yet the most critical areas of influence still remain the fundamental ones of home, self, and school, at the stages of development preceding adulthood. How children are socialized and how they perceive themselves and their competency are critical to the development of talent. Sharing what we know about these patterns of influence and what more we need to know is crucial to the work of educating gifted and talented learners.

These, then, are the issues we will grapple with in the following 14 chapters. These chapters are divided among three parts—the home, the self, and the school—reflecting the three greatest spheres of influence on gifted learners. Each part opens with an overview of the material to be covered in its chapters, as well as an illustration of its themes in the form of a short prose piece written by a student. The students' essays convey the spirit of the particular type of influence under discussion in the chapters and thus vivify each part of the book. It is our sincere hope that the significance of each influence is amplified and clarified in such a way as to foster greater understanding of the complexity of the talent development process.

REFERENCES

Benbow, C., & Stanley, J. (1983). *Academic precocity: Its nurturance and consequences.* Baltimore, MD: Johns Hopkins Press.

Bloom, B. (1985). *Developing talent in young people.* New York: Ballantine Books.

Clark, R. (1984). *Family life and school achievement: Why poor black children succeed or fail.* Chicago: University of Chicago Press.

Cox, J., Daniel, N., & Boston, B. (1985). *Educating able learners: Programs and promising practices.* Austin: University of Texas Press.

Csikszentmihalyi, M., & Larson, R. (1985). *Being adolescent: Conflict and growth in the teenage years.* New York: Basic Books.

Getzels, J. W., & Csikszentmihalyi, M. (1976). *The creative vision: A longitudinal study of problem finding in art.* New York: John Wiley.

Goertzel, M., & Goertzel, V. (1962). *Cradles of eminence.* Boston: Little, Brown.

Harnischfeger, A., & Wiley, D. W. (1981). *Minority education 1960–1980: Grounds, gains and gaps* (Vol. 1). Evanston, IL: Northwestern University, ML-Group for Policy Studies in Education.

Kulieke, M. (1985). *The effects of residential integration on children's school and neighborhood environments, social interactions, and school outcomes.* Unpublished doctoral dissertation, Northwestern University.

Nicholls, J. G. (1983). Conceptions of ability and achievement motivation: A theory and its implications for education. In S. G. Paris, G. M. Olson, & H. W. Stevenson (Eds.), *Learning and motivation in the classroom.* Hillsdale, NJ: Lawrence Erlbaum.

Oden, M. H. (1968). The fulfillment of promise: 40-year follow-up of the Terman gifted group. *Genetic Psychology Monographs, 77,* 2–92.

Renzulli, J. (1977). *The enrichment triad.* Wethersfield, CT: Creative Learning Press.

Rowe, M. B. (1984). Paper presented at Argonne National Laboratories in Pre-College Science Education, Lemont, IL.

Rubin, H. H. (1980). Longitudinal investigation of factors influencing the development of educational goals among low-income blacks. (Doctoral dissertation, Northwestern University). *Dissertation Abstracts International, 41*, 4177.

Snarey, J., & Vaillant, G. (1985). How lower- and working-class youth become middle-class adults: The association between ego defense mechanism and upward social mobility. *Child Development, 56*, 899–910.

Stanley, J. (1980). On educating the gifted. *Educational Researcher, 9*, 8–12.

Sternberg, R. (1985). *Beyond IQ*. Cambridge: Oxford University Press.

VanTassel-Baska, J. (1988, April). Case studies of disadvantaged gifted learners. Paper presented at the meeting of the American Educational Research Association, New Orleans, LA.

Whitmore, J. R. (1980). *Giftedness, Conflict, and Underachievement*. Boston: Allyn & Bacon.

PART I

INFLUENCE OF THE HOME

The family has been viewed as the most important influence on the development of talent and ability. The construct of "family" includes the family structure, such as number of members and siblings; the family climate or general atmosphere within the home; and the relationships among family members. The chapters in this part of the book emphasize the role of the home, values, and homelife in the development of talent.

In chapter 2 Wendy Roedell points out the need to identify and nurture intellectual talent in early childhood. She presents a developmental perspective on young, able children, noting that gifted children often show disparities in their developmental level in different areas. She highlights the preschool as a proper learning environment for introducing advanced content and skills to gifted young children. At the same time, young children's social and physical needs, which may lag behind their intellectual development, also need attention.

Joyce VanTassel-Baska in chapter 3 presents a description of the basic demographics of talent-search participants and their families. Her data indicate overwhelmingly that these adolescents come from higher-income backgrounds with small, intact families and have well-educated parents. Such family backgrounds have helped establish high levels of academic interest and aspiration in gifted students, as clearly evidenced by the data in this chapter. Students show multiple interests and talents extending to computers, music, and athletics; and at the age of 13 or 14 these adolescents aspire to advanced levels of education and are confident in their career direction.

In chapter 4, Marilynn Kulieke and Paula Olszewski-Kubilius examine many dimensions of family life, including values, family climate, and parental actions, and their impact on the ability, achievement, and self-concept of gifted adolescents. Their results show that aspects of the family environment are differentially associated with student outcomes. Family climate variables and verbally espoused values are more potent factors for student achievement, while parental enactment of values appears to be the more salient influence on students' self-perceptions. Also, different patterns of relationships between variables were obtained for males and females.

Joyce VanTassel-Baska in chapter 5 considers case studies of gifted adolescents who come from economically disadvantaged circumstances. Her analysis reveals the existence of many adverse factors such as divorce, distressed marriages, as well as low socioeconomic status in the lives of these youngsters. In addition, the case studies highlight the importance of the family, extended-family members such as grandparents, and other adults, including teachers, in communicating important messages such as the value of education, commitment, and hard work to adult success.

Out of the four chapters in this section, several key issues emerge. One of these is the notion that some form of adversity or a seemingly inhibiting or detrimental factor, which exists within the family structure or happens to the individual, can and does somehow work in a beneficial, generative manner. Seen in retrospect, this adversity factor has generally been facilitative of talent development. It is evident in the case studies reviewed by VanTassel-Baska and in much of the literature cited by Kulieke and Olszewski-Kubilius. The range of handicaps includes physical deformity, divorce, severe economic disadvantagement, cultural disadvantagement due to race or sex, parental loss, parental rejection, or tense family relationships. The adversity factor is found in much of the case study literature on gifted individuals, most notably in the descriptions of eminent individuals in *Cradles of Eminence* (Goertzel & Goertzel, 1962). As Kulieke and Olszewski-Kubilius point out, while acute factors of disadvantagement have often been found in the lives of eminent individuals, they are uncharacteristic of gifted individuals who do not attain eminence, but are nevertheless quite successful and personally fulfilled, such as those in the Terman sample.

What is perhaps most interesting about the existence of such adversity in the lives of gifted individuals is the notion that somehow it operates to motivate them to achieve or to dedicate themselves to a cause or field with tremendous intensity and commitment. It may engender emotional growth and maturity that pave the way to creative achievement and without which an individual would not make the transition from cognitive potential to creative production referred to by Albert (1978). It is the psychological interpretation given to the adversity that is significant. Such interpretations, although they are part of the individual, are probably influenced by the cultural, political, and social milieu in which the individual is living; the views of parents or significant others and the degree of identification between the gifted individual and these others; and the personal way in which the individual sees the world, makes connections between events, and sees himself or herself (e.g., as a victim or as a "doer").

Thus, the identifiable adverse factor must be examined in light of the meaning attached to it, which is related to the individual's own definitional structures, cognitive processes, and self-attributions. Research will need to focus on the reasons why different individuals interpret the same events differently and on the personal qualities that predispose some individuals to make facilitative as opposed to inhibiting interpretations of such events.

A second issue arising from the chapters in this part has to do with the roles and expectations placed upon a gifted child within the family. Kulieke and Olszewski-Kubilius refer to literature that suggests that parental expectations regarding achievement vary with gender and birth order, and their research demonstrates the differential responsiveness of males and females to family environment. These expectations, combined with a family history of involvement in a field or with parental talents in an area, plus a child's ability, provide a context for the development of the talent of particular individuals within the family. Albert (1978) refers to this as an intense focusing of socialization pressure on a particular child. This may be a beneficial situation for a child, but it can very often be detrimental for another child in the family who is also talented.

We know from genetic theory and research that it is not unlikely that more than one child in a family will be talented in a particular domain, but it may be that only one child can occupy a particular psychological space in the family at a time. Parents may need to say, "This is our bright child; this is our athletic one," thus differentially applying labels or attributions so as to individualize and distinguish children from one another. Also, a family has a limited number of resources (parental time, attention, money) and may only devote these to one child, the one who by luck (birth order and sex) fits their expectations about who should be talented or the achiever in the family. In addition, as gleaned from the case studies of VanTassel-Baska, parents give to their children their unfulfilled dreams and work hard to see them attained through a child they identify with. Thus, parental expectations regarding the roles of individual children appear to be a critical operative factor in the talent development process. Future research should address the match between parental expectations and the degree to which gifted individuals are responsive or sensitive to parental wishes or to fulfilling either parent's dreams for them.

The third issue that emanates from the chapters in this part has to do with the family as a system of relationships. Albert (1978) refers to giftedness as an organizer for family life and a determining factor of family relationships. It thus provides structure for parental involvement and expectations as well as for sibling relationships. Roedell points out the impact that identification and recognition of talent in young children can have on a family. Piechowski (see chapter 6) indicates that the mother is usually the parent who initially recognizes talent in her child, while fathers are more often disbelieving. The resulting importance of the mother in the lives of eminent individuals has been amply documented in the literature. What is apparent is that the gifted individual has an impact on the family system, the nature of which is dependent upon the extent of recognition of the talented child, parental adeptness at responding to multiple children, and the power lines within the family.

A final issue has to do with the history of the family. In the case studies presented by VanTassel-Baska, we see evidence of gifted children who are planted in a historical context and come from an indigent family background or an immigrant background. They are given the message that they have a certain responsibility to alter the family's position, a message often communicated by a grandmother. These children are told to get an education, to get ahead, so they won't have to work for others, so they won't have to work as hard as their parents or as laborers, and so they will have a better, easier life.

While the burden of moving the family out of its present socioeconomic position can be placed onto a gifted child, children from more advantaged circumstances may bear the burden of carrying out the family tradition in a particular field (e.g., statesmanship). This is supported in the literature reviewed by Kulieke and Olszewski-Kubilius. And, as suggested earlier, parents can transmit their unfulfilled aspirations to their children and their children's generation. Thus, in many respects, the gifted individual is vulnerable to pressures that can cross generational lines.

In reading the four chapters in this part, one is struck by the complexity of giftedness. When seemingly adverse factors turn out to be facilitative, it is difficult to predict who will achieve fame and renown or will contribute creatively and who will not.

These chapters on the family also clearly implicate the self as an important dimension in the development of talent. While we may point to characteristics that are found in the families of the gifted, these have significance only because children are differentially responsive to family environments and parental influences.

Student Perspective: Male, 18 years old

This is the story of my intellectual development, from birth through freshman year of college. It starts, logically enough, with my parents. They have been the single greatest (positive) influence on my intellect so far. They have always taken a very positive and nonpushy attitude toward my development; their attitude has always been, "We will support you as fully as possible in whatever you choose to do; just do it to the best of your abilities, and we will be happy." They have proven true to their promise, and have always managed to support me in everything, gently nudging me to do better without pushing or pressuring me. (I simply cannot work if I'm pressured . . . it cramps my style.) When I was very little, I remember them reading to me, getting me books of all kinds (all of which I devoured), and, when I had learned to read, listening to *me* read to them. All through high school, and so far this year, they have taken the role of guiding me in my decisions on classes, major, and so forth, but only when *asked*. They have never tried to foist their decisions about my future on me; according to Dad, it wouldn't be any use anyway, since I would do what I wanted no matter what. Instead, they have tried to help *me* decide what is best for myself. As a result, I have always believed that I can do absolutely anything I want to in life—which now makes it hard for me to choose one specific area to explore in depth. All in all, I couldn't ask for better parents, with a better attitude.

Next in strength of influence come my teachers. I've been supremely lucky to have a barrage of great teachers in my career—teachers who have challenged me to learn and grow, who haven't let me slide by on little effort, or get out of assignments with my personality. My seventh-grade science and high school English teachers come to mind as exemplary. They have been friends and guides to me.

Last come my friends, such as they are. I don't mean that to sound insulting or superior, but the fact is that I have never been a particularly outgoing person among my peers. I have friends, to be sure, and I don't stay locked in my room all day; it's just that I am an essentially private person, especially with respect to my intelligence. Throughout elementary school, I knew I was brighter than other kids, but I didn't mind much—I had a very understanding set of friends. To them I was "the Computer," a sort of intellectual guru to whom everyone came for advice. That was a great time for me, as I felt no stigma attached to my intellect.

In seventh grade, it wasn't quite as good; the people in my classes leaned toward the jock types and "mainstream learners." There weren't many opportunities to display my knowledge without getting at least a stare or two. Ever since seventh grade, I've had to fight with myself to keep from completely suppressing my intelligence to appear "normal."

It got easier to be myself in eighth grade, when I transferred to a special school geared toward, though not exclusively made for, the gifted. Here I was, for the first time, challenged to keep up with the other members of my class as well as with my own personal ideals. I could no longer drift by without effort. My friends in middle and high school included those who respected my intelligence, and those who were suspicious of it. In addition, there was a third group: those on my intellectual level, with whom I could have meaningful discussions and *real* arguments. It was great. That group saved me from total intellectual decay, and also made me a bit more extroverted. Having friends of all three of these types hasn't exactly made me subvert my intelligence; rather, it has made me adjust without compromising myself. I try not to show off, spouting out knowledgeable items solely for effect; nor do I deliberately hold back. . . . Instead, I try to find a happy medium, and be honest with myself. After all, the only person I'll have to live with *all* my life is me.

REFERENCES

Albert, R. S. (1978, Summer). Observations and suggestions regarding giftedness, familial influence and the achievement of eminence. *Gifted Child Quarterly, 28*(2), 201–211.
Goertzel, M., & Goertzel, V. (1962). *Cradles of eminence*. Boston: Little, Brown.

CHAPTER 2

Early Development of Gifted Children

Wendy C. Roedell

Efforts to identify and serve intellectually and academically gifted students have increased over the past several years. Many of these efforts, however, are directed toward children in late elementary school or after. Educators often seem to believe, as parents sometimes do, that children cannot be gifted until they have mastered basic academic skills, are old enough to begin independent study projects in the fourth-grade program for the gifted, or score at high levels on the SAT during the seventh-grade talent search. As one Seattle early childhood educator said, "We keep watering the flower, and forget about the seed." A comprehensive understanding of the nature of giftedness requires developmental perspective on the changing nature of intellectual and academic abilities, with a focus on the emergence of abilities that change over time and are manifested in different ways at different developmental stages. This perspective begins with a look at the early development of giftedness in young children and includes important implications for child-rearing and educational practice.

Parents, as their children's first teachers, can offer educators a wealth of information on the types of advanced abilities evidenced by gifted children as well as the types of educational activities that spark these children's interests. Yet educators frequently ignore this information, assuming that they, as "professionals," have a more accurate understanding of what children need. An effective approach to the identification and nurturance of giftedness

The research reported here was conducted while the author and Dr. Nancy E. Jackson were associate investigators on the Seattle Project, founded and directed by Dr. Halbert Robinson at the Child Development Research Group (now called the Center for Study of Capable Youth), University of Washington. Thanks are due Dr. Charles Stillman, for his work on many of the analyses reported here, and all members of the Child Development Research Group staff. The Seattle Project was supported in part by grants from the Spencer Foundation, the Ford Foundation, and the Office of Gifted and Talented, U.S. Office of Education.

in young children demands a cooperative partnership between home and school, characterized by mutual respect and an ongoing sharing of ideas and observations about the children involved.

One parent reported that, when she went to talk to her school principal about special programming for her gifted kindergartner, he said, "Don't worry, Mrs. Jones, just put her in the school, and soon she'll be just like everyone else." Certainly the goals of public education are not to make each student become "just like everyone else." Most educators want to encourage diversity in the student population and to support the development of unique talents. Talent development cannot occur, however, unless talents are identified and plans are made for specific educational challenges. Parents provide a crucial link in the process.

The Seattle Project at the University of Washington, begun by Halbert Robinson in 1976, sought to find answers to the question of whether intellectual and academic talent can be identified in children younger than age 5 (Robinson, Jackson, & Roedell, 1977; Roedell, Jackson, & Robinson, 1980). In addition, the project addressed the question of whether or not intellectually advanced children could benefit from special programming during the preschool/kindergarten years. During the course of the project, it became apparent that early identification and programming for highly able students is not only possible but desperately needed.

The overwhelming community response to the Seattle Project indicated surprisingly large numbers of highly gifted young children for whom no appropriate program existed. Parents were eager to find a professional who would listen sympathetically to their concerns about their children's advanced abilities and would offer assistance in choosing an appropriate educational setting to support their children's development. Anyone working with families of intellectually precocious young children soon recognizes that urgent needs exist in several areas. Early childhood educators must be made aware of the special capabilities of gifted young children and children whose intellectual and academic skills are developing at a faster than average rate must be identified as early as possible. In addition, early childhood programs must be developed to serve young children who have already mastered much of the standard preschool and early primary curriculum. Finally, there needs to be planned continuity in educational programming from preschool through college, to nurture the special talents of intellectually and academically advanced students.

In many school districts, parents and educators frequently seem to be at odds about the best educational placements for young gifted children entering the school system. Versions of the following conversation can often be heard when young gifted children start school. "Bill doesn't belong in kindergarten!" the parent cries. "Look, he's reading at the fourth-grade level and has already learned two-column addition." The teacher or principal, having already decided this is a "pushy parent," replies, "Well, Mrs. Smith, Bill certainly doesn't belong in first grade; he hasn't learned to tie his shoelaces, he can't hold a pencil properly, and he had a tantrum yesterday in the hall."

The problem in this continuing controversy is that both parties are usually correct. Some gifted children entering kindergarten have acquired academic skills far beyond those of their age-mates. Such children master the academic content of kindergarten when they are 3 years old. However, their physical and social development may be similar to that of other 5-year-olds, making an accelerated placement a mismatch as well. The usual solution is to place a child like Bill in a program matched to his weaknesses, rather than to his strengths. Bill usually ends up in kindergarten, where his advanced intellectual development becomes a frustration to his teacher, an embarrassment to his peers, and a burden to Bill.

Educators justify this placement by saying, "Bill needs socialization—he's already so far ahead academically, he doesn't need anything in that area." There are two major problems with this rationale. First, educators are essentially telling such students that there is no need for them to learn anything in school. There is even an element of penalty: "We're not going to teach you any more—you already know too much." Teachers who have to deal with that child later on in school will wonder why the child remains unmotivated and seems to be "turned off" to school. Usually they blame the child or the parents; rarely do they attribute this lack of motivation to the educational process that slammed the door on the child's early enthusiasm for learning.

The second problem is revealed by examining the "socialization" experienced by a brilliant 5-year-old like Bill in a kindergarten class of 25 to 30 students. A major component of early socialization involves a child's feeling that she or he is accepted by others—teachers and children alike. If the teacher does not validate a gifted child's advanced abilities and intellectual interests by making them part of the ongoing curriculum, the child experiences no feelings of acceptance from the teacher. If, as is highly likely, this child makes the additional discovery that she or he is quite different from most classmates and that communication is extremely difficult because of differences in vocabulary and modes of expression, then the child misses peer acceptance as well. In fact, this first school experience, which should furnish the impetus for future enthusiasm about learning, can be a dismal failure for the brilliant child in a lock-step kindergarten program. Such children may develop behavioral problems or psychosomatic symptoms (stomachaches, headaches), causing parents to confront the school with justifiable concern.

Often these children hide or deny their abilities, so as to fit in better with the other children. One first-grade teacher told of a child who was already reading at the third-grade level when she entered kindergarten. Her abilities remained undetected until she was in the first grade and went to the school library to check out a book. She was told by the librarian that she could not have the book she wanted because she obviously would not be able to read it. It was not until her mother wrote a note to the school asking that her daughter be allowed to use the library that teachers had any inkling of this child's advanced abilities.

Programs for the gifted in many school districts are designed to meet the needs of older students. Children in kindergarten are rarely included in such programs, which generally do not begin until third or fourth grade. Programs for preschool-age children are even more rare. Most curriculum approaches in education for the gifted assume that such learners are self-directed, independent students capable of carrying out extensive projects with minimal assistance. The result is that many gifted young children simply do not fit into any existing program option. The obvious solution for gifted young children is a program designed to challenge each child's strengths while at the same time providing experiences for development in weaker areas.

IDENTIFICATION

Many school personnel are held back from addressing the educational needs of gifted young children by fears about identification. What if the system misses a "truly gifted" child who has not yet demonstrated underlying giftedness through possessing advanced academic skills?

Part of this fear comes with the prevailing notion that identifying gifted children requires looking into a crystal ball to identify the "leaders of tomorrow." According to this new labeling, affixing the magic "gifted" label to a child should mean accurately predicting a future Edison, Churchill or Marie Curie. In effect, educators often are really looking for future gifted adults. Trying to predict which children are going to be eminent at some later time is clearly an impossible task, particularly when children are quite young. What democratic teacher wants to look around a group of 5-year-olds and decide which of them will become a "leader of tomorrow"? Better to identify no one than to risk making a mistake of this magnitude.

This problem can be resolved if educators give up crystal-ball gazing and start concentrating on each child's abilities and the immediate developmental need for special programming that these may engender. Four-year-olds who have known all the colors since they were 18 months old, who read at the third-grade level, and who have the vocabulary of an 8-year-old obviously need something different from the usual preschool or kindergarten curriculum. It makes sense to identify and meet those immediate needs. It doesn't really matter how the child developed these advanced abilities—whether it was early teaching, early experience, genetic endowment, or whatever. What matters is that the child's existing level of competence should be matched by appropriate educational experience. This does not mean that every child identified for programming at age 4 or 5 will automatically need continued programs, although it is highly likely, nor does it mean that children who do not demonstrate their giftedness in advanced skills at an early age should be deprived of programs later on. It only means that when advanced skills exist and can be identified, they should be nurtured as early as possible.

There are several points to bear in mind when developing a system for identifying these advanced skills in young children (Roedell et al., 1980). The first step, of course, is to consider carefully the type of program that is to be offered. The identification system must mesh with the goals of the program in that the program must include some provision for challenging the talents and abilities that have been identified. In addition, the information used in identifying young children's advanced abilities should come from a variety of sources, so that children will have multiple opportunities to demonstrate their most advanced skills. Since young children's performance is likely to be variable, casting a wide screening net is most likely to capture evidence of advanced abilities. Useful information can be obtained from parents and teachers and by noticing the child's performance on different types of tests. Furthermore, questions asked through tests or questionnaires must be difficult enough to document unusually advanced performance; hence, out-of-level testing will most likely be necessary. For example, administration of a school readiness test will not identify the 4-year-old who can read at the third-grade level.

Information from these various sources should be combined in such a way that extraordinary performance can be acknowledged, even if it is not documented by all sources of information. The strategy should focus on looking for examples of a child's best performance, wherever it is found. The hint of extraordinary ability in a very young child should be taken quite seriously, since performance in other areas of the screening system may have been suppressed by inattention or other sources of unreliability.

Testing

Tests used to identify young children for an intensive, advanced academic program should be chosen to measure both academic skills and intellectual ability. Preschool-age children, of course, must be tested individually. As children become somewhat older (age 5 or 6), it may be possible to administer group tests if the groups are kept small.

In assessing the abilities of young gifted children, it is wise to look beyond test information. However carefully a test is administered, children with advanced mental competencies may not demonstrate the full extent of their abilities during a test session. This is particularly true for preschool-age children. Part of the unreliability of young children's performance arises from the fact that they may not be at their best during a test session administered by an unfamiliar adult in new and different surroundings. Some children may be more interested in playing their own games with the test materials than in following the tester's directions. When a child performs well on a standardized test, there is little doubt about the child's advanced abilities; however, when a child does not perform well, it is difficult to determine the reason(s). It may be due to lack of ability, but lack of concentration, effort, or self-confidence may also be the cause.

Information from Parents

Children's developing competence can also be observed in their everyday behavior. Because parents have the best opportunity to observe young children's ongoing behavior across a variety of settings, they make excellent partners in the identification process. At the Seattle Project, parents produced consistently reliable descriptions of their children's favorite activities and often recalled detailed instances of outstanding performance that indicated unusually advanced skills. A questionnaire was developed asking parents to give a short description of their child's precocious behavior and to respond to a series of yes/no questions regarding specific attainments in language, spatial ability, memory, reading, and mathematical understanding. A positive relationship was found between parent questionnaire information and children's test scores at age 4 and 5, regardless of whether the parent information was obtained concurrently with test performance or at an earlier age. In fact, questionnaire scores at age 2 or 3 predicted later test performance just about as well as did early test scores (Roedell et al., 1980).

What kinds of things do parents notice about their children's developing abilities? Early verbal ability can be detected from parental reports of early emergence of complex sentences and advanced vocabulary. One mother reported that at the age of 2 her daughter habitually used such complex sentences as "I'm trying to figure out where I left my dancing shoes" and "I want to take a look at this story to see what kinds of boys and girls it has in it" (Roedell et al., 1980).

In many cases, early reading ability seems to arise spontaneously without active teaching by parents other than responding to their children's interests and answering questions. Many parents will say that their child is reading and that "it's not my fault." Often parents experience negative reactions about their preschooler's reading ability, from neighbors and others. "Why have you pushed that child to read?" people say, when in fact it is usually the child who has pushed the parent. For example, one parent described her 18-month-old son's determined efforts to learn to read by spending hours arranging and rearranging alphabet blocks, continually asking his parents, "What does this spell?" His efforts resulted in fluent reading ability at age 2. Other parents would say, "I don't know how he learned to read; all of a sudden he picked up a book and started reading it!"

Occasionally, parents will comment on their child's ability with numbers. One parent described her 3½-year-old son's ability to add numbers between 1 and 10. She told him that his cousin was 2 years younger than he, and he said, "Oh, when she is 3, I'll be 5, and when she is 4, I'll be 6. . . ." He continued adding up to age 12. When asked if her child could count to 20, another parent reported, "He only gets lost when he gets to 10,000."

Another noticeable behavior of intellectually advanced young children is their ability to make connections between areas of learning. For example, one 4-year-old boy had been studying about sets in math. Later, someone asked him what he wanted to be when he grew up. "Let's see," he said, "Maybe I'll be a doctor; no, I think I'll be a fireman; no (intersecting set) I'll be a paramedic!"

In short, young children with advanced intellectual skills do everyday things that are notable. Given the right questions, parents can and will describe these notable behaviors; however, they usually do not possess the educator's broad perspective of general child development. While parents bring to the identification partnership accurate information about their own child, educators bring valuable information about how that individual child's skills compare with those of other children. Parents describe behavior; educators determine whether the behavior is advanced or average.

UNEVENNESS OF DEVELOPMENT

In designing an identification system and program effort for young gifted children, it is important to remember that these children very often do not develop evenly. In fact, young gifted children frequently show peaks of extraordinary performance, rather than equally high skill levels in all cognitive ability areas.

Intellectual and Academic Aspects

Even a somewhat narrow focus on the intellectual and academic aspects of giftedness does not assure a homogeneous population. The child who learns to read at age 3 or who shows unusually advanced spatial reasoning ability, for example, may not be the child with the highest IQ or the earliest language development. This diversity, of course, persists and increases as children grow older. In the talent-search population, for example, some students score high on the math subtest while others excel on the verbal (Keating, 1976). Unique patterns of development can be observed within a group of gifted children, and uneven development is frequently evident in the pattern of a single child.

In some cases, it seems as though children's abilities develop in spurts, guided by changes in interest and opportunity. A boy from the Seattle Project provides a case in point. The Peabody Individual Achievement Test (PIAT) was used by the project to document advanced academic performance in preschool children, even though percentile norms are not available for that age group. At age 4, Bruce scored at the first-grade level on the math subtest and at the third-grade level in reading recognition. His mother reported that he had started reading before he was 3 years old, and, while he was slightly advanced in math, reading was the skill he spent most of his time practicing. Future test performances showed fairly even development in these areas, up until Bruce's kindergarten year. At that point, Bruce began to lose interest in reading and shifted his attention to math. He commented that he didn't enjoy reading much, even though he knew most words. However, he did enjoy computing three-column addition problems in his head and spent lots of time with all of the mathematically oriented activities in the classroom. When his teacher decided he was ready to learn about multiplication, she spent a few minutes explaining it to him. He responded by saying, "Oh, so 5 times 5 must be 25, and 3 times 6 must be 18, and . . ." Clearly he had been doing multiplication for some time but had not been able to label the process. When Bruce took the PIAT at age 6, he spent a great deal of time figuring out all of the math problems and scored at the seventh-grade level on the math subtest (Jackson, 1988). While this PIAT score certainly does not indicate that Bruce knew all of the mathematics taught in the first 6 years of elementary school, it is clear that he was able to figure out quite a bit for a 6-year-old. It is also clear that he moved from being moderately advanced in math to unusually advanced in a very short time. His test scores at age 4 showed no indication that he would be so advanced in math at age 6.

Other children have shown equally uneven patterns of development. Reading, for example, might develop almost overnight. Children who know all their letters and letter sounds by age 2½ may remain at that level for some time, perhaps until age 4 or 5, and then in a matter of months develop fluent reading skills at the third- or fourth-grade level. Parents may become concerned when their child, who has demonstrated superior letter recognition skills for years, fails to begin reading as early as expected. Understanding the unique developmental patterns often present in gifted children can help parents, and teachers as well, adjust their expectations of academic performance in young children to a more reasonable level.

Physical and Social Skills

Another area of unevenness in the development of gifted young children is found in the relationship between advanced intellectual development and development of physical and social skills. In the area of physical development, recent researchers have refuted Terman's findings of superior physical development among the gifted. Hildreth (1954) and others have noted that the supposed physical superiority found among gifted children may be due to the fact that most of the children in the older studies came from upper socioeconomic neighborhoods, where nutrition and health care practices tended to be superior to those in the general population. When socioeconomic status is controlled, these differences disappear. One study of gifted preschool children (Leithwood, 1971) did find relationships between Binet IQ and children's ability to perform complex motor tasks, although there was no relationship between IQ and simple motor tasks involving such skills as strength and balance. The evidence seems to indicate that intellectually gifted children's performance in the physical domain may only be advanced to the extent that the physical tasks involve cognitive organization.

Likewise, at the Seattle Project, intellectually advanced children tended to possess some advanced social-cognitive skills but did not necessarily demonstrate those skills in their social behavior. For example, 3- and 4-year-old children whose IQs were at or above 130 showed advanced understanding of the constancy of gender across time and situations (Miller, Roedell, Slaby, & Robinson, 1978). Intellectually advanced preschool children were also advanced in their ability to conceive of many different solutions to hypothetical social conflict situations (Roedell, 1978). When administered the Preschool Interpersonal Problem-Solving Test (PIPS) developed by Spivack and Shure (1974), children with higher IQs had more ideas about ways to solve social conflicts and ways for children to interact cooperatively. However, these advanced social-cognitive skills were not reflected in children's behavior. Children with more ideas about ways to interact cooperatively did not, in fact, engage in more cooperative behavior when they were observed in the preschool classroom. Cooperative interaction did increase overall during the year, as children participated in a program that emphasized social interaction skills. Guided social interaction experience was necessary to help these children translate their advanced intellectual understanding into concrete behavior.

It is not uncommon to find gifted young children experiencing a vast gap between their advanced intellectual skills and their less advanced physical and emotional competencies. For example, 4- and 5-year-old children may converse intelligently about abstract concepts such as time and death and read fluently at the fourth-grade level, yet find it difficult to hold a pencil or to share their toys with others. Sometimes young children's advanced skills bring them in contact with information they are not emotionally ready to handle. One father described coming upon his 4-year-old daughter reading the Bible. She closed the book with a terrified look on her face and said, "I'm reading the 'Book of Revelations,' and boy, is it scary!"

Often these uneven developmental levels can lead to extreme frustration, as children find that their limited physical skills are not sufficiently developed to carry out the complex projects they imagined. These children may throw tantrums or even give up on projects without trying. Adult guidance in developing coping strategies can help such children set more realistic goals for themselves and learn how to solve problems effectively when their original efforts do not meet their high expectations. Adults, too, can be misled by children's advanced verbal ability or reasoning skill into expecting equally advanced behavior in all areas. It is unsettling to hold a high-level conversation with a 5-year-old who then turns around and punches a classmate who stole her pencil. Sometimes young children's age-appropriate social behavior is interpreted as willful or lazy by parents and teachers whose expectations are unrealistically high. Further research is clearly necessary to tease out which aspects of social development might be advanced as a result of advanced intellectual development.

Temperament

One additional factor that influences the expression of children's advanced abilities is behavioral style or temperament (Thomas & Chess, 1977). A brilliant child possessed with a particularly flamboyant style might frequently be the center of involvement in a classroom, while another equally brilliant but quiet and unassuming child might receive less attention. Some teachers may, in fact, tend to overlook the abilities of the quieter child who is hesitant to become involved in new situations (Gordon & Thomas, 1967).

Responses of parents of children in the Seattle Project to a questionnaire developed by Thomas and Chess (1977) indicated wide variation in gifted children's temperament characteristics. Initial analyses indicated that children with higher IQs tended to be slightly more persistent and have longer attention spans than children with lower IQs. However, the overlapping range between the two groups was wide (Roedell et al., 1980). Teachers and parents should not forget that advanced intellectual skills are not always accompanied by particular temperament styles.

Checklists used in identifying gifted children often include characteristics that reflect temperament rather than actual skills or abilities. Such checklists should be used with caution, particularly with young children. A child who is not responsive to new stimuli, persistent, well organized, or enthusiastic about learning new things may well be the one whose real strengths are overlooked and ignored. A little encouragement in the early years might be necessary to help such children develop the habits of persistence and achievement orientation that will allow them to make the most of their skills. Gifted adults do not spring into the world fully formed, with fully developed abilities, creativity totally unleashed, and their determination firmly forged.

Given these sources of extreme variability, the only accurate generalization that can be made about the characteristics of intellectually gifted young children is that they demonstrate their unusual intellectual skills in a wide variety of ways and that they form an extremely heterogeneous group with respect to interests, skill levels in particular areas, social development, and physical abilities.

PROGRAM DEVELOPMENT

Developing a program for such a diverse group is indeed a challenge. Model programs exist throughout the country which offer successful examples of academically challenging options for young intellectually gifted students. The Child Development Preschool/Kindergarten, started by the Seattle Project, is one example (Roedell et al., 1980). In New York, the Astor Program developed by Virginia Ehrlich for 4- to 6-year-olds has been adopted in several public schools (Ehrlich, 1979), and the gifted program on the Hunter College campus provides another model for working with the very young. Public schools in the Chicago area have also developed programs for academically gifted children, starting in kindergarten.

Public school identification of academically advanced children should begin at the time parents register their children for kindergarten. As pointed out earlier, schools should encourage parents to share their observations of their children's behavior and their perspectives on their children's educational needs. Further screening could be accomplished for those children initially identified by parents. Teachers might also make efforts to identify advanced children during the early part of the year. Such students might be placed in a special classroom or be clustered in the classrooms of trained teachers who could devise programs for them in the context of the regular kindergarten.

An early childhood program for advanced learners need not commit a school district to identifying all of their gifted students at age 5. A district-wide K–12 program might develop in stages, with appropriate screening procedures at each level. Children whose gifted potential has not yet been demonstrated in advanced behavior can be placed in gifted programs later on, as their giftedness matures. To accommodate them, a district would be wise to plan for increased numbers at older grade levels.

In areas where early childhood programs for gifted children are not available, parents must assume the responsibility for initiating dialogue with school personnel regarding possible options for nurturing their child's unusual abilities. Parents whose children have some unusual characteristics that will affect their learning needs have an obligation to share that information with educators, just as educators have an obligation to listen carefully to parent concerns. Since many gifted children will hide their abilities so as to fit in more closely with classmates in a regular program, teachers may not be able to observe advanced intellectual or academic abilities directly. If a kindergartner enters school with fluent reading ability, the parent should share this information at the beginning of the year, instead of waiting until the end of the year to complain that the teacher didn't find out that the child could read. When parents and teachers pool their observations of a child's skills, they begin to work together to develop appropriate educational options for nurturing those abilities.

Individualization

Ideally, any effective educational program should provide an optimal match between the entry level of learners and the instructional level of learning experiences. One of the few psychological truths educators and psychologists agree upon states that the most learning occurs when an optimal match between the learner's current understanding and the challenge of new learning material has been carefully engineered. When the entry level of learners is generally high but extremely diverse, an appropriate program must be highly individualized. Children should be encouraged to progress at their own learning rate, which will result in most cases in subject-matter acceleration. The program should be broadly based, with planned opportunities for development of social, physical, and cognitive skills in the informal atmosphere of an early childhood classroom.

Many intellectually gifted children master the cognitive content of most preschool and kindergarten programs quite early. They come to school ready and eager to learn concepts not usually taught until an older age. However, academic tasks designed for older children often require the learner to carry out teacher-directed activities while sitting still and concentrating on written work sheets. Young children, no matter how bright they are, require active involvement with learning materials and often do not have the writing skills required for above-grade-level work. One primary task of the teacher, then, is to make appropriately advanced content accessible to young children, taking into account their typical social and physical skills. Lessons can be broken into shorter units, activities presented as games, and many concepts taught through inquiry-oriented dialogue and experimentation with manipulatable materials. Language experience activities in reading (e.g., Allen & Allen, 1969, 1970) and the use of manipulatable math materials as described in *Mathematics Their Way* (Baratta-Lorton, 1976) are good examples of appropriate curriculum approaches.

In looking for an appropriate program for their gifted preschooler, then, parents must be aware of the learning needs of young children and not be misled by so-called experts who advocate rigid academic approaches with an emphasis on rote memorization and repetition. Rather, wise parents will look for open-endedness, flexible grouping, and opportunities for advanced activities in a program for their intellectually gifted child.

Opportunities for Peer Interaction

In addition to offering challenges for advanced abilities and creative opportunities for growth in all developmental areas, a major function of a program for highly gifted young children is to help them discover their true peers at an early age. Somehow our current method of organizing schools has led us to believe that a child's peers consist of all other children the same age. In fact, the word *peer* refers to individuals who can interact on an equal plane around issues of common interest (Lewis & Rosenblum, 1975). For children who are significantly different from other children their own age in skills and interests, finding true peers in a regular school classroom may prove difficult. In fact, many gifted children have different sets of peers, depending on what activity they are pursuing. They may have one set of peers on the soccer field, another set when playing in the school orchestra, and still a different set when discussing literature or solving mathematical problems.

Parents of gifted children frequently find that, while their child can get along with other children in the neighborhood, an intense friendship is likely to develop with a more developmentally equal peer met in a special class or interest-based activity. Such parents may be dismayed to discover that this "best friend" does not live next door but across town, and they may wonder whether or not to give in to their child's pleas for inconvenient visits. Probably one of the most supportive activities a parent can engage in is to help a child find a true friend and make the effort required to permit the friendship to flower.

The importance of true peers cannot be overestimated. Preschool- and kindergarten-aged children are just beginning to make their first social contacts, to define themselves in relation to other children. A 3-year-old who can converse like a 6-year-old may feel pressured to make adjustments to fit in better with agemates. For example, one 4-year-old boy was constantly frustrated because when he would make appointments to meet his friends, they would be late because they couldn't tell time. When he wrote a note to his friends to tell them he couldn't play that day, he later tore it up and explained to his mother, "I forgot—they can't read."

While adaptation is important, gifted young children also need the give-and-take of interactions with others of equal ability, where they can find acceptance and understanding, the keys to the development of successful social skills and positive self-concept. Ronald, a 5-year-old in the Seattle Project's kindergarten, explained it well when he said, "Do you know why Bob is my best friend? Because he's the only one who understands the kind of guy I really am."

Sequencing

Of course, development of program options for young gifted children is not the complete answer. Bits and pieces of programs offered at some grade levels and not at others cannot begin to address the continuing educational needs of these students. When the academic content of early childhood programs for gifted students is appropriately matched to these children's advanced abilities, and when the pace is adapted to their accelerated learning rate, then these students will be learning concepts usually taught to much older children. Provision must be made, then, for continuous programming throughout the grades, if students are not to be decelerated in their learning. Students who are learning fourth-grade material in the second grade should not have to repeat it in the fourth grade. A K–12 accelerated scope-and-sequence program will allow for this needed continuity in academic skill development and will also provide a planned sequence for introducing process skills such as critical thinking and problem solving.

In school districts where an accelerated K–12 program has not been established, parents may need to work closely with the schools to insure educational continuity for their gifted children. For example, if the kindergarten teacher has worked out a way for a child to attend a first-grade reading group, then the parent may need to consult the first-grade teacher the following year to be sure the child is still moving ahead at an appropriate place in the curriculum. The more unusual the child's abilities, the more essential is parental involvement in the schooling process. In addition to negotiating with the school system for the most reasonable educational placements for their child, parents may need to supplement the school situation with classes, activities, or tutorials that take place outside the classroom situation.

SUMMARY

Intellectually advanced children can be identified at an early age using a combination of information from parents and test scores. These gifted children often enter school having mastered most of the academic curriculum of the primary grades. A regular preschool, kindergarten, or even first-grade program is often an inappropriate placement, since children develop best when learning experiences are matched to their advanced skill levels and rapid learning rate. Parents and educators in working together can develop mutual understanding of the educational needs of individual gifted children and can develop effective programs that combine the informal style of early childhood education with access to advanced content and ideas. Just like their older counterparts, young gifted children need opportunities to challenge their intellectual abilities and develop to the next level in their academic skills, in a developmentally appropriate educational context that allows them to learn in the company of their intellectual peers. Effective nurturance of giftedness in the context of home and school can only be achieved through a developmental perspective that begins with the child's earliest years and continues with appropriate educational experiences throughout the child's educational life.

REFERENCES

Allen, R. V., & Allen, C. (1969). *Language experiences in early childhood.* Chicago: Encyclopedia Britannica Press.

Allen, R. V., & Allen, C. (1970). *Language experiences in reading* (Vols. 1 & 2). Chicago: Encyclopedia Britannica Press.

Baratta-Lorton, M. (1976). *Mathematics their way: An activity centered mathematics program for early childhood education.* Menlo Park, CA: Addison-Wesley.

Ehrlich, V. Z. (1979). A model program for educating gifted four- to eight-year-old children. *International Journal of Early Childhood, 2,* 115–123.

Gordon, E. M., & Thomas, A. (1967). Children's behavioral style and the teacher's appraisal of their intelligence. *Journal of School Psychology, 5,* 292–300.

Hildreth, G. (1954). Three gifted children: A developmental study. *The Journal of Genetic Psychology, 85,* 239–262.

Jackson, N. E. (1988). Case study of Bruce: A child with advanced intellectual abilities. In J. M. Sattler (Ed.), *Assessment of children's intelligence and special abilities* (3rd ed.) (pp. 676–678). San Diego, CA: J. M. Sattler.

Keating, D. P. (1976). *Intellectual talent: Research and development.* Baltimore, MD: Johns Hopkins University Press.

Leithwood, K. A. (1971). Motor, cognitive and affective relationships among advantaged preschool children. *Research Quarterly, 42,* 47–53.

Lewis, M., & Rosenblum, O. A. (1975). *Friendship and peer relations.* New York: John Wiley.

Miller, J., Roedell, W. C., Slaby, R., & Robinson, H. F. (1978, April). *Sex-role development in intellectually precocious preschool children*. Paper presented at the annual meeting of the Western Psychological Association, San Francisco, CA.

Robinson, H. B., Jackson, N. E., & Roedell, W. C. (1977). *Identification and nurturance of extraordinarily precocious young children* (Annual report to the Spencer Foundation). Seattle: University of Washington, Child Development Research Group. (ERIC Document Reproduction Service No. ED 151 095)

Roedell, W. C. (1978, August 30). Social development in intellectually advanced children. In H. B. Robinson (Chair), *Intellectually advanced children: Preliminary findings of a longitudinal study*. Symposium presented at the annual convention of the American Psychological Association, Toronto.

Roedell, W. C., Jackson, N. E., & Robinson, H. B. (1980). *Gifted young children*. New York: Teachers College Press.

Spivack, G., & Shure, M. B. (1974). *Social adjustment of young children*. San Francisco: Jossey-Bass.

Thomas, A., & Chess, S. (1977). *Temperament and development*. New York: Brunner/Mazel.

CHAPTER 3

Profiles of Precocity: A Three-Year Study of Talented Adolescents

Joyce L. VanTassel-Baska

While studies of eminence have provided a rich literature that examines the factors that may have accounted for high-level adult performance, another strand of work has attempted to view giftedness prospectively. The nature of highly gifted learners has always been a question of great interest. We are intrigued as a society by the phenomenon of giftedness, but we tend to see it as an aberrant form in nature, an unusual and rare mutation that springs full-blown like Venus from sea foam. Certainly our view of prodigies is very much like this, but so also is our view of general intellectual ability in the extreme. We speak of quantitative learning differences that become qualitative differences when a build-up of knowledge has occurred. Berliner (1986) refers to this notion as "catastrophe theory." Feldman (1986) views the phenomenon in chess prodigies as "developmental leaps," where young chess students at ages 10 and 12 can outperform older adult chess masters because they have been able to focus their attention and intellect very sharply in one field. Krutetskii's work (1976) with highly gifted mathematicians also asserts a powerful ability to intuit the process by which complex problems are solved.

As I examine the literature on highly gifted students in both verbal and mathematical academic areas, I am struck by the similarity of the personal profile, regardless of the area of academic strength. Looking at key variables such as family background, interests, aspirations, and accomplishments, a pattern of precocity begins to emerge. Such students not only have learning traits that differ from those of their age peers, they also appear to have an identifiable social and psychological context in which learning occurs. This pattern appears to be stable across several studies (Benbow & Stanley, 1983; Hollingworth, 1942; Terman, 1925; VanTassel-Baska, 1983).

METHODS AND PROCEDURES

As part of an annual Midwest Talent Search (MTS) application process, I collected background demographic information regarding students and their families. The 1982 regional finalists comprised the first group for whom such data was collected, analyzed, and reported (VanTassel-Baska, 1983). Subsequent data-collection efforts have focused on a different population of high-scoring students, those who have attended a special program at Northwestern University during the summer following their identification through the MTS. Some, but not all, of these students were regional finalists. Consequently, the 191 students from 1982 represent a higher-scoring group overall than those from 1983 and 1984 ($N = 150$ and 256, respectively). These differences may be seen as follows:

1982   SAT-M$\geq$630 or SAT-V$\geq$580
1983   SAT-M$\geq$500 or SAT-V$\geq$430
1984   SAT-M$\geq$500 or SAT$\geq$430

A questionnaire was used to collect the data, with one section completed by the students and another completed by the parents. Percentage of return

Table 3.1   General Interests of MTS Students 1982–1984

	% of Students Selecting Item		
General Student Interests	1982	1983	1984
Sports	32	35	59
Music	31	30	58
Computers	27	31	58
Collections	19	20	37
Reading	18	22	78
Games/puzzles	17	13	54
Academic areas (i.e., math, science)	8	15	58
Writing	7	9	34

Note: These data represent multiple responses; thus, numbers reflect the percentage of the total population responding for that year to each item.

ranged from 64% in 1982 to 82% in 1984. The mean was 74%. A simple numerical and percentage approach to reporting the data was used consistently over the 3-year-period.

RESULTS

The results of the data reported on in this chapter are grouped according to the following categories: student interests, student aspiration level, student accomplishments, family background, early academic development, and the educational practice of acceleration. For 1984, data on ethnic background, family income, and attitude toward school are also reported.

For comparative purposes across the 3-year period, results for each category are reported in percentages only, since the number of student responses fluctuated by year. Males have been disproportionately represented in the top-scoring group each year, and this disparity is also reflected in the student population attending summer programs at Northwestern. Among our survey respondents, males outnumber females by approximately 2 to 1 in each year:

	1982	1983	1984
Males	69%	67%	63%
Females	31%	33%	37%

Student Interests

The 3-year data (see Table 3.1) reflect a stable set of interests for talent search students. The variation that does occur across years largely results from more students indicating more interests. This tendency, however, may be an artifact of a change in the questionnaire, which was revised to a forced-choice format in 1984. Multiple interests were very evident for students across all 3 years. Preference order shifted significantly in 1984 toward reading, and in 1984 many more students indicated a preference for reading adventure, math/computer-related, history, and reference sources, in comparison to earlier years. Other reading preferences remained stable, with science fiction being the most preferred genre over the 3-year period. Again, marked increases in 1984 are probably due to questionnaire artifact.

In school-based experiences, the interest patterns in academic areas were very consistent over the 3-year period studied. MTS students clearly enjoyed mathematics far more than any other school subject, regardless of their tested area of ability, and continued to cite science as their second-favorite area of study. Over the 3-year period an average of 53% of MTS students selected mathematics as their favorite subject, while 17% selected science and 11% selected language arts. Other subject areas were selected by fewer than 9%. New subjects in the curriculum, such as computer science, were indicated as preferences but not by large numbers of students.

Student Aspiration Level

The aspiration level of MTS students at junior high age may be interpreted as very high, with over 60% of the group each year aspiring to the highest educational level attainable within any given field (see Table 3.2). Consistently, all the MTS students saw themselves as future college graduates, with almost 90% going on to advanced schooling and graduate degrees.

Student Accomplishments

Midwest Talent Search students demonstrated a strong sense of their own capability and accomplishment in fields outside of the academic endeavors for which they had been recognized (VanTassel-Baska, 1983). Music was one of the major outside areas cited as a talent area by almost a quarter of the students, and mathematical talent was cited most frequently, with 63% identifying it as a talent area in 1984. Other areas in which MTS students identified talent included art, writing, sports, language, computers, solving problems, science, spelling, drama, and debate. Since the 1984 questionnaire

Table 3.2   Aspiration Level of MTS Students for Advanced Education 1982–1984

| | % of Students Selecting Item | | |
Aspiration Level	1982	1983	1984
Doctorate	46	42	46
Advanced professional degree (i.e., law, medicine)	15	20	30
Master's	23	24	16
Bachelor's	12	9	7
High school	0	0	0
No response	5	5	1

Table 3.3 Educational Level of MTS Parents, 1982–1984

Educational Level	Mothers (%)			Fathers (%)		
	1982	1983	1984	1982	1983	1984
Doctorate	5	4	5	32	30	26
Advanced professional degree	-	4	4	-	-	19
Master's	22	25	27	20	27	9
Bachelor's	38	40	38	24	17	19
Two-year technical college	10	8	13	7	10	8
High school	23	12	7	15	8	5
Elementary school	2	-	-	1	-	-
No response	0	7	6	0	7	7

provided specific choices, more students were willing to cite more outstanding accomplishments in more areas than in previous years. This may represent an artifact of the form rather than a substantial shift in increased student self-esteem.

Family Background

A recurring theme throughout the literature on talent development is that of the nurturing family system (Albert, 1980; Bloom, 1985; Clark, 1984). Clearly, the MTS students substantiated the important role of the family in their responses over the 3-year reporting period. As shown in the following list, although the number of intact families in the group declined slightly, overall the percentage was significantly higher than in the general population (National Opinion Research Center, 1980).

	1982	1983	1984
Both parents	95%	91%	85%
Just father	1%	1%	3%
Just mother	4%	8%	12%

In addition, the educational level for both parents of MTS students has remained consistently high, and the number of other children living in the household relatively low. As shown in Table 3.3, over 30% of the fathers from year to year reported having attained either a doctorate or an advanced professional degree in medicine or law. Over half of the fathers attained at least the level of a master's degree, as did a third of the mothers. Averaging across years, 77% of the fathers and 71% of the mothers had at least a 4-year college degree.

As shown in Table 3.4, the average number of children for MTS families was 2.6 and over half of the participants in the sample were the oldest child in the family structure. Averaging across the 3 years, about 7% were only children, 25% the youngest child, and 14% the middle child. The birth-order findings were consistent with the early literature (Hollingworth, 1942; Terman, 1925), which found the gifted child to be typically the oldest child in the family.

Academic Development

Regarding early academic development, the data on these MTS students were consistent across the years. On the average, 72% of these students were reading prior to formal school instruction at age 6, and 56% were doing basic mathematical operations prior to age 6. It is important to note, however, that the higher-scoring 1982 group reported higher percentages for early reading tasks than did subsequent groups. While 82% of 1982 students were early readers, only 67% of the 1983 and 1984 groups were. In early math mastery, however, the reverse was true. Over twice as many students from 1983 and 1984 (69%) exhibited this advanced behavior, when compared to the 1982 sample (31%).

In the area of special programming, 80% of the MTS students received special provisions, while 20% received no extra educational opportunities in school. Averaging across the 3-year sample, the students' advanced behavior

Table 3.4   Family Size and Birth Order for MTS Students, 1982–1984

Birth order and	% of Students Selecting Item		
number of children	1982	1983	1984
Oldest child	53	54	51
Only child (0)	5	7	9
Middle child	15	18	10
Youngest child	26	20	29
Twin	2	1	1
Average number of children per MTS family	2.7	2.5	2.6

was evident in the home for 78% of each year's group, but only 17% of families took advantage of grade acceleration as an intervention in school.

Additional 1984 Questionnaire Results

In 1984, ethnic data were also collected on each student. The breakdown by percentages for families in this category is as follows: white, 69; Asian, 24; black, 4; Hispanic, 1; and not reporting, 2. There was an overrepresentation of Asian students and an underrepresentation of other ethnic groups in this sample, based on percentages found in the overall population (National Opinion Research Center, 1980).

The 1984 questionnaire also collected new data on MTS student attitudes toward school. The majority of these students experienced school as a favorable learning environment that was interesting and challenging to some extent. Approximately 20% of the students disliked school and found it boring; 39% found it easy.

Data were also collected to assess family income levels. Of the 249 families who reported family income, 191 (76.7%) reported income above the $28,000 mean income reported for all families nationally (Bureau of Labor Statistics, 1983). Of those, 102 families (41%) reported income in excess of $70,000. Forty-nine families (20%) reported income below $20,000, a level which may be labeled economically disadvantaged.

By comparing the income levels of mothers and fathers within families, we see striking differences. Only 9 of the mothers (4%) earned over $50,000, while 99 (40%) of the fathers did. A total of 144 (58%) of the mothers earned below $10,000 per year, indicating either only part-time employment or no work outside the home.

These income data are interesting when compared to findings in an incidence study on disadvantaged gifted talent search students in the Midwest (VanTassel-Baska & Chepko-Sade, 1985). In that study, 13.5% or 2,692 of the 20,000 students participating in the 1985 MTS (i.e., all students registered to take the SAT) came from families with incomes below $20,000. To find an even higher percentage attending a special summer program may indicate that needy students are not only being identified for talent search services but are actually receiving them, at least through summer experiences where scholarship opportunities have been established.

DISCUSSION

Different cohorts of high-scoring Midwest Talent Search students have demonstrated a remarkable stability with respect to their interests and aspiration levels. There has been little deviation of the cohort groups on any dimension for which data were collected. It would be reasonable to assume, therefore, that we are observing a consistency based on traits of the academically talented, well documented in the early literature of the field (Hollingworth, 1942; Terman, 1925). Interests in reading, collections, music, and so forth were all clearly delineated as interests of the intellectually gifted 65 years ago; only the technology of computers has been added to the interest list for the 1980s. The rich diversity of the interest patterns also echoes these earlier studies.

The clear preference cited for mathematics as a favorite school subject and science as the second choice in all 3 years should have implications for in-school programs for the gifted, particularly for the content areas educators may choose for programming. Currently, language arts–oriented programs abound, but few school science programs for the gifted are in existence, especially at the elementary level. Mathematics is typically handled by mild acceleration of content, amounting to Algebra I by eighth grade. More systematic programming efforts in these areas would build on the strong interest pattern discerned in this study.

What can account for the high aspiration level of these students in respect to advanced schooling? The data seem to suggest at least three reasons:

1. These students have succeeded well in schools, have tested well, and have had advanced opportunities. Such success with academic work reinforces the desire to continue that success at a higher level.
2. These students believe they have talent in some area. Perceived self-competence at a level they themselves would label "talent" breeds a sense of confidence to aspire to the highest levels.
3. These students generally come from families with strong educational backgrounds and interests. There is a high value placed on education in the home and on the need for opportunity to learn.

These three hypotheses are, of course, mutually reinforcing and help to create a climate in which aspirations can be realized.

As indicated earlier, the families of MTS students exhibited characteristics that have been found to be supportive of talent development. They were intact, well educated, and generally small in size. Parents were aware of their children's development over the years and, particularly in the case of mothers, were able to clearly delineate age markers for certain types of advanced behavior such as reading and mathematical manipulations.

These students were advanced in reading and mathematics prior to any formal educational efforts on their behalf. The majority were reading at least

2 years early and doing mathematics at similar early stages. While most had had special program experiences, only a small percentage had been accelerated in school, a finding that is understandable, given the prevailing social opinion on the issue of acceleration, but mildly disappointing, given the educational level of these parents and the solid research base for such intervention (Kulik & Kulik, 1984).

It seems clear that educators have largely believed that high-level talent, academic or otherwise, tends to emerge from families of economic means. This is not because economic means alone account for a facilitative and nurturing family background, but rather because such means allow for educational access to opportunities beyond the sphere of public education and over time represent an accruement of educational advantage. While this fledgling effort to examine the income level of talent search families provides limited evidence to counter prevailing studies (Bloom, 1985; Jencks, 1972), particularly since the clear majority of high-scoring talent search students come from families of economic means, it does raise the issue of the need for special support mechanisms in schools for economically disadvantaged students. This group represents a sizable minority worthy of educators' attention and concern.

IMPLICATIONS AND CONCLUSIONS

These talent search families exhibit a strong sense of self-reliance and assertiveness. In order to become involved with the project, families must pay fees, spend time completing forms, and subject their child to a 3-hour test on a Saturday. A family that supports such an enterprise must be well organized, goal directed, and willing to act, sometimes based on limited information. Furthermore, for those students who attend the summer program, even more family sacrifice is necessary in terms of money and commitment.

While the family pattern that emerges from these data is encouraging with respect to nurturing talent, the available schooling programs are less so. Almost half of the parents in 1983 reported that they felt the school programs were inadequate, and almost 40% of the 1984 student respondents found school to be "easy." For the majority of students from the 1982 sample, no special programs were available until junior high school.

While the talent search students in this study represent a small percentage of students in any given school setting, educators nevertheless need to address some of the issues implicit in the data regarding school-based program opportunities and services. The following questions may be useful in framing these issues:

1. What should be the core program in reading and mathematics for students coming to school at age 5 with mastery of basic skills in those academic areas?
2. How might the practice of acceleration become commonplace for groups of academically talented learners at various levels of development?
3. What should be the identification process used to find academic talent early?
4. What criteria should be used to judge the adequacy and appropriateness of school programs for the gifted?
5. What assurances are there in school policy that academically promising students from family patterns different from the majority in the MTS sample will receive the attention and encouragement they need to meet with school success?

Until school personnel are willing to tackle these questions, there is little reason to believe that research findings will change to any great extent regarding what happens to talented students in the schools of this century.

REFERENCES

Albert, R. (1980). Family positions and the attachment of eminence: A study of special family positions and special family experiences. *Gifted Child Quarterly,* *24*(2), 87–95.

Benbow, C., & Stanley, J. (1983). *Academic precocity.* Baltimore, MD: Johns Hopkins University Press.

Berliner, D. (1986). Catastrophes and interactions: Comments on "the mistaken metaphor." In C. J. Maker (Ed.), *Defensible programs for the gifted: Critical issues in gifted education* (Vol. 1, pp. 31–38). Rockville, MD: Aspen Press.

Bloom, B. (Ed.). (1985). *Developing talent in young people.* New York: Ballantine Books.

Bureau of Labor Statistics. (1984). *Detailed population characteristics: U.S. summary based on the 1980 census.* Washington, DC: U.S. Department of Commerce, Bureau of the Census.

Clark, R. (1984). *Family life and school achievement: Why poor black children succeed or fail.* Chicago: University of Chicago Press.

Feldman, D. (1986). *Nature's gambit.* New York: Basic Books.

Getzels, J., & Csikszentmihalyi, M. (1976). *The creative vision: A longitudinal study of problem-finding in art.* New York: John Wiley.

Hollingworth, L. (1942). *Children with IQ's above 180.* New York: World Book.

Jencks, C. (1972). *Inequality.* New York: Basic Books.

Krutetskii, V. (1976). *The psychology of mathematical abilities in school children*. Chicago: University of Chicago Press.

Kulik, J., & Kulik, C. (1984). Effects of accelerated instruction on students. *Review of Educational Research, 54*(3), 409–425.

National Opinion Research Center. (1980). Chicago, IL.

Sternberg, R. (1985). *Beyond IQ*. Cambridge: Oxford University Press.

Terman, L. (1925). *Genetic studies of genius* (Vol. 1). Stanford, CA: Stanford University Press.

VanTassel-Baska, J. (1983). Profiles of precocity. *Gifted Child Quarterly, 27*(3), 139–144.

VanTassel-Baska, J., & Chepko-Sade, D. (1985). *An incidence study of disadvantaged and gifted learners in the Midwest*. Unpublished research report.

CHAPTER 4

The Influence of Family Values and Climate on the Development of Talent

Marilynn J. Kulieke and Paula Olszewski-Kubilius

The family has been cited as a critical component in the translation of talent, ability, and promise into achievement for gifted individuals. The family provides the context for the transmission or enculturation of general values. This often occurs indirectly by parental actions or modeling of certain behaviors, or directly by verbal espousal of particular values. These values can include the importance of achievement, success, and hard work; or of being involved in activities; or of being independent and self-sufficient. Parents may also act directly in the talent development process by selecting certain activities for their children; monitoring, organizing, and prioritizing children's time; or setting, communicating, and reinforcing standards for performance.

In addition, parents can create a general climate within the home that varies on dimensions such as child-centeredness, family cohesion, openness of expression, and emphasis on control, rules, structure, and organization within the family. Family interaction patterns and the focus of family resources on the talent development process are other dimensions that will vary in families.

These indirect and direct aspects of the family culture are constructs that can be used to describe families in general, but they may also differentiate families of gifted individuals from others. In this chapter, our review of previous research on the families of the gifted offers some insights regarding the value of each of these constructs. We will also present our own, more detailed contemporary study of the families of gifted and talented students.

REVIEW OF RESEARCH ON FAMILY CHARACTERISTICS

Values Espoused by Parents

An important characteristic of families of gifted individuals is the values espoused by parents, particularly surrounding achievement and success. Bloom (1985) found that the parents of his talented athletes, musicians, and artists emphasized to their children doing one's best, being successful, winning, striving for excellence, and developing task persistence. Getzels and Jackson's (1962) work revealed that parents of high-IQ children emphasized academics and placed more pressure on their children to achieve scholastically, compared to the parents of highly creative children. Sheldon (1954) reported that the parents of intellectually gifted children (IQs > 170) emphasized academic achievement, and this was also espoused by the grandmothers, who stressed and encouraged the accruement of academic awards and honors among their gifted grandchildren. This cross-generational communication of values has also been noted by Albert (1971, 1978). Mac-Kinnon's (1965) work indicated that creative architects recalled that their parents espoused the value of cultural and intellectual endeavors, success, ambition, diligence, the development of talent, and joy in work. Kahl's (1953) research suggests that boys who come from "common man" backgrounds and who achieve in school adopt their parents' view of the work world and particularly their father's espousal of education as the key to success and getting ahead, compared to boys who do not achieve scholastically. Thus families of high achievers directly espouse the value of academic success and produce children who enact that value.

Bloom's (1985) research suggests that other values such as using free time actively and productively or encouraging sports and other recreational pursuits are also espoused by parents to offspring.

Values Enacted by Parents

Families can verbally espouse certain values or emphases, but some of the research literature has spoken to how parents actively and directly enact those values for their children. For example, Getzels and Jackson (1962) noted that parents who emphasized scholastic achievement for their high-IQ children were more vigilant about checking their children's homework. Similarly, McGillivray (1964) reported that parents of high-IQ, high-achieving seventh graders provided desks for children to study at, set standards for grades, and were more knowledgeable about education, compared to parents of high-IQ nonachievers. MacKinnon's (1965) families of creative architects provided rich cultural experiences for their children and modeled early an emphasis on drawing by participating in this activity themselves and by providing materials for their children and encouraging their artistic endeavors.

Bloom (1985) found that his parents similarly checked children's homework and monitored practice time. They sat in on piano lessons and swimming meets. In addition, they often provided the initial introduction of the child to the talent field, participated in it themselves, and provided early instruction for the child in the area. Albert (1980) also found that parents of eminent individuals such as statemen and politicians steered their children into their own talent fields and provided the child's first "taste" of it.

Thus, parents of gifted individuals not only espouse the value of certain activities, fields, or achievements, but they model attitudes and behaviors that foster achievement, direct the interests and activities of their child to these areas, model participation and achievement within the talent areas, and monitor and structure their children's time and participation.

General Family Climate or Environment

Another way in which families influence the talent development process has to do with the general climate of the home. The home environment includes the attitudes of parents toward children, relationships among family members, parental philosophies about child rearing and parenting, and the way that family life is structured and ordered.

There is little research that looks specifically at parenting style for gifted individuals, but it does offer some ideas about important parental behaviors that are conducive to talent development. Nichols (1964) assessed the parenting styles of mothers of National Merit Scholarship finalists and found that the children of authoritarian mothers obtained better grades in school and more favorable ratings by teachers. An authoritarian parenting style was also associated with greater conformity in thought and expression by children and a lack of originality. Similarly, other researchers have found that creativity in children is associated with less conventional parenting styles (Getzels & Jackson, 1962), parental expressiveness of affection toward the child, and avoidance of parental dominance (Weisberg & Springer, 1961). Parents of creative children expected less conformity to parental values (Weisberg & Springer, 1961), and parents of creative architects allowed their children more freedom and were extraordinarily respectful of them. (MacKinnon, 1965).

The relationships among the family members of gifted individuals have received some attention in the research literature. Several studies document family relationships for creative individuals that were tense and "less than harmonious." Albert (1978) suggested that creative individuals came from homes with "wobble" among family members and that these families were capable of living together with more tension among members. Roe (1953) cited that, among her groups of eminent scientists, social scientists' family relationships were described as tense, particularly those between the gifted individual and his or her parents. MacKinnon (1965) similarly reported that his creative architects came from homes where there was a lack of closeness between members, including the child's relationship with both parents. Weisberg and Springer (1961) found that the families of creative fourth graders did not feel that members depended upon one another for emotional support.

Some research has looked specifically at the relationship between gifted individuals and their mothers. Helson and Crutchfield (1970) found that creative mathematicians perceived that they received unusual warmth and affection from their mothers. The researchers hypothesized that the mathematicians were probably more open to the "feminine" side of their personalities as a result of the closeness. In the Berkeley Growth Study, Brooks (1973) found that men who as boys had artistic interests described their mothers as distant, tense, worrisome, and somewhat rejecting of them during childhood. Albert (1978) suggested that creative individuals often came from families where there was an imbalance in the relationship between their parents, especially where the mother had the dominant personality and was particularly focused on the gifted child. Bloom's (1985) study of gifted musicians, athletes, scholars, and artists indicated unusually closely knit, cohesive families and very close relationships between gifted individuals and their parents, particularly the mothers who were often most closely involved in getting the children to their lessons.

Thus, the research literature indicates that family relationships for creatively gifted individuals are often strained, tense, and imbalanced. Explanations offered for the facilitating effect of these environments on creative achievement and expression are similar to those offered for the influence of parental loss. Children are freer of affectionate ties to family members, which in turn lessens identification with parents and parental values and allows the individual greater freedom for personal expression and development. On the other hand, the literature also suggests that an unusually close parent/child relationship, particularly between mother and son, is also conducive to the development of talent. Albert (1978) suggests that the homes of creative individuals are characterized by a climate that is "tense but secure." On the other hand, it is doubtful that a very conflictual home environment would be conducive to creative achievement, though there is little research on this with regard to gifted children. Such homes may be very detrimental to academic achievement in particular, with interpersonal conflicts siphoning energy away from intellectual pursuits and studying.

With the literature on the gifted, there is some evidence that parents of creative individuals demand less conformity to parental values (Colangelo & Dettmann, 1983; MacKinnon 1965; Weisberg & Springer, 1961), whereas the parents of high-IQ children socialize more strongly for conformity to conventional values (presumably their own), particularly around achievement and success (Getzels & Jackson, 1962). Weisberg and Springer (1961) found evidence that parents of creative children emphasized the open expression of individual views and feelings among family members, and MacKinnon's (1965) sample of creative architects came from homes where parents emphasized the development of a personal code of ethics and values rather than the adoption of the parent's values. This emphasis on developing a personal code is consistent with a loosely knit family environment or one where identification with parents has been disrupted or is not strong.

Other characteristics of the families of gifted individuals are an encouragement of curiosity and active exploration by the child (Roe, 1953; Walberg et al., 1981). Walberg et al. found that 82% of the biographies of a sample of eminent individuals indicated that their families encouraged exploration of the environment and supported their curiosity.

The research evidence around the child-centeredness of the homes of gifted individuals is equivocal. Bloom's (1985) work indicated that the homes of his gifted sample were extremely child-centered. The gifted child's activities, lessons, and so forth were the organizer for family activities and family resources. VanTassel-Baska (1983) found that, even though the mothers of top scorers on the Scholastic Aptitude Test (SAT) were well educated, most were homemakers, focusing their time and energy on the lives and activities of their children. McGillivray (1964) found that the parents of gifted children exhibited high levels of involvement with them. Getzels and Jackson (1962) noted that the homes of high-IQ children tended to be more child-centered than the homes of highly creative children. Albert (1978) reported that the parents of creative individuals had their own interests, hobbies, and activities and focused less on the children as the center of family life.

Another aspect of the family environment studied by researchers is the emphasis on structure and routine in the home and the extent to which family functioning is governed by rules. MacKinnon's (1965) work with creative architects indicates that discipline was consistent and predictable within their homes and there were rules of conduct for children. Similarly, Walberg et al. (1981) found that families of eminent individuals had clear parental expectations for conduct. Brooks (1973) noted that, although artistic males came from homes with tense family relationships, they were also well ordered and organized. McGillivray (1964) found that the parents of intellectually gifted children emphasized routine responsibility for children in the home. Thus, despite the presence of disharmony among family members and tense parental relationships, these families also provided well-ordered, structured, and organized family environments. Parents also tended to provide direct organization and structure for children by choosing activities for them, planning their nonschool time (Sheldon, 1954) and prioritizing their activities (Bloom & Sosniak, 1981; McGillivray, 1964).

One area on which there is little direct evidence of family influence is parental acceptance of the child's behavior. Weisberg and Springer (1961) reported that parents of creative children were more accepting of their child's behavior, particularly regressive behavior. On the other hand, children who were academic achievers were found, at least in one study (Getzels & Jackson, 1962), to have parents who were less accepting and more critical of their children's behavior, compared to parents of creative children.

In the remainder of this chapter we will report on our study of high-achieving adolescents and their families. We will examine the relationships between family characteristics—family values espoused, family values enacted, and family climate—and student aptitude, achievement, and self-concept.

METHODOLOGY FOR STUDY OF GIFTED ADOLESCENTS AND THEIR FAMILIES

Design

The 1985 and 1986 summer programs for academically able students at Northwestern University provided the subjects for the study we undertook. Participants included the students themselves and their families. There were 193 families involved, 63 from the 1985 program and 130 from the 1986 program. The students had either a score of 430 or greater on the Scholastic Aptitude Test verbal subtest (SAT-V) or a score of 500 or greater on the Scholastic Aptitude Test mathematics subtest (SAT-M). The majority of the students came from an eight-state region in the Midwest.

Ninety-nine of the families had male students, while 90 were the families of females (in 4 cases sex was not reported). The students' grade levels ranged from 6 to 12, although the majority of students were in grades 7 through 10. The sample was 69% Caucasian, 23% Oriental, 4% black, and 4% other. These families were predominantly middle to upper income; 64% had household incomes of over $50,000 per year.

During the summer program, students completed the Self-Perception Profile for Children developed by Harter (1985) and the Family Environment Scale developed by Moos and Moos (1981). These were administered by their instructors. Six months after the summer program ended, parents were sent and asked to complete two questionnaires: the Family Environment Scale and the Family as Educator Questionnaire, the latter developed at North-western University (Olszewski, Kulieke, Willis, & Krasney, 1985). Approx-imately 63% of the 1985 parents and 30% of the 1986 parents returned the surveys.

The Family Environment Scale was developed by Moos and Moos (1981) as a measure of the social-environmental characteristics of families. There are 10 subscales which assess three underlying domains or sets of di-mensions—relationship dimensions, personal growth dimensions, and sys-tem maintenance dimensions. We have recategorized the subscales into the three types of family variables that were being studied—family values es-poused, family values enacted, and family climate. The achievement subscale fit into the "family values espoused" category. The intellectual, cultural, and active/recreational subscales fit into the "family values enacted" category. Fi-nally, the expressiveness, conflict, control, organization, cohesion, and in-dependence subscales fit into the "family climate" category. The results reported are those from the parents' forms. Reliability estimates for the sub-scales ranged from .61 to .78.

The Family as Educator Questionnaire is a 47-item, seven-page ques-tionnaire that was developed to assess the family's contribution to the talent development process. The constructs assessed in this survey were as follows: stress or emphasis on achievement; education and intellectual activities in the family; parents' own participation in and pursuit of intellectual activities; child-centeredness of the home; and parental involvement with the child's talent area and in the child's education. Several subscales were developed from these items, and each was assigned to one of the three categories that were studied. Under the "family values espoused" category were scales on parents' verbalized expectations for child's achievement, parents' verbal em-phasis on succeeding, expressed importance of academic activities, and ex-pressed importance of nonacademic activities. The "family values enacted" category consisted of subscales related to the family's playing academic games and participating in cultural activities, and the parents' modeling aca-demic and nonacademic activities. The "family climate" subscales were re-lated to openness around intellectual expression; parental monitoring and discipline; consistency, order, structure, and organization; and the priority given to the child's activities in the household.

There were three categories of outcome measure used in this study—aptitude, achievement, and self-concept. The SAT, which is typically taken by college-bound high school juniors and seniors, was used as the measure of aptitude. The second outcome measure, achievement, was measured using the gain between the pretest and posttest on the standardized achievement tests used in the classes (College Board Achievement Tests in biology, chem-istry, Latin, literature, and writing; the Cooperative Algebra Test in mathematics). Finally, self-concept was measured using three of the six self-concept subscales developed by Harter (1985), namely, social acceptance, academic self-concept, and global self-worth.

The analytic strategy used for this study was a correlational approach. Pearson product-moment coefficients were computed between each of the family environment variables and the student aptitude, achievement, and self-concept outcomes.

Questions

This study addressed two questions. First, we investigated whether the three major categories—family values espoused, family values enacted, and family climate—were related to the aptitude, achievement, and self-concept of academically talented adolescents. Second, we investigated whether there were different relationships between these variables for males and females.

FINDINGS ON THE RELATIONSHIP BETWEEN FAMILY CHARACTERISTICS AND STUDENT OUTCOMES

As a first step toward assessing the relationship between family charac-teristics and student outcomes, we computed the percentage of statistically significant relationships between family environment variables and aptitude, achievement, and self-concept. Although this analysis is problematic due to spurious correlations, it will give an estimate of the extent to which these two sets of variables are related to each other. The results of these computations are shown in Table 4.1.

When the entire table is examined, it appears that the greatest percent-age of correlations is found between self-concept and family values enacted. The next highest percentage appears in the correlation between all outcomes combined and, again, family values enacted. The third highest percentage (13% for both males and females) appears where aptitude and achievement measures intersect with family values espoused. There are some noteworthy sex differences. Aptitude and achievement measures are more frequently re-lated to family values enacted for females compared to males. Family climate, however, is more frequently related to self-concept for males than for fe-males. As can be seen in Table 4.1, there are virtually no differences in the percentage of significant relationships for males and females when totaled across all family environment variables and all outcome measures. Overall, these figures show that family values enacted is the category having the great-est percentage of relationships to outcome variables.

Table 4.1   Percentage of Significant Relationships Between Family
Environment Variables and Measures of Aptitude, Achievement, and
Self-Concept, by Sex[1]

Family Variables	All Outcome Measures		Aptitude and Achievement Measures[2]		Self-Concept Measures[3]	
	Males	Females	Males	Females	Males	Females
All Variables	11	11	7	12	7	9
Family Climate	9	6	7	9	12	3
Values Enacted	16	20	3	16	33	25
Values Espoused	7	7	13	13	0	0

[1]The percentage is based on the number of Pearson Product Moment Correlation Coefficients
that are significant at $p < .05$, over the number possible.
[2]Three aptitude (SAT-total, SAT-M and SAT-V) and one achievement (change in score from
pretest to posttest) variables were studied.
[3]Three self-concept variables were studied; global self-worth, academic competence, and
social acceptance.

Family Values Espoused

Family values espoused are expectations and beliefs that we theorize are
related to academic achievement. Parents' emphasis on academic achievement, their expectations for their children's further education, the amount
of emphasis they place on success and competition, and their feelings about
the importance of academic and nonacademic activities are all variables that
were studied. These variables were grouped into two categories, parents'
stress on academic achievement and education, and the importance of activities for the family.

Stress on Achievement and Education. Table 4.2 shows the correlation between student outcome variables and parents' stress on academic
achievement and education. It can be seen from this table that there are many
more significant relationships between parental values and student achievement outcomes than there are for the other outcome variables. Parental emphasis on academic achievement was associated with higher achievement for
females in the summer program. Higher expectations regarding the child's
eventual level of education and a stress on competition were both associated
consistently with lower achievement for all students in the summer program,
and the latter had a particularly negative impact on males. This suggests that

there needs to be a balance between expectations for achievement and emphasis on winning.

Regarding all the aptitude outcomes, there were few significant relationships obtained. Academic career expectations and competition were positively related to SAT-M for males.

Parents' expectations for a child and that child's aptitude and achievement may well be intertwined. Although correlational analysis does not suggest causality, it is clear that a child's ability and achievement will impact parental expectations, and vice-versa. Males and females generally show the same patterns and directions of relationships, although some are significant and some are not. It appears that parents' expectations for their children's

Table 4.2 Correlations Between Student Outcomes and Parents' Stress on Academic Achievement and Education

Parents' Values Espoused	Aptitude			Achievement[1]	Self-Concept		
	SAT-total	SAT-V	SAT-M		Global	Academic	Social Acceptance
Emphasis on academic achievement							
All parents	-.05	-.06	-.03	.23**	-.00	-.08	-.07
Parents of males	-.02	-.09	-.03	.14	-.03	-.04	-.10
Parents of females	-.05	-.04	-.03	.32**	-.00	-.13	-.06
Academic career expectations							
All parents	.09	-.01	.12*	-.15*	-.03	-.07	.08
Parents of males	.13	-.02	.17*	-.09	-.03	-.07	.13
Parents of females	.10	-.01	.16	-.21*	-.04	-.07	.05
Emphasis on succeeding							
All parents	-.00	.04	-.03	-.04	.08	-.03	-.09
Parents of males	-.10	.07	-.21	-.05	.12	-.12	-.05
Parents of females	-.07	.03	-.08	-.14	.04	-.14	-.21
Stress on competition							
All parents	-.06	-.11	.18*	-.29**	-.01	.07	-.04
Parents of males	-.19	-.03	.33**	-.50**	-.08	.05	-.04
Parents of females	-.05	-.17	.08	-.10	-.08	.07	-.13

[1] Change in score from pretest to posttest. The College Board Achievement Tests were used in biology, chemistry, Latin, writing and literature. The Cooperative Algebra Test series was used in mathematics.
* $p < .05$
** $p < .01$

Table 4.3 Correlations Between Student Outcomes and Importance of Activities to Parents

Parents' Values Espoused	Aptitude			Achievement[1]	Self-Concept		
	SAT-total	SAT-V	SAT-M		Global	Academic	Social Acceptance
Importance of academic activities							
All Parents	-.06	.06	-.05	-.11	-.02	.09	.10
Parents of males	-.01	.05	-.06	-.19	-.05	.03	.06
Parents of females	-.09	.08	-.07	-.03	-.10	.15	.13
Importance of Nonacademic activities							
All parents	.10	.07	.09	-.23*	-.01	.07	.13*
Parents of males	.05	.07	.01	-.19	-.02	.08	.14
Parents of females	.11	.05	.13	-.29**	-.03	.06	.14

[1] Change in score from pretest to posttest.
* $p < .05$
** $p < .01$

education are related to their children's ability. It is interesting to note that there are no significant relationships between a child's self-concept and any of the categories of parental stress on achievement and education.

Importance of Activities to the Parents. Table 4.3 shows the correlations between parents' feelings about the importance of activities and the student outcome variables. Achievement in the summer program shows the strongest relationship with these parental variables, but the only significant results were found in the nonacademic area. Stress on nonacademic activities is associated with lower levels of achievement in the summer program for females. The only other significant correlation obtained was between the importance of nonacademic activities and students' self-perceptions of social acceptance.

These findings concerning nonacademic activities confirm the results reported in the next section on parental modeling of nonacademic activities. It appears that an environment where nonacademic activities are valued is detrimental to a child's achievement but helpful to a child's feelings of acceptance by peers.

Family Values Enacted

Variables that were classified as "family values enacted" relate to the activities and actions occurring within a family, particularly those of parents.

The assumption regarding this cluster of variables is that they suggest or are indicative of underlying values and priorities. The family values enacted variables broadly consisted of two kinds: participation and involvement in activities with an academic orientation and participation and involvement in activities with a nonacademic orientation.

Academic Orientation of Family. Family academic orientation refers to the family's participation in cultural and intellectual activities (see Table 4.4). The first category, intellectual orientation, is weakly related to SAT-V for males and females combined. It is also negatively related to the males' social

Table 4.4 Correlations Between Student Outcomes and Academic Orientation of Family

Parents' Values Enacted	Aptitude			Achievement[1]	Self-Concept		
	SAT-total	SAT-V	SAT-M		Global	Academic	Social Acceptance
Family intellectual orientation							
All parents	-.07	.18*	-.04	.06	-.10	-.06	-.08
Parents of males	-.10	.17	-.02	.06	-.10	-.11	-.23*
Parents of females	-.04	.12	-.17	.04	-.05	-.21	-.17
Family plays academic games							
All parents	-.06	-.08	-.03	.23**	-.01	-.02	-.10
Parents of males	-.08	-.12	-.03	.10	-.00	-.14	-.08
Parents of females	-.04	-.06	-.01	.34**	-.04	-.09	-.13
Family participation in cultural activities							
All parents	-.08	-.08	-.06	.09	.06	-.04	.03
Parents of males	-.16	-.17	-.11	.07	.15	-.15	.11
Parents of females	-.04	-.07	-.00	.12	.01	-.01	.00
Parental modeling of academic reading							
All parents	-.01	.07	-.05	-.04	.08	.00	-.05
Parents of males	-.02	.04	-.06	-.05	.12	.01	-.24*
Parents of females	-.03	.09	-.03	-.12	.06	.00	-.11
Parental modeling of academic hobbies							
All parents	-.09	.13*	-.03	-.08	.13*	.11	-.05
Parents of males	-.02	.08	-.10	-.02	.21*	.08	-.20*
Parents of females	-.24*	.21*	-.20*	-.12	.03	.13	-.10

[1] Change in score from pretest to posttest.
* *p* < .05
** *p* < .01

acceptance, or the child's perceived ability to make and have friends. Family participation in academic games is related to achievement during the summer program for females only. There are no significant correlations between the third value, participation in cultural activities, and any of the student outcomes.

Parental modeling of academic activities, with regard to both reading and hobbies, is related to several outcome variables. For males, the parental modeling is positively related to social acceptance and global self-concept. For females, parental modeling of hobbies is associated with higher SAT scores.

In summary, our data suggest that the academic orientation of the home, as reflected in the actions of the parents, influences males and females differentially. It appears at first that modeling of academic pursuits positively relates to how male children feel about themselves and in relation to others. However, when the family provides an environment that offers male children many intellectually oriented activities, it appears that males may feel less connected socially to their peers, possibly because of less need to receive support from peers. This contrast suggests that there needs to be balance in terms of the overall intellectual environment of the family, such that it is supportive of intellectual pursuits but not so consuming that a male child may become isolated from others.

For females, the academic/intellectual environment of the home is generally related to aptitude and achievement, rather than self-concept. Our data suggest that providing an academically oriented environment for females is facilitative of their achievement strivings, as least as measured on standardized tests.

Nonacademic Orientation of the Family. Table 4.5 shows the relationships between nonacademic behaviors in the family and the outcomes of aptitude, achievement, and self-concept. An active climate in the home, which stresses participation in pursuits related to recreation and leisure, appears to be related positively to academic self-concept for males, and positively to feelings of social acceptance for males and females combined.

Parental modeling of nonacademic reading is positively related to global self-concept for males and negatively related for females. It also relates negatively to social acceptance for females.

There are several significant relationships between nonacademic hobbies and the outcome variables. For males, the greater the number of parents' nonacademic hobbies, the lower their SAT-M score. There is also a strong negative relationship between parents' nonacademic hobbies and females' achievement during the summer program. Males show positive relationships between parental participation in nonacademic hobbies and global self-

Table 4.5 Correlations Between Student Outcomes and Nonacademic Orientation of Family

Parents' Values Enacted	Aptitude			Achievement[1]	Self-Concept		
	SAT-total	SAT-V	SAT-M		Global	Academic	Social Acceptance
Active recreational orientation							
All parents	-.06	-.02	-.11	-.13	-.02	-.05	.19*
Parents of males	-.03	-.06	-.09	-.10	-.04	-.24*	.16
Parents of females	-.14	-.08	-.14	-.17	-.14	-.17	.25*
Parental modeling of nonacademic reading							
All parents	.05	.10	-.01	-.07	-.02	.06	-.08
Parents of males	.03	.04	-.01	-.01	-.23*	.13	-.07
Parents of females	.03	.13	-.07	-.16	-.20	.01	-.24*
Parental modeling of nonacademic hobbies							
All parents	-.04	.07	-.12*	-.17*	.17*	.08	.00
Parents of males	-.12	.01	-.19*	-.01	.30**	.01	.20*
Parents of females	.02	.11	-.07	-.34**	.03	.18*	-.20*

[1] Change in score from pretest to posttest.
* $p < .05$
** $p < .01$

concept and social acceptance. A positive relationship is shown between nonacademic hobbies and females' academic self-concepts, while a negative relationship is apparent between social acceptance and this parental factor.

It appears that the nonacademic orientation of the family is most related to students' feelings about themselves and how others accept them. While this is so for both males and females, there are also differences between them, in that the greater the nonacademic orientation for males, the better they feel about themselves. For females, on the other hand there is generally a negative relationship between nonacademic participation and feelings toward self. Nonacademic participation, as modeled by parents, may stimulate children to involve themselves similarly in such activities. This may provide intellectually talented males with other avenues for gaining acceptance with peers. Why this may not be the case for female children is unclear. It could be that intellectually oriented females experience conflict when parents participate in many nonacademic activities while they themselves are concentrating their efforts on schoolwork. There are many possible intervening variables, including the degree to which children are influenced by and model what their parents do.

The generally weak correlations between nonacademic orientation and achievement and aptitude outcomes suggest that a family environment that stresses nonacademic activities may not give a strong message to children that high levels of achievement are critical and important.

Family Climate

One aspect of family climate studied was family communication, which was defined in terms of openness of expression within the family with regard to feelings, intellectual exchanges, and conflict. The second aspect of family climate was comprised of family control, structure, and organization and included the following specific subcategories: emphasis on rules governing family functioning; emphasis on routines; support received from family members; encouragement of acting independently; parental monitoring and discipline; consistency, order, structure, and organization; priority of child's activities in the household; and child's ability to manage time.

Table 4.6 presents the correlations regarding family communication.

Table 4.6   Correlations Between Student Outcomes and Family Communication

Parents' Values Regarding Family Climate	Aptitude			Achievement[1]	Self-Concept		
	SAT-total	SAT-V	SAT-M		Global	Academic	Social Acceptance
Openness of expression of feelings in family							
All parents	-.04	-.01	-.05	.12	-.04	.09	-.00
Parents of males	-.03	-.00	-.05	.15	-.12	.18	-.06
Parents of females	-.07	-.06	-.05	.09	-.03	.01	-.06
Openness of intellectual expression							
All parents	.09	.06	.09	-.21**	.11	.08	.20**
Parents of males	.08	.08	.07	-.14	.16	.10	.20*
Parents of females	.06	.03	.06	-.29**	.06	.08	.19*
Openness of expression of conflict and disagreement							
All parents	-.10	-.18*	-.01	-.24*	-.09	.07	-.09
Parents of males	-.20	-.27*	-.10	-.19	-.18	.07	-.23*
Parents of females	-.00	-.08	-.06	-.30*	-.04	.07	-.12

[1] Change in score from pretest to posttest.
* $p < .05$
** $p < .01$

Family Communication. Open expression of conflict and disagreement between family members is negatively related to SAT-V for males and to achievement for females (with the males following the same trend). It is positively related to males' social acceptance. Openness of intellectual expression also negatively relates to achievement for females (with the same pattern holding for males) and is positively related to social acceptance for both males and females. Expression of feelings showed no significant correlations with outcomes.

Thus, there appear to be two outcome variables that are influenced most strongly by family communication; child's achievement in the summer program (negatively) and the child's social acceptance (positively). These findings might be explained in several ways. The research on the family characteristics of the gifted has suggested that the development of creativity is associated with a family environment where there is "wobble" and a more frenetic climate that emphasizes the development of a personal code and individual opinion. Children who are creative may be less oriented toward traditional school achievement and accruement of academic awards. It may be that a segment of the summer program participants have high aptitude but are less concerned with traditional achievement markers. The positive relationship between openness of expression and social acceptance suggests that children from such families may be more extroverted, more peer oriented, or better able to communicate and socialize with peers.

Family Control, Structure, and Organization. Table 4.7 shows the correlations between student outcomes and family control, structure, and organization. It appears from this table that a greater emphasis on rules governing family functioning is associated with lower aptitude (SAT-V and SAT-total). However, a family climate that promotes independent functioning and places priority on the child's activities is positively related to SAT scores.

Parents' emphasis on consistency, order, structure, and organization in the home appears to relate negatively to achievement for females, as does child-centeredness (priority on child). For both males and females, the ability to manage time well is associated with higher achievement in the summer program.

An emphasis on independent functioning is related negatively to social acceptance for males, while parental monitoring and discipline are positively related. High priority on the child's activities shows positive relationships with global self-concept and social acceptance for males and females combined.

This series of variables centering on family control, structure, and organization shows many interesting relationships. It appears that families who do not emphasize rules, do encourage children to act independently, and do

Table 4.7 Correlations Between Student Outcomes and Family Control, Structure, and Organization

Parents' Values Regarding Family Climate	Aptitude			Achievement[1]	Self-Concept		
	SAT-total	SAT-V	SAT-M		Global	Academic	Social Acceptance
Emphasis on rules governing family functioning							
All parents	-.18*	-.19*	-.13	-.17	-.04	-.06	.11
Parents of males	-.21*	-.20	-.18	-.21	-.15	-.05	.08
Parents of females	-.18	-.13	-.17	-.15	-.13	-.20	.10
Emphasis on routines							
All parents	-.03	-.01	-.06	-.04	-.08	-.05	.03
Parents of males	-.13	-.08	-.14	-.04	-.08	-.17	.01
Parents of females	-.13	-.11	-.11	-.14	-.12	-.08	.02
Support received from family members							
All parents	.05	.11	-.01	.02	-.04	-.01	-.13
Parents of males	.07	.10	-.03	.00	-.03	-.03	-.15
Parents of females	.00	.08	-.07	.03	-.00	-.03	-.06
Encouragement of acting independently							
All parents	.17*	.16*	.14	-.05	-.05	-.00	-.16
Parents of males	.12	.15	.07	-.17	-.10	-.09	-.31**
Parents of females	.18	.14	.17	-.08	-.03	-.13	-.00
Parental Monitoring and Discipline							
All parents	-.03	-.02	-.06	-.04	-.08	-.02	.10
Parents of males	-.11	-.01	-.16	-.04	-.06	-.02	.20*
Parents of females	-.06	-.06	-.03	-.05	-.10	-.06	.00
Consistency, order, structure, and organization							
All parents	.09	.06	.09	-.16*	-.03	.11	-.05
Parents of males	.07	.03	.08	-.00	-.02	.07	-.18
Parents of females	.05	.06	.04	-.27*	-.02	.14	-.03
Priority of child's activities in household							
All parents	.12	.06	.13*	-.20**	.13*	.09	.15*
Parents of males	.14	.11	.13	-.13	.14*	.07	.12
Parents of females	.08	.03	.09	-.29**	.13	.15	.17
Child's ability to manage time							
All parents	-.01	-.06	-.05	.24**	-.05	.01	-.10
Parents of males	-.09	-.13	-.04	.21*	-.01	.01	-.15
Parents of females	-.06	-.02	-.08	.26*	-.09	.01	-.06

[1] Change in score from pretest to posttest.

* $p < .05$

** $p < .01$

make a child's activities a priority tend to have children with higher aptitude measures. It may be that parents who know that their children are bright create a family environment in which they allow the child to have more responsibility. It may also be that children who are more internally oriented and self-disciplined have higher aptitude scores, since they feel that they can better control their environment and their learning. The results with regard to social acceptance for males are also important. The negative impact of encouraging male independence and the positive impact of monitoring and great child-centeredness suggest that there may be some positive social effects of a tightly organized family environment.

SUMMARY

The research literature on the families of gifted children, reviewed in this chapter, yields several conclusions:

1. While there is little direct work on the values espoused by gifted or creative individuals, their parents tend to espouse values related to the importance of academic achievement, working hard, success, and being active and persistent.
2. Parents not only espouse such values but act directly to inculcate them by directing their children along certain paths and into particular domains and disciplines and by modeling behaviors conducive to talent development.
3. Family climate variables such as quality of relationships between family members, cohesiveness, parental acceptance of the child, and stress on conformity to parental values are very interesting because they differentiate among families who produce creative individuals and those who produce high-achieving, scholastically competent individuals.

Our study of academically talented youth at Northwestern University yields the following findings about the talent development process:

1. It appears that the greatest number of relationships are found between family values enacted and self-concept for both males and females. In contrast, espoused values showed little relationship to students' self-perceptions in this study. Family values enacted also showed several relationships with aptitude and achievement measures.
2. When the outcome variables (aptitude, achievement, and self-concept) are examined, it is apparent that both achievement and self-

concept (especially social acceptance) are related to many different family environment variables, while aptitude as measured in this study had few relationships to family variables. Females show the greatest number of relationships for achievement, and males show the greatest number for social acceptance.

It is apparent from the set of findings yielded by this particular study and the literature reviewed that the role family values and climate play in the development of abilities and skills is complex. Even though one element in the family is related positively to an element in the talent development process, that same element may be related negatively to another outcome. In our data this is particularly noticeable where those variables that relate positively to ability and achievement may relate negatively to self-concept, and vice versa. Although these data do not show causality, they do suggest that family values and climate variables may work in different ways to emphasize personal, social, and/or intellectual orientations for talented students. This suggests the need for balance among the different family influences, with the activities that the family actually encourages and engages in being most related to outcome variables.

The study reported in this chapter is based on a particular type of gifted student, the academically talented student. They are extremely talented, given their high scores on the SAT. This research both supports and contradicts some of the work done by others in the field. It also adds some additional information about three different aspects of talent development, namely, aptitude, achievement, and self-concept. This work needs to be replicated with different samples, exploring in more depth some of the variables that might be influencing the talent development process.

REFERENCES

Albert, R. S. (1971). Cognitive development and parental loss among the gifted. *Psychological Reports, 29*, 19–26.

Albert, R. S. (1978). Observations and suggestions regarding giftedness, familial influence and the achievement of eminence. *Gifted Child Quarterly, 28*(3), 201–211.

Albert, R. S. (1980). Family positions and the attainment of eminence: A study of special family positions and special family experiences. *Gifted Child Quarterly, 24*(2), 87–95.

Bloom, B. S. (Ed.). (1985). *Developing talent in young people*. New York: Ballantine.

Bloom, B. S., & Sosniak, L. A. (1981, November). Talent development. *Educational Leadership*, 86–94.

Brooks, J. B. (1973). Familial antecedents and adult correlates of artistic interests in childhood. *Journal of Personality, 41*, 110–120.

Colangelo, N., & Dettmann, D. F. (1983). A review of research on parents and families of gifted children. *Exceptional Children, 50*(1), 20–27.

Getzels, J. W., & Jackson, P. W. (1962). *Creativity and intelligence.* New York: John Wiley.

Goertzel, M., & Goertzel, V. (1962). *Cradles of eminence.* Boston: Little, Brown.

Harter, S. (1985). *Manual for the self-perception profile for children.* Denver, CO: University of Denver.

Helson, R., & Crutchfield, R. S. (1970). Mathematicians: The creative research and the average Ph.D. *Journal of Consulting and Clinical Psychology, 34,* 250–257.

Kahl, J. A. (1953). Educational and occupational aspirations of "common man boys." *Harvard Educational Review, 23*(3), 186–203.

MacKinnon, D. W. (1965). Personality and the realization of creative potential. *American Psychologist, 20,* 273–281.

McGillivray, R. H. (1964). Differences in home background between high-achieving and low-achieving gifted children: A study of 100 grade eight pupils in the City of Toronto public schools. *Ontario Journal of Educational Research, 6*(2), 99–106.

Moos, R. H., & Moos, B. S. (1981). *Family environment scale.* Palo Alto, CA: Consulting Psychologist Press.

Nichols, R. C. (1964). Parental attitudes of mothers of intelligent adolescents and the creativity of their children. *Child Development, 35,* 1041–1049.

Olszewski, P., Kulieke, M. J., Willis, G. B., & Krasney, N. (1985). *The family as educator questionnaire.* Evanston, IL: Center for Talent Development, Northwestern University.

Roe, A. (1953). *The making of a scientist.* New York: Dodd, Mead.

Sheldon, P. M. (1954, February). The families of highly gifted children. *Marriage and Family Living,* pp. 59–67.

VanTassel-Baska, J. (1983, Summer). Profiles in precocity: The 1982 Midwest Talent Search finalists. *Gifted Child Quarterly, 27*(3), 139–144.

Walberg, H. J., Tsai, T., Weinstein, T., Gabriel, C. L., Rasher, S. P., Rosecrans, T., Rovai, E., Ide, J., Trujillo, M., & Vukosavich, P. (1981). Childhood traits and environmental conditions of highly eminent adults. *Gifted Child Quarterly, 25*(3), 103–107.

Weisberg, P. S., & Springer, K. J. (1961, December). Environmental factors in creative function: A study of gifted children. *Archives of General Psychiatry, 5,* 64–74.

CHAPTER 5

The Role of the Family in the Success of Disadvantaged Gifted Learners

Joyce L. VanTassel-Baska

There is a common belief that most academically talented learners come from a middle to high socioeconomic background that reinforces natural ability by creating access to important educational opportunities. Studies have focused on the importance of the home in developing achievement patterns, attitudes, and talent (Bloom, 1985; Clark, 1984). Social psychology research has demonstrated that a father's education and occupation are the strongest determinants of the socioeconomic level his children will attain (Jencks, 1972), and that only 1.8% of the children of manual laborers enter the professions (Sennett & Cobb, 1972). Other research has noted the effects of advanced educational levels in accounting for higher income and more prestigious positions in our society (Jencks & Brown, 1975). Still other research has focused on the dynamics of mature coping strategies as important variables in upward mobility for the low-income individuals who do break through the barrier of socioeconomic class (Snarey & Vaillant, 1985).

Recent research with gifted junior-high-age students in the Midwest (VanTassel-Baska & Willis, 1988) found that students whose family income was below $20,000 per year scored significantly lower on the Scholastic Aptitude Test (SAT) compared to higher-income students. These students represented an able population (i.e., all the students in the study were in the top 5% in achievement nationally), and 15.2% of them came from lower socioeconomic levels.

Clearly there is a sizable proportion of poor but able students who are at risk for not maximizing their potential during their years in secondary school and beyond, due to the complexity of factors associated with low income. Yet many eminent individuals have emerged from unstable homes and impoverished environments (Goertzel & Goertzel, 1962). A contributing factor in success emerges from a study of immigrants who were matched in

terms of ability and poverty. The difference between those who were successful and those who were not was the interpretation they rendered to poverty
in their lives (Csikszentmihalyi & Beattie, 1979).

What influences the talent development process for gifted students who
attain high-level academic success in school in spite of their disadvantaged
background? How similar or different are those influences from those affecting talented students who are more advantaged? In an attempt to answer
these questions, a series of case studies was undertaken. One set examined
background factors associated with advantaged gifted learners, while another
examined background factors associated with disadvantaged gifted learners.
It is this latter set of case studies that is reported on in this chapter.

One of the hypotheses in conducting these case studies of disadvantaged
gifted students and their families was that individuals and institutions other
than the family may play more significant roles in these students' lives than
in the lives of their more advantaged peers. Furthermore, it was hypothesized
that the "adversity factor" (i.e., being raised in a low-income home, having
only one parent, being a member of a minority group) may be a powerful stimulus for some individuals to succeed beyond expectations for their
socioeconomic level in society. To test these hypotheses with an adolescent
group, the heuristic model introduced at the beginning of this text (see Figure 1.1) was used. The model presupposes that the talent development process rests on three major types of influence in a child's life: institutional,
interpersonal, and intrapersonal. Each of these types of influence contributes
to the talent development process in different ways, and each is a necessary
but not sufficient condition for the process. The model also presupposes that
the influences in closest proximity to the child have the greatest impact; thus,
the child's inner resources would be more influential than environmental institutions, which are more peripheral. Similarly, individuals close to the child
would exert a greater influence than the entire family system.

METHODOLOGY

Defining Adversity

There are many ways that life adversity may be defined. Most would
agree that it includes one or more of the following factors: low socioeconomic
status (SES), handicapping conditions, minority status, and disrupted or abu-
sive family life. It may also include other circumstances and special life
events. In this study, all of the subjects came from family patterns that could
be termed adverse in some way. Intergenerational family patterns were
probed in an effort to view the issue over the span of three generations. The

purpose of exploring the theme of adversity was to highlight the role that it played in the context of the family structure and the possible implications that it may hold for the future of the adolescents under study. Furthermore, by focusing on talented students who were disadvantaged, it was possible to discern key patterns or themes of influence in their lives that differed from those in the lives of gifted students who were not similarly disadvantaged.

Sample

Fifteen case studies were completed for disadvantaged gifted adolescent students who attend or had attended public school in the Midwest. They distinguished themselves for their academic talent by scoring in the top range on the Scholastic Aptitude Test for their age group (SAT-M $\geq$ 500 and SAT-V $\geq$ 430). Less than 1% of that age group would be expected to score at that level in a given year. In addition, these students all had been identified as disadvantaged in respect to available family resources and other conditions in their lives.

School Setting

All of these students were enrolled in self-contained centers for the gifted by the time they reached junior high school. Although student-teacher ratios in these classes were approximately 28 to 1, the individual attention offered to students was considerable. The programs were highly academic in nature, and homework each night was a program requirement.

In the high school program component, which many of these students had already entered, honors and advanced placement (AP) courses were readily available and had about 30% of the overall student population enrolled in them. Four years of instruction in six foreign languages were offered; two languages were offered from seventh grade on. Both AP physics and AP calculus were offered. Sixty-four percent of the student population from these schools attended at least a 2-year college; about half matriculated to a 4-year institution. Each year, about 10% of the graduating class completed college-level work while in high school. Opportunities for internships, extracurricular competitions, special seminars, independent study, and academic counseling were also available through the schools these students attended.

Data Collection

The case study method I employed used questionnaire administration and follow-up interviews, both of which were carried out with the student subjects, at least one parent, and a school person, in order to obtain triangulation of information (Denzin, 1962; Yin, 1986). Student, parental, and school district permissions were obtained in order to carry out these interviews. Students were interviewed at their school sites, as were most parents. In a few cases, parents were interviewed by telephone. One approach to reporting on the cases was to synthesize all of the issues and views of parents, schools, and the students themselves and integrate them into a case history.

This has been done with four of the cases deemed the most interesting. A second approach was to organize the data by themes or issues that characterized the key responses. These central themes were then analyzed and discussed.

INDIVIDUAL CASE STUDIES

The following four case histories were selected because of their diversity with respect to family background issues. Each provides a different perception of the role of the family in student success.

Case Study #1: "Life consists of memories, doing things, and some joy."

Sujo is an 11-year-old seventh grader who already has demonstrated extensive and diverse talents. Trained in Suzuki violin since age 2, she performs regularly in recitals. She also sings with a major opera company and is purported to have perfect pitch. Sujo has also excelled academically, winning citywide and statewide competitions in mathematics, science, and Latin. She writes poetry and hopes to publish someday. While disavowing a career in music, she wishes to pursue journalism as a field of study, which she hopes will culminate in becoming a professor. She states, "I can imagine myself being a successful young journalist, portraying reality at its worst and its best." Sujo has been accelerated in school by one year by virtue of early entrance. Her favorite subject is mathematics, and she rates herself very high in that area. She is a straight-A student, although somewhat indifferent to school. She was learning both Korean and Esperanto before the age of five, and has participated in many university-based programs.

Sujo is the second child of a Korean mother and Caucasian father. The other child is her brother, who is 13. Her father was married previously and has eight other children by his first wife. Both parents are college graduates, the father attaining a master's degree. The mother is a full-time homemaker. Although the father earns a good salary, much of the money goes to support his "other family." Sujo's father was orphaned as a young teenager and lived much of his adolescent years in foster homes. He was resourceful and bright, but bitter about his circumstances. His own parents had been well educated and modestly well off. Sujo's mother came from a family of three brothers. She was very close to her mother, very dependent like Sujo is on her. She aspired to be a lawyer, but the family was poor and tradition dictated that her brothers would complete college before she would as a female child. Despite the Korean War and other obstacles, however, she maintained a double major in college and helped put her brothers through college. Eventually she came to the United States as a student of photography and a church organist. Yet she was always "sorry not to have had a real chance to develop my own ability."

Sujo's mother reports that Sujo has always been an apt learner, more organized and quicker than other children her age. She has always enjoyed doing work and was never very interested in play; she still reads many books, having begun at the age of 3. She maintains a homework ritual each day: "Work first, spend time checking and editing work, ask father to check work, and then do other things." Reluctantly, however, her mother admitted that Sujo is now displaying some "pubertal procrastination."

Sujo is a dreamful child, frequently fantasizing herself as a "princess in a castle." She has a tendency to withhold her problems, coping with them by withdrawing into reading or writing activity. Her mother describes Sujo as a good-natured child with a determined mind; a child who always wants to do her best; and a child of high moral character, often giving her own rewards to others. Motivation for action, however, is clearly externally controlled, with her mother pulling the strings: "Just like the elephant—one trick, one banana." Her mother's wish is for Sujo "to be content inside, to feel loved, so that she will feel free to stretch for learning." Leisure time is spent viewing educational television or enlightening films, or traveling. Sujo has been to 18 countries and plans to visit China this coming year. As Sujo sees it, "Life consists of memories, doing things, and some joy."

The overriding attachment figure for Sujo is her mother. By the admission of both, each worships the other. Her mother delivers what she calls her counsel or lectures to Sujo, which are comprised of three main themes:

1. Work toward long-term goals.
2. Work is the core of life; there are no short cuts.
3. Work at an even pace, eating three meals a day.

At 6 years of age, Sujo observed, "Mama not beautiful like fashion model but has wisdom." She likes her older brother very much, but she feels he rejects her. Other attachment figures have been men of great learning and educators. She commented on her regard for such men because of their scholarly and "calm" attitudes. She has experienced a crush on one teacher, for example, who answers all her questions and relates well to her. Her music teacher has also been an important influence, encouraging her to continue music lessons and often good-heartedly cajoling her to practice more to bring him honor.

The mother recalls Sujo's first-grade teacher as most important because she was "strict but effective." Teachers in recent years have been most valued because of their willingness to take a personal interest in Sujo. Sujo seeks out contacts with professors, whose company she likes at the same time she is awed by them. At this stage of Sujo's development, her mother actively seeks out teachers of reputation who can provide the best education for her daughter. Both children have been taken to many cultural events, usually by their mother. She feels that school contributes only 50% to her daughter's education; the other half is accomplished through outside programs and opportunities.

Case Study #2: "I enjoy writing about people and life in general."

Jack is now 13 years old and completing his seventh-grade year. He has had poetry published in the anthology for young writers of his school system. Mathematics is his favorite subject, and he aspires to a career in architecture. He hopes to earn a master's degree. His current science fair project was entitled, "Can Computers Do Factorials?" He has participated in special computer classes offered at a national laboratory and has had a long-term interest in programming on a home personal computer. He also enjoys sports and drawing. He entered a self-contained program for the gifted at first grade and has participated in it ever since. He has been an able student in the A–B range, is well-liked by his teachers and peers, and admittedly enjoys everything about school.

Jack is the seventh child in a family of 12 children, 10 of whom still live at home. The size of this family with several members simultaneously in college has put a large financial burden on its resources. The high parental expectations for each of the children have been largely realized in good school achievement. The father's occupation as a computer consultant has occasioned considerable travel and absence, which have been balanced by the mother's role as primary caretaker. Family income becomes a significant issue in view of the educational, medical, and personal expenses of 14 people. Both parents are college graduates; the father holds a master's degree. The mother has been primarily a homemaker, involving the children in creative activities such as grinding wheat for homemade bread.

The grandparents on both sides of the family came from rural backgrounds, and both grandfathers were blue-collar workers for a number of years. Neither set of grandparents was educated beyond high school; on the maternal side, education for the grandfather and grandmother ended after fifth and eighth grade, respectively. Jack's mother was the youngest of four children and only the second in the family to attend college. Although she always did well in school and had the highest average in her class, her parents did not value her continued education. However, she "adopted the attitude of her teachers" and prepared to become a teacher. Emotionally she did not feel she could handle classroom teaching, having been fired twice for being unable to maintain classroom discipline. Jack's father was the oldest of 14 children. He went to college as a strong reaction to his own father's hard life of working several jobs to make a living for the family. He once remarked to his wife that he would not have married her without his having a college degree, as he saw it as an economic necessity for the future. His mother (Jack's grandmother) was a "closet poetess" who has now gathered hundreds of her poems into books. Although lacking in formal training, she is thought of by her daughter-in-law as "very verbal and smart."

Of all the children in his family, Jack has had the most physical trauma, with fractures of the clavicle, arm, and leg. Recently he was discovered to have diabetes and now manages his own insulin injections.

For such a large group, Jack's family seems close, participating frequently in family get-togethers such as picnics and beach parties. Jack is very close to one of his older brothers, who is studying to be a nuclear physicist, and to his father. He is easily angered by his mother and appears troubled not to have access to things his friends have. His mother describes him as somewhat materialistic. While Jack receives attention in the family pattern, his mother could not remember early behaviors that he exhibited, only commenting that he had a good vocabulary and was an early reader. Each of the 12 children in Jack's family show signs of unusually high ability, all scoring in the highest range on individual intelligence tests.

Jack brings an intense quality to his involvement in all his activities, and this has put him at the top of his class. Sports such as Little League, swimming, soccer, and other "leisure" activities receive the same concentrated effort. He is currently writing a book and hopes to become a writer as an adult. His interests are broad in range, and family outings and large gatherings are particular favorites. He has used a paper route to earn his own spending money and help pay for his contact lenses. He frequently will do chores around the house before asking for a ride to some event, but most of the time he uses his bicycle for transportation. He views little television, preferring active participation in many differing projects.

His mother characterizes Jack as having excellent power of concentration from earliest age and as being an intense, determined competitor in sports and academic activities. He does not complain about homework or the academic challenge in school and has been a consistently high performer.

Jack credits several of his teachers in the early grades for providing the kind of encouragement for independent study that has helped him develop his general ability and writing talent. His older brother has been a scholarly role model for him, and his father's occupation as a computer consultant seems a major influence on him at this point. He is especially sensitive to his father's approval, challenging his mother verbally in ways that would not be attempted with his father. He is described as the most fascinating of their 12 children, since he is continually involved in activities that are creative, interesting, and productive.

His fifth-grade teacher, who demanded a large volume of written work and self-discipline with that activity, was particularly influential in his early writing efforts. Publication of his poem in the school district anthology when he was in fifth grade was an honor that has encouraged him to begin larger works such as his current book. He claims to "enjoy writing about people and life in general." The mother is amazed by his tenacity with this effort and his ability to be a self-starter for many projects. He has responded positively to all the academic challenges that have been presented him by teachers and finds ways to accomplish his advanced workload with a minimal expenditure of time.

Jack has sought out friends who come close to his cognitive level for out-of-school activities. His involvement with friends is essentially connected to projects such as producing a film or working on developing a computer program. He does have one friend who has been a popular student, with whom he attends parties. The family has been a major source of support, with the large number of older siblings providing academic and personal role models for him.

Case Study #3: "School is great!"

Nolan is a ninth grader who has been an A–B student throughout his school career and received academic achievement awards every year. He placed second in the high school in a recent math contest. He has participated in a special citywide music program over the past 3 years, learning to play the trumpet. He also placed in the top 10 in the city in the academic talent search competition. He plans to tutor younger students this summer in mathematics at his former elementary school.

Nolan is black and the second oldest of six children. He lives with his siblings and his mother and father in a single-family home. His maternal grandmother lives downstairs. Although both parents are currently unemployed, are on welfare, and have not finished college, they value education highly. The father speaks of his maxim for his children, "Reading is knowledge," and feels that the home environment has provided motivation for Nolan to do well, "a nudging for excellence." The father serves as the president of the elementary school PTA and has been a political activist in the school system. By his own admission, he "knows what goes on" and monitors his children's education very closely.

Nolan's mother and her family came from the South, where she was raised by her grandmother until she was 14 years old, when she moved to the North to join her mother who had remarried. Nolan's mother warmly described her grandmother, who lived until she was 100, as "strict, making me go to school every day—she really wanted me to have an education." She is the oldest child of four; she and her sister both went on to take college courses, but her brothers went into the service and then straight into jobs. Both her mother and stepfather had finished high school and encouraged their children to get an education. On the paternal side of Nolan's family, his grandfather completed eighth grade only, but his grandmother went back to school when Nolan's father was a small boy to get her high school diploma and also attended some college classes. As his father describes, "One stopped short and stayed short; the other started short but then said 'not enough!'" She worked in nursing homes and at practical nursing until retirement. Nolan's father is the youngest of three brothers. In the South, he was a cook and worked for a tobacco company; in the North, he was a chauffeur, a stoker at an electric company, and a machine oiler. "Not better, just different," he remarks of the shifts.

While Nolan is described by his father as lacking good study habits, often waiting until the last minute to finish a school project, he does credit him with good reading behaviors, "reading virtually anything and everything from the time he was a small boy." Nolan currently has three loves: music, mathematics, and his computer. He often spends hours at home, working out special problems on the computer and then comparing solutions with his best friend. Nolan aspires to attend college and perhaps go into mathematics or computers. His father is vague in respect to his son's aspirations, commenting that the family "jokes about it every once in awhile." Nolan is described by his father as having been a fearful child, frightened of bugs and snakes in the garden. Some of that behavior has subsided with age. His father also characterizes Nolan as willful, wanting his own way in all situations and putting his personal needs before the rules of the house. Nolan's way of dealing with the world, according to his father, is to appear blasé, not to let things get to him. If he does have problems, he escapes "back to computer heaven." Nolan is described by his father as "moving toward independence," with age removing some of his earlier fears. Nolan and a younger sister are known as the "smart ones" in the family, although his response to the label is one of nonchalance. Leisure time is spent either at the computer or watching the "Transformers" television cartoon series. His father attributes Nolan's accomplishments thus far to "genes and reading habits."

The father feels Nolan is closest to his younger sister, who shares many characteristics with him, including his love of reading. A science teacher at the elementary school was rather significant for Nolan, in that "he taught him things . . . that he didn't know." His second-grade teacher was credited for recognizing his academic ability and recommending he attend a special school. Nolan has two close friends with whom he spends time working on projects and talking on the telephone. Negative reactions to some school personnel were forthcoming from the father.

Family experiences center around the neighborhood, with frequent trips to "Mickey Dee's" (McDonald's) and church, although the father does not attend the latter. Occasionally the family plays board games, particularly Monopoly. Amusement parks also rate high as family entertainment.

According to his father, Nolan reacts against the prevailing peer culture, largely by ignoring it. At the father's urging, Nolan signed up for the summer jobs program, "to make sure he's not on the streets." The younger daughter, however, is becoming influenced by her peer group, and socializing with friends is becoming a predominant activity for her.

His father cited Nolan's high score on the SAT as a major boost in Nolan's self-confidence. "He has not looked back since," stated the father proudly.

Case Study #4: "Learning is the greatest experience."

Wanda is a 14-year-old high school freshman. She is the youngest child of four in her family. Maintaining a B$^+$ average, she has excelled academically at this stage of her development, particularly in mathematics. She aspires to the doctorate and cites accounting as a career interest. Not only is mathematics her favorite subject, it also is her favorite hobby and a self-recognized talent area. Annually since sixth grade she has entered math competitions, usually placing well. She has attended special summer programs at several universities and currently takes courses in modeling. She has performed in movies and has had dancing and theatrical lessons.

Wanda is the youngest child in a low-income black family. Both parents are high school graduates and are self-employed in their own small upholstery shop. Their three older children are all in college. A brother and sister also reside at home. Family experiences typically consist of watching television, playing games such as checkers, eating out, and attending movies. Occasional vacations are spent in Florida.

Wanda's grandparents on both sides were farmers in the South and also high school graduates. They warned their children to "stay in school; it is the only way to get ahead." Wanda's mother, the third child of six, left the South with an aunt at age 18 to come north to work. Her father, one of three children, moved north a few years later, and her mother and he soon married.

College appeared out of the question for both of Wanda's parents, as "money was not the best."

Wanda is a very well-motivated child, according to her mother. She always does her homework and goes to sleep without parental urging. Asked why, she replies, "I like to be #1!" She has always been very alert and has enjoyed studying. An independent child by nature, she likes doing things for herself but occasionally will share problems with her mother or an older sister who lives at home. Wanda is very involved with many activities and enjoys staying busy. She is seen as "the baby of the family," with 5 years separating her from her next sibling. She has always related better to older people than younger ones.

Wanda has one very close friendship, which has lasted for over 3 years. She and her friend spend time bike riding, running track, and doing special school projects together.

In addition to the summer programs, Wanda has taken extra classes at area universities and cites all of these programs as significant to her feelings about her competence as well as valuable for the opportunity to meet different people. She considers learning to be her greatest experience.

Interpretation of the Cases

While these four case histories present the diversity of the small study group in respect to sex, ethnic origin, family constellation, and circumstances of disadvantagement, they also exemplify certain commonalities found in all our case studies, including those not presented here. Let us examine some of these common elements.

All of the students interviewed come from families who served as major sources of encouragement and influence. They all had limited peer interaction and involvement, with most such interactions emerging out of common academic or school-related interests. Each of the students had at least one strong parent who monitored the child's progress through school very closely. In the majority of cases, that parent was the mother; in a few, it was the father, or both mother and father. All of the case study subjects evidenced high-achievement needs and had practiced goal-oriented behavior over a period of years. All emerged out of a familial pattern of negative circumstance in some way, usually traced beyond their parents' generation, yet passed on to these students through the powerful inculcation of resultant parental values. The basic message did not differ greatly from one ethnic group to another, from one family circumstance to another. It read: "You must work hard, get an education, and achieve what your parents and grandparents did not, even though they, too, were bright and eager. You will have the chance that we did not have. Don't waste it."

Parental aspirations, expectations, and standards for their children's achievement appeared relatively high in all the cases, although a few subjects appeared to have very "watchful" parents from an early age onward. Family work habits, routines, and priorities were in evidence for all cases, but adherence to a ritual of routine around a given child's talent area was seen in only a few of the cases. In the area of family activities and resources being brought to bear on a child's talent, some families showed evidence of great involvement while in others the students pursued their academic interests separately.

The parents in this study also seemed very self-conscious about the academic talent displayed by their children, much more so than was evidenced by parents in the Bloom study (1985), for example, where the family interests and child's talent area naturally converged. In several cases in our study, the parents appeared to be experiencing vicariously the academic success of their children, which may explain their hyperawareness.

These families demonstrated valiant attempts to be equitable with their time and attention to all their children. In two cases, the parents saw all their children as highly able and therefore did not feel a need to respond differentially. In another, the parents viewed their child as having a highly valuable quality not possessed by others in the family and therefore stressed each child's "talent." The closeness of the family system in another case minimized comparisons between two boys. In only one family did there appear to be attempts to show deferential treatment to the academically gifted child.

Finally, these parents appeared to represent the critical element in their children's current and future talent development. Even though many of them were not well educated or financially comfortable, they exerted a powerful influence over their children's lives. Opportunities such as school programs and university experiences were accessed through the parents, who acted as gatekeepers for such activities. No individual or institutional influences outside the family have emerged as being similarly powerful in the lives of these adolescents. It will be interesting to see—over time—how, when, and if the inner resources of these students and significant events outside the family begin to outweigh the strong parental influence currently operating.

CASE STUDY THEMES

A second kind of analysis was conducted on the collected case studies. In addition to commenting holistically on a few individual students, I identified key themes that characterized the group. These themes represent in some instances important deviations from what has been found to characterize the lives of advantaged learners. The following section of this chapter amplifies on them, using quotations from students to substantiate the interpretations.

Attitudes Toward School

The case studies revealed students who were highly successful in the school context. All were A students, many the best in their classes. Individual comments revealed a generally positive attitude toward their school experience. When these students had been accelerated, they generally felt positively about the experience. A straight-A student who skipped first grade put it this way:

> Skipping a grade is what you do when you're ahead of the class and there's no way that the teacher or the class can do anything more for you. My sixth-grade math teacher gave me encouragement. She worked hard to get me what I needed.

Another described the experience as follows:

> The principal at my old school helped me get into here. You know I skipped third grade. If I hadn't done this, I'm sure I would be bored and frustrated, wishing I was doing something else. If a child thinks he can fit into a higher grade and can handle the work, then I think skipping a grade is the way to go.

Being engaged in worthwhile academic activity seemed important to these students also, with a number of them citing the importance of summer experiences or other special activities.

> My involvement with the yearbook was the most rewarding experience in school because I enjoyed knowing that I helped put something together that everyone is going to remember.

> To me, a summer without being in one kind of program is boring. During the summer I am more able to study on my own and you have more time to think about what you've learned. I like shorter events. I like the competitiveness of it. With academics, you're not competing against somebody else, you're really just doing your best.

One student saw school as a kind of retreat into her own world:

> School is just about the only place where a repressed chatterbox like me can live in its [her] own world.

Family Life

The family life of these students varies considerably yet is marked by the fact that they all live in low-income circumstances. Many of these students come from families where divorce has left an emotional and economic impact that is still being felt.

My parents are divorced. I have a sister (8 years old) and two stepsisters (9 and 7 years old). I don't get along well with my stepmother and I call her my "step-monster"—not to her face, though. My stepmother seems to lead my dad's life, but I can't do anything about it.

The most significant experience that has affected my view of myself was my parents' divorce. It really changed my life. When I was little, they're right when they say a child thinks it's all his fault, because I did, too—everybody does. It changed my views on everything. I would watch "Dallas" and I was always hoping J.R. and Sue Ellen would get married after a divorce, . . . but I know it won't. I went to the social worker at school and that helped a little bit, but what really helped was time. Time really heals.

The importance of the extended family for these students emerges consistently in their commentary. The most dominant figure in all of this is the maternal grandmother, who many times has much responsibility for raising the child and providing the central source of nurturance. It is frequently through the grandparents' generation that the value system of the family is transmitted.

My mother had me when she was 15 years old, and my aunt adopted me. My mother was not a very good student and neither was my father—he was 19 years old when I was born. My aunt started going to art school, so I moved down south to live with my grandmother. I love my family, and if my aunt didn't adopt me or if my grandmother didn't take care of me, there's no telling where I'd be, probably in a foster home. . . . Since I've been with my grandmother, my life has been fairly consistent. My cousin is the closest thing to a sibling that I've lived with. All of us eat dinner together. I respect my grandmother a great deal. She'll be 70 years old this year.

My grandmother graduated as valedictorian of her high school, and I want to do that, but she didn't go on to college after that. All my grandmother says is to do real good and to get straight A's to get into good colleges.

My grandmother's smart. She has priorities, her opinions. She's 80 years old. I see her sort of a lot for 2 weeks in the summer. We talk about books we've read (which are the same).

Among nuclear family members, the mothers of these students emerge clearly as the most influential in their lives—as a source of encouragement and inspiration as well as caregiver.

Mom is always encouraging us to do things. She always talks about when she was growing up she didn't have it and whether we want to take advantage of it or not, she's going to make us. She always gives the choice, and she won't make us do something if we really don't want to. She'll explain what's good about it, and we'll discuss ways to make it different.

My mom is very independent, and she has had the strongest influence on my academic development. She'll say, "I know you can do it. You're so smart, of course you can do it." She's so encouraging. She had also taught me to be independent. I've taken care of the house for so long that I feel on my own—that I can do it. I started babysitting when I was 7 years old, and I started getting jobs that paid over $4 an hour when I was 10 years old.

The influence of a male figure in the home was also cited, especially by girls, as having a profound influence on achieving well in school.

My dad can't read. He wants me to be the best I possibly can be. He doesn't get mad at me if I get a B$^+$. He'll tease me, tell me I better do better and get an A next time—and I do.

Once I brought home a B in math on my report card, and my grandfather asked me why I received such a low score. Since then I have never received another B.

Family size also appears to influence these students' view of themselves, their environment, and the major influences in their lives.

Having so many siblings is kind of a pain, but it also can be fun because there's always something to do. I spend most of my time with my family, either eating meals or playing games. The size of my family is different from most families in the neighborhood. Also it seems like kids in other families can do just about anything they want, and it's somewhat more restricted in my house. As far as influencing me academically, my oldest brother in graduate school has won three (school) gold medals in math and one in science. He's really smart, and I thought, if I could put what I have to work, I could go pretty far.

While family members, collectively as well as individually, can be seen as pivotal positive forces in the lives of these successful students from disadvantaged backgrounds, they also serve as confusing role models. While students may receive encouragement for good grades and achievement in school, future aspirations may be tied to the family history.

I don't want to be a doctor. What I really want to do is cook. My grandmother—my whole family—cooks really well. However, I do like getting recognized for my schoolwork. My family is extremely proud of me, and my brothers will brag to their friends about my report card.

Teachers

The role of teachers in the lives of these students also appeared to be pivotal in helping to shape their self-perceptions and in providing them with a sense of competence in their academic life.

Math teachers have influenced me in a significant way. They were nice and not too picky. They gave you challenges, but they're not too hard. They don't push you to do things you know you can't do. Having good teachers is really what makes the difference. You can turn someone who has a learning disability into someone who's really smart, if you help them and don't push too hard; and if you give them good self-esteem that they can do it, they'll try harder.

This teacher's ideals were to study while you were in elementary school, high school and college, and then play around afterwards and have fun. I liked her a lot. She was very good. I really miss her now. She was unique, and she cared about people. She was one teacher that remembers what it was like when she was a kid and can understand why things are so hard, and can be understanding yet be strict and firm enough not to hand things to kids on silver platters [but] make them work for things.

Procrastination

A negative characteristic evident in many of these students is a propensity toward procrastination. They have been successful despite this behavior, yet they recognize that it is not a good pattern to follow. The presence of this characteristic in these students' profiles also points up their lack of planning for their academic work.

I have good work habits when I want to, but I often procrastinate and have a history of completing tasks successfully at the last minute.

I'm a procrastinator, although I think about the assignment a lot before I start it. If I start a project the night before it's due, it turns out to be much better that way because of my anxieties. Somehow the best always comes out last.

Peer Culture

Individual peers appear to have a significant influence on these young people, although there is little recognition of the peer culture as a dominant influence. Peers serve several purposes for these students, mainly as confidants who will listen to their problems and as inspirations for doing well in school and related areas. These students also tend to select peers carefully.

I need people. Just trying to think what I'd be without my closest friends is scary. You know, religion plays a large role in my life. I don't go to church, though. Everyone has me to come to, but sometimes I don't have anyone to go to.

I have two best friends; we really have become better friends, sort of like a rubber band flexing. We're all really alike. We're all smart, play an instrument, and like computers and role-playing games. Like mine, their parents are divorced and we're the oldest in our families. They're [friends] supportive, and if you make a mistake they'll say, "Well, you tried hard." They would say I was nice, smart, and sometimes a little too sensitive. They helped me be more social; that's how I started playing basketball and softball. Friends are very important to me, because you need friends, as they're someone to talk to, someone to lean on.

Economic Disadvantagement

Surprisingly, these students complained very little about socioeconomic hardship. Several of them lived in homes where neither parent was employed, and few of their parents had attended college. Most homes had an income level well below $20,000. However, a few of the students perceived the importance of having a more substantial income, to have access to specific material goods in which they were interested, such as college, clothes, and travel.

My family's financial background has made me work harder for my future. I want to go to a big university and get a degree so I can use it to make a lot of money. A lot of people at my school are on the poorer side, although most of my friends are upper-class. I go to their houses and see two or three cars parked in the driveway, a bigger house, a better way of living. I have better clothes recently because I've been baby-sitting. I might become a doctor or a lawyer—they make money.

I do want to be secure, not just financially secure. I know I'm not going to be in the streets.

Community

Many of these students characterized their communities as mixed environments, where they saw clear distinctions in the nature of the population and were very aware of socioeconomic differences.

On one side of the street you'd see a nice house with nice people, and on the other side you'd see lower-income people with no telephone and things like that. The lower-income people are really religious, while the higher-income people are really hard workers and get up at six in the morning, which I can't do. Most people in our area don't mix well, but everyone minds his own business.

I live in a really interesting neighborhood in the middle of the block. At one end of the block, there's the lake and all those glamorous high-rises with all the rich people. At the other end of the block, is where people just hang out. I have lived in the same building now for 9 years.

Positive community influences were scarce in these case studies; however, one influence emerged in the form of a female pastor who clearly was serving as a role model for this female subject:

It's not that she's different from male pastors; it's that she's different from everybody else and, to make it, she had to be better than the others. Most people did accept her, although a couple of people quit going to church. I have respect for her both because of her sex and her position.

Achievement Motivation

These students appear to share a high need for achievement, some of which appears to be intrinsic but much of which is extrinsic at this stage of their lives.

When I do well, I tell myself, "that's good." When someone else says it and reinforces it, I feel even better. When I met with my counselor and she told me that my test scores are competitive with the nation, it was encouraging to hear that I was that high up, so that made me work harder and achieve my best.

Doing well on the first math contest I entered was a key event in my life, because it made me keep trying because I enjoyed it.

Coping Strategies

Many of these students reveal a strong inner sense of how to handle their problems and how to think about themselves in ways that enhance their specialness.

I will try and see what's wrong, will tell myself that things aren't so bad, and will see what I can do to pick myself up again.

The time I spend alone is important. That's how I get to sleep at night, just thinking, meditating, reflecting about who I am, trying to find myself. If I hardly have time for this, I find time. It makes it easier to get along with people and with yourself instead of saying everyone else is wrong.

Summary

As can be seen from these key themes, the importance of the family institution is very great. Even in cases where there has been a divorce or other separation, the significance of extended families is cited. For girls in these case studies, the role of the grandmother as surrogate parent appears critical. These disadvantaged gifted students found educational institutions to be fairly important in their development process, allowing them access to opportunities otherwise denied them. School staff played an important role for many, particularly influential teachers encountered at various stages of development. Acknowledgment of ability, encouragement, and guidance characterized the important role that such individuals played in the lives of these students. In the area of personal resources, it is clear that these students all showed high achievement motivation, exhibited successful coping strategies at this stage in their development, and appeared to be self-directed learners.

The negative patterns of behavior observed from the case study data revolve around two areas. Procrastination appeared as a pattern in several of the cases. In the long term, it could negatively affect the talent development process, leading to underachievement at later ages. The other area of negative behavior discerned was the lack of future planning, especially a lack of specificity regarding next steps in planning for the students' entry into college. This vagueness was apparent from both parent and student interviews. While the value system and aspiration levels in these families indicated college as the next step, there was little understanding of the process by which college would become a reality. This situation could lead to the speculation that some of these students may be deprived of the best college education because of lack of appropriate information and assistance at a critical stage of development.

CONCLUSION

These 15 case studies of disadvantaged gifted students have provided rich insights into their individual and collective patterns of development, from the perspective of adolescence. How they will traverse the next stages in the talent development process remains to be seen; however, it is clear that they are armed with many of the same resources found among more advantaged populations—a supportive family that values education and work, individuals who provide encouragement and guidance, and an inner sense of direction that manifests itself in high achievement.

REFERENCES

Bloom, B. (1985). *Developing talent in young people*. New York: Ballantine Books.
Clark, R. (1984). *Family life and school achievement: Why poor black children succeed or fail*. Chicago: University of Chicago Press.
Csikszentmihalyi, M., & Beattie, O. (1979). Life themes: A theoretical and empirical exploration of their origins and effects. *Humanistic Psychology, 19* (1), 45–63.
Denzin, N. K. (1962). *The research act*. Chicago: Aldine.
Goertzel, M., & Goertzel, V. (1962). *Cradles of eminence*. Boston: Little, Brown.
Jencks, C. (1972). *Inequality*. New York: Basic Books.
Jencks, C., & Brown, M. (1975). The effects of high schools on their students. *Harvard Educational Review, 45*, 273–324.

Sennett, R., & Cobb, J. (1972). *The hidden injuries of class*. New York: Random House.

Snarey, J., & Vaillant, G. (1985). How lower- and working-class youth become middle-class adults: The association between ego defence mechanism and upward mobility. *Child Development, 56,* 899–910.

VanTassel-Baska, J., & Willis, G. (1988). A three year study of the effects of income on academically able students. *Gifted Child Quarterly, 31*(4), 169–173.

Yin, R. K. (1986). *Case study research: Design and methods*. Beverly Hills, CA: Sage.

PART II

INFLUENCE OF THE SELF

The four chapters in this part of the book illustrate the uniqueness of gifted and eminent individuals and the constellation of personality dimensions and personal characteristics that differentiate them from others.

Michael Piechowski in chapter 6 studies developmental potential and the emotional growth and development of gifted children. He presents student quotations from qualitative data to frame ideas about the nature and depth of individual gifted students' feelings about themselves. The outcomes are intriguing, reflecting variations in self-insight, self-actualization, emotional growth, creativity, responsibility, and conventionality.

In chapter 7 Thomas Buescher and Sharon Higham describe findings from two developmental studies conducted with over 700 young adolescents who participated in a talent search program. This study examines the ways adolescents cope with being gifted. The results suggest that, overall, the students in the sample respond in positive ways by using their talents to help others or finding other labels for themselves in or outside of school. Coping strategies appear to be influenced by age, sex, and participation in programs for the gifted.

Paula Olszewski-Kubilius and Marilynn Kulieke in chapter 8 examine the personality dimensions of academically talented adolescents, using a variety of instruments. The gifted students are compared to norming groups of same-age students, and gifted females are compared to gifted males. The results of the study showed that the gifted students were different from their same-age nongifted peers on several dimensions and generally presented a very positive picture of mental health and adjustment. They were more intellectual and theoretical, tended to desire leadership positions and possess leadership qualities, were internally oriented, and showed better than average psychological adjustment and lower levels of tension and apprehension. Many more differences were found between gifted and nongifted students than between gifted females and males.

In chapter 9, Joyce VanTassel-Baska provides insights regarding individual characteristics that seem to be necessary, but not in themselves sufficient, for gifted individuals to reach the level of eminence. The interplay of intelligence, family background, and individual characteristics is described and substantiated from a review of relevant literature. Her conceptions of the necessity for activation of successive links in the total system poses an interesting challenge to parents and educators who seek to develop talent to the highest degree.

There are several issues that emanate from this collection of chapters on self. Chapter 7 demonstrates the wealth of gifts possessed by the individuals in the various research studies. These gifted adolescents were multitalented and had interests and talents in areas beyond academics. In chapter 8 the authors demonstrate that their subjects were psychologically well adjusted. They distinguished themselves from their nongifted counterparts by having higher scores on positive personality dimensions such as independence, altruism, and assertiveness. These students were above the norm on their ability to cope. All in all, the students appeared to be blessed in many ways. They were psychologically healthy and wealthy, and able to develop their talents with the aid of supportive families.

Yet chapter 7 points out the problems experienced as a result of these many blessings. Students struggled with problems of perfectionism, competitiveness, unrealistic appraisal of their gifts, rejection from peers, confusion due to mixed messages about their talents, and parental and social pressures to achieve, as well as problems with unchallenging school programs or increased expectations. The very families who provided support and nurturance, who gave so much to their talented children, also expected much in the way of achievement and success in return. The same was true of teachers. These students with varied interests had difficulty deciding what to study or become involved with and how to make decisions about which talent area to make a life's commitment to. They felt guilty about being so talented and/or worried about appearing too different from other students.

The basic pressure often experienced by gifted students is that they have been given "gifts" in abundance and so must give of themselves in abundance. Gifted students have difficulty owning their abilities, because often it is subtly implied that they belong to parents, teachers, and society. Thus, despite the overall picture of health and successful adjustment, and the uniqueness of the personalities of gifted students, they, too, experience problems centered on finding and identifying friends, a course of study, and, eventually, a career. The developmental issues that all adolescents encounter exist also for gifted students, yet they are traversed with their special needs and characteristics complicating the path.

Gifted females appear to be especially vulnerable to the pull of cultural expectations that drive them toward seeking peer acceptance rather than leadership and the full development of their abilities. Chapter 8 demonstrates the degree to which gifted females are internally focused in their orientation to the world, clearly in contrast to the cultural expectations for being extroverted, social, and people oriented. How does one pay attention to one's own inner callings and yet fit into a society with very different role expectations? Future research may need to look at how students make compromises between their own needs and the expectations of others and how developmental tasks such as identity formation are accomplished by gifted adolescents. Also, we need to examine the underlying attributes of the self that determine the susceptibilities of students to be unduly concerned, at the expense of their talents, with the expectations of peers, parents, or cultural norms. In our efforts to help gifted students achieve and develop, via socialization from parents and teachers about the importance of success, high grades, or making a contribution, do we inadvertently foster conformity, susceptibility to what others think, or a self-identity that is not truly owned but dependent on others? These aspects of the self may be predictors of students who are at risk for the adjustment problems mentioned.

Finally, we address in this part the paradox of eminence and the role of the self in producing it. If the individual's perception of events and adverse circumstances can play a crucial role in shaping eminent behavior, as Van Tassel-Baska suggests in chapter 9, then perhaps we should consider focusing more attention on promoting self-knowledge, emotional strength, and coping skills rather than using an academic standard as the basis for our ideas about the development and nurturance of talent.

Student Perspective: Male, 28 years old

For most of my formal schooling, I went to public schools. In fifth grade I had a teacher who was really fine, a paragon of what teachers should be. Tremendously interested, she had no sense of hostility toward students who were very bright, no sense of jealousy. It was something she really shared in and was delighted by. In fact, she was so committed to our particular class that she actually moved from fourth to fifth grade with us, which in our school system was unprecedented. In fifth grade she decided that it would be interesting for me to take some tests, not tests at sixth- and eighth-grade levels (things that I could probably do very well on) but SATs, which are designed for eleventh and twelfth graders. I was in fifth grade at the time and 10 years old. I was given quite a battery of tests, and my resultant scores were high.

Based on my scores, I went to work at the Maryland Academy of Science. It was very interesting. By today's standards of education for the gifted, the program was incredibly crude. What we did was to learn computer programming. What did that mean? It's amazing to me, now that I'm an old-timer with computer programming, that 10 years ago what that really meant was using a computer by Wang Laboratories which is now outdated. They had a machine that was about the size of a portable stereo, and it worked like a toaster. What we did was punch out holes in cards and stick these cards in the machine, and it really worked like a sophisticated calculator, very crude and awkward. My first product was learning to program some algebra, like how to solve $2X + 1$, a technological breakthrough. I did this for a couple of months, basically exhausted the limit of the resources there, and then went and talked to a well-known psychologist about my work, future plans, and acceleration.

As an educational strategy, acceleration usually works, not only for 4 or 5 years of skipping, as in my case, but 1 or 2 years, which is pretty healthy. However, it was quite natural for me to skip from sixth grade into the eighth grade, because in my region there were five elementary schools that fed into a particular junior high, so one was likely to lose one's friends in the shuffle, anyway. So for me to move from sixth to seventh would have been traumatic in terms of losing friendships, but moving from sixth to eighth was no big change. I had a relatively normal time, took typical courses, and was virtually indistinguishable, physically or emotionally, from the kids I was in school with. Then I skipped into eleventh grade in high school; that was a bigger leap. I spent one year in high school—basically crunched high school into 1 year and took things like tenth-grade English and twelfth-grade calculus, and a whole range of courses. I was also on the wrestling team. Then I went to college. So it was just 4 years of acceleration. I had taken some college courses and a number of AP exams, which are of course highly recommended for students who are able, so I was able to finish college in five semesters. And then when I graduated in December, I went off to work as a reporter for about 6 months and then came to graduate school at the University of Chicago, and it took me 4 years to finish there, which is actually kind of fast by Ph.D. standards, especially for the University of Chicago. (In the divinity school there, the average Ph.D. student spends about 10 to 12 years.)

Clearly, skipping grades can be somewhat traumatic, so it's useful to engineer it so that there is a natural break, so that losing the attachments to friends, teachers, or a particular school comes when it would probably happen anyway.

Generally, gifted students are torn between two kinds of senses and pressures. One is that they are supposed to get high test scores and raise their hands to questions if they know the answers. Obviously, whether one is in sports or arts or science, one feels that pressure. And the other pressure is that one wants to conform and the students in seventh grade tend to frown upon the kid in the back of the class who's constantly raising his hand to every question, making the rest of them look bad. So there's this conformity pressure as well that exists, and it's very difficult for gifted students to achieve appropriate balance.

Gifted students' reactions to this fit into one of two categories. On the one hand, they tend to rebel and handle this pressure by externalizing it or being very loud and vocal about excelling, even at the expense of upsetting peers and angering teachers and administrators. The other outcome, which may be even worse, is that students withdraw quite a bit, and the desire to conform outweighs everything. Even though they know the answer, and they put their hand halfway up, if people around are frowning or smirking, the hand comes down.

I went through both stages. When I was in eighth grade, some administrators in the school very conscientiously sent around letters to most of my teachers asking, "Do you think this kid is capable of being skipped into eleventh grade, without inflicting damage on himself or the school?" Science was especially rough because it was very low level. At the time I was just dipping into physics, although I later taught it to myself so I could take the AP exam. Since I knew I was capable of doing some high-level science, experiments like burning sugar to watch the carbon come out was a little rudimentary for me. Thus my strategy was not to do any work at all. I had tremendous fun with my lab partner, doing tricks and things, and acting as if I didn't have any ability. Mr. Eisner, my science teacher, couldn't tell whether I had tremendous ability or if this was my way of expressing dissatisfaction. So he wrote a letter saying that I was actually incapable of doing serious science and instead of looking at pushing me forward, he recommended that the school should keep me in the eighth grade another year. Two years later, I was taking junior-level physics at Hopkins, so he clearly wasn't right. But one can understand the confusion a nice, normal teacher would feel at the prospect of a student who's rebelling in this way.

One of the most important characteristics of gifted people is an absolutely burning sense of curiosity, coupled with a thirst and a hunger for knowledge. Sometimes you temper it in the classroom by not raising your hand that often, or bugging the teacher with requests for outside reading. So there's a flame that's turned down, as it were, by various social pressures, but it really is a terrific force. You get a sense of this drive from being around gifted people, the sense that they want to know more, the sense that there's hundreds of things out there to know, numerous problems to be solved, and almost a perfectionistic sense that it's their job to do it. Someone was telling me that there was something on PBS about Richard Feynman, who's a Nobel laureate and well-known physicist at Cal Tech. The thing that absolutely enthralled him about watching the program wasn't the physics or the substance of it, but that Feynman took tremendous interest in all this knowledge out there to be developed that's not apparent to the naked eye on the surface, and in understanding how it all works. He had a terrific time conveying this information, stumbling over his words and conveying the feeling that the most important thing in the world was knowing these things and getting other people to know them. Presumably in his younger years, knowing that there were worlds out there to conquer led to ferocious scientific curiosity.

This capacity of gifted people to grab hold of knowledge and make it work for them is a key element in their make-up. Helping students unlock this "inner tiger" should be the goal of all educators who work with the gifted.

CHAPTER 6

Developmental Potential and the Growth of the Self

Michael M. Piechowski

Eagle and Hawk with their great claws and hooked heads
Tear life to pieces; vulture and raven wait for death to soften it.
The poet cannot feed on this time of the world
Until he has torn it to pieces, and himself also.

Robinson Jeffers, *Memoranda*

In the developmental trajectory of human life, each phase is viewed as a preparation for the next one. Adulthood, the productive participation in the human community, is often viewed through the prism of an ideal norm. In their study of adolescence, Csikszentmihalyi and Larson (1984) expressed this view as follows: "A community needs people who are self-confident, motivated to achieve yet respectful of others, who are adaptable, original, and at peace with their own selves, more than it needs students who score high on tests" (p. 199).

But is it possible to be original, adaptable, and at peace with oneself, yet at the same time be a sensitive barometer of the undercurrents, conflicts, future trends, and tensions in society? Hardly. Rather, we must consider that such qualities are sorted out into different types of personality arising during different developmental circumstances. It is safe to say that individuals who are self-confident, achieving, adaptable, considerate toward others, and possibly even at peace with themselves come for the most part from families characterized by a distinctive style of parenting, which Baumrind (1970) called authoritative (Colangelo & Dettmann, 1985; Cornell & Grossberg, 1987). Originality, though not necessarily absent, is not the distinguishing characteristic here. Development of such individuals tends toward more or less stable patterns; it is less likely to be subject to frequent moves and uprootedness, and to feelings of being different, alien, or out of step with one's generation.

Individuals who look for the unseen links in the structure of knowledge or in the fabric of a culture, to whom it is always important to find new patterns and to create new meanings, to see what no one has seen, to understand what no one has understood, to uncover what is hidden, who live to create, tend to come from a different kind of family. Their families tend to be less cohesive but more permissive (Domino, 1979; Getzels & Jackson, 1962). Their development is likely to be subject to disruptive changes, be it loss of a parent or a move to a new city or even to a new country and a new culture. The individual, and a gifted one especially so, brings into this contextual matrix something of her or his own: talents, special abilities, a level of energy, and a level of intensity. These personal qualities do not come as one package. The nature and magnitude of talent, the type and assortment of abilities, the area of concentration of energy (e.g., intellectual or emotional, or both) and its direction (inward, as in introversion, or outward, as in extroversion), and the type of intensity (as in the subjective intensity of feeling or in a performer's ability to project it) are so many different components whose particulars are unique to each individual. The personal qualities of how intensely things are experienced are gathered under the rubric of *developmental potential.*

DEVELOPMENTAL POTENTIAL

Developmental potential (Dabrowski, 1972; Piechowski, 1986) includes talents and abilities, plus five primary components: psychomotor, sensual, intellectual, imaginational, and emotional capacities. Conceived broadly as five dimensions of psychic life, these primary components have many possible expressions:

1. Psychomotor (P)—movement, restlessness, drivenness, and an augmented capacity for being active and energetic
2. Sensual (s)—enhanced differentiation and aliveness of the sensual experience
3. Intellectual (T)—avidity for knowledge, discovery, questioning, love of ideas and theoretical analysis, and search for truth
4. Imaginational (M)—vividness of imagery; richness of associations; facility for dreams, fantasies and inventions, animisms, and personifications; and liking for the unusual
5. Emotional (E)—great depth and intensity of emotional life expressed in a wide range of feelings, compassion, attachments, a heightened sense of responsibility, and self-examination

Heightened intensity of experiencing is a quality in talented people. In fact, it is one of their strongest characteristics, manifested in varied and sometimes extraordinary ways. For example, for painters, "visual stimulation, reaction to things seen is intense, sometimes almost painful" (Roe, 1975, p. 167). For writers, emotions can be overwhelming in their range and intensity: "I feel too much, sense too much, am exhausted by the reverberations" (Sarton, 1970, p. 12). Enhanced imagination, passionate curiosity, extended range of intense feelings, and heightened energy are all signs of strong developmental potential (Piechowski, 1986). The question is, potential for what kind of development?

There are two basic kinds of development which may or may not be combined. One is the development of talent in the broad sense of creative work, be it scientific, artistic, or expressive performance. The characteristic of heightened intensity or experiencing represents the kind of endowment that feeds, nourishes, enriches, empowers, and amplifies talent. A study of artistically and intellectually gifted adults showed that both groups scored much higher than a comparison group on the dimensions of enhanced feeling, imagination, and intellectual passion (Piechowski, Silverman, & Falk, 1985). The artistically gifted subjects were particularly strong in the emotional dimension and imagination.

The other kind of development is personal growth guided by powerful ideals. It is characterized by moral questioning, existential concerns, and methodical self-judgment that guides the individual in the work of inner psychic transformation. This type of development, especially when intense and sustained, produces self-actualizing growth of the kind observed in spiritual leaders and other individuals of high moral character (Piechowski, 1986). The study of emotional growth in adolescents can help us to identify better the *potential* for this type of development, which in turn will lead us to better ways of nurturing the growth of self. In the terms of the paradigm presented here, the growth of self is a process by which a person finds an inner direction to his or her life and deliberately takes up the work of inner transformation.

THE GROWTH OF SELF: TWO TYPES OF MATURATION

The self develops in terms of the knowledge of one's separate identity, particularly one's attributes, traits, and skills; and in terms of self-awareness, i.e., the awareness of how others see and appraise one, and self-consciousness, which is the knowledge of one's inner self. Mature self-awareness entails a sense of continuity of the self over time, a sense that the qualities defining the self are unified (rather than being like so many loose pieces); as well as the sense of mutual understanding with others, that is, that the way I see myself is congruent with the way another who knows me sees me (Harter, 1983).

The most important developmental patterns in the adolescent advance toward self-understanding are

1. The shift from physicalistic to psychological conceptions of self
2. The increasingly volitional and self-reflective nature of self-understanding
3. The emergence of stable social-personality characterizations of self
4. The tendency toward the conceptual integration of diverse aspects of self into a unified self-system [Damon, 1983, p. 320]

These patterns are not completed by every adolescent; in fact, for many the process may continue well into adulthood. Integration of the self into a unified system is what Erikson (1968) described as the achievement of identity.

The processes characteristic of development of self-understanding appear in gifted adolescents early and can be articulated by some of them in a highly sophisticated manner. However, the typology of maturity that we found was twofold (Piechowski, Colangelo, Grant, & Walker, 1983). One type resembles Peck and Havighurst's (1960) rational-altruistic type, while the other is introspective, emotionally intense, and points to inner psychic transformation of the kind described by Dabrowski (1967, 1972).

The rational-altruistic type is in some ways akin to the foreclosure identity described by Marcia (1980). These individuals establish their identity without going through a developmental crisis. In Peck and Havighurst's (1960) description, such a person is

"rational" because he assesses each new action and its effects realistically, in the light of internalized moral principles derived from social experience; and he is "altruistic," because he is ultimately interested in the welfare of others, as well as himself. . . . He wants everyone to work constructively in some area and produce results useful to everyone. He sees relations with others as pleasant, cooperative effort toward mutual goals. . . . As an adult, he assumes an appropriate share of responsibility in his role as a member of a family, community, nation. . . . He reacts with emotion appropriate to the occasion. This does not mean he is unemotional, for he is enthusiastic about promoting what is good and aroused to prevent what is bad. [p. 8]

This describes many gifted youngsters and the mature and responsible adults they eventually become. Notice that this picture stresses adaptation to social reality, a reality governed by laws and conventions, contracts and agreements. Although cooperative and democratic participation is stressed, this is still only an *external* social reality. Character development in terms of such adaptation cannot produce the kind of personal growth that results in radical inner change, which is necessary to achieve autonomy and a clear vision of universal ideals. There are other realities, then, which are *emotional* and *individual*. Maturation in terms of these realities entails emotional growth through developmental crises and represents the second introspective type of development. Some gifted children become engaged in this type of growth rather early. For many, however, introspective-emotional growth receives too little attention. Recognizing and cultivating this type of maturity in individuals for whom it is often denied any importance is the motivation for the work presented in this chapter.

STUDY OF MATURATIONAL PATTERNS

The purpose of the study described here was to find individual patterns of emotional development. In this 2-year study, conducted in collaboration with Nicholas Colangelo at the University of Iowa, self-reports were collected from gifted youngsters who at the beginning of the project were 12 to 17 years old (Piechowski et al., 1983). The subjects were recruited from programs for the gifted in several junior and senior high schools in the state of Iowa. The youngsters were given an open-ended questionnaire with items asking them what evoked in them strong positive feelings, what stimulated their minds, what was their conception of self, and other such questions. The items were designed to tap the five primary dimensions of developmental potential mentioned earlier (Piechowski, 1979).

There were 19 youngsters who agreed to participate in the two-year follow-up. In most cases the individual features of emotional growth emerged when comparing the content of the responses from the first round with the second or follow-up round. There appeared two highly distinct and two less distinct patterns. Pattern A mirrored Peck and Havighurst's (1960) rational-altruistic type. Adolescents in this category seemed to mature predictably, in keeping with the demands of school and career as well as their active service to the community. Pattern B, the other distinct form, manifested itself in intense emotional growth and much less emphasis on academic and social achievement. Pattern C was less distinct in that it lacked the intensity and depth of Pattern B. Pattern D subjects showed no apparent growth issues. Pattern A was represented by three subjects (all age 19 and in college at the time of the follow-up), patterns B and C by seven subjects (ages 14 to 18), and pattern D by two subjects (ages 14 and 18). The study is exploratory,

meant only to suggest future lines of investigation, and the analysis of the
material is of necessity impressionistic and intuitive. Because our interest
here is in gaining insight into the growth of self, we shall focus our attention
on the contrasting features of patterns A and B.

Pattern A: Rational-Altruistic

In pattern A we notice concentration on the tasks at hand, hard work,
and a sense of social responsibility. The responses are quite similar across the
2-year span. Here are a young female's answers, at ages 17 and 19, to the
question, "What has been your experience of the most intense pleasure?":

> My experience of most intense pleasure in academics so far has been
> when I did very well on a college entrance test. Because I did well
> then, I received many more honors since that have brought pleasure.
> [age 17]

> My experience of the most intense pleasure was graduation day. I was
> leaving high school and moving ahead to college. On that day, I was
> recognized for my achievements. Besides the recognition, it was a per-
> sonal victory—all that hard work had payed off, I had accomplished
> what I wanted to do. [age 19]

She answered the question, "What do you like to concentrate on the most?"
as follows:

> The things I like to concentrate on (center activities around) are in the
> order of importance: family, church and school, work. I like these
> things because they are the main thing in my life right now. The thing
> I like to concentrate on (think about) is myself. It may be egotistical
> but I am involved in so many things that I hardly have time to sit down
> and just think about myself—how things are, make decisions, decide
> my activities for the weekend, etc. [age 17]

> It seems that I concentrate on the most whatever is at hand that is ap-
> pealing at the time. Academically I like to concentrate on those sub-
> jects I know I will use someday or that I can apply in day to day life.
> [age 19]

In replying to the question, "If you ask yourself, 'Who am I?' what is the
answer?" she wrote:

I am a 17 year old girl who is smart, dependable, responsible, tall, hardworking, but lazy at times, kind, active in clubs, has high ideals, who functions best in organized environment, somewhat slow, involved, and tired. [age 17]

I am an intelligent young woman who enjoys being with others and who likes to do things for them. I like to learn and I like to do things well. I am a person who likes things to be clearly defined—I want to know what is expected of me in a given situation. Right now, I am someone who is making difficult decisions about the future and what I really want to do with my life. [age 19]

In these responses we see a strong goal orientation. The framework is rational and altruistic. Satisfaction comes from involvement in many activities, service to others, and seeing clearly what ends it all serves. In another place she said, "I dislike activity that has no purpose." Such response could have come from a self-actualizing "doer" (Maslow, 1971), and, although we do not see here much emotional intensity, rich imagination, or intellectual thirst for knowledge, it is worth remembering that Eleanor Roosevelt, who had all these traits, also disliked activities that had no purpose.

Pattern B: Introspective-Emotional

The type of emotional growth represented by pattern B has several characteristics. Not all of them have to be present at once, but, in the subjects from whose responses the examples below are drawn, at least four out of six of the following qualities are present in each case:

1. Awareness of growing up and changing; awareness of different growth possibilities or paths that are open
2. Awareness of feelings and conscious attention to them; interest in others and empathy toward them
3. Feelings of unreality present occasionally, marking periods of particularly intense emotional growth
4. Inner dialogue and self-judgment, at times quite severe
5. Searching or problem-finding; asking questions that are basic, philosophical, existential
6. Awareness of one's real self

Unlike many adolescents who either live for the moment or worry about the future, we find rather early in a number of gifted children an awareness

of their personal growth as well as anticipation and making ready for what is
to come. One girl expressed it in several ways:

> I think about what I am going to do when I get older. They are good
> thoughts. I seem to want to rush into life. . . . I fantasize about people
> I will meet in the future, places I will visit, friends I will make, where
> I will live. . . . I dream about being an adult. . . . It's sort of funny
> how us children dream about being older, and dream about the future
> and the adults dream about the past and being young again. [age 12]

> I dream about how my life will be when I grow up. I dream lots and
> lots of ways I could be. [age 14]

At 17, in response to a question about what he pays attention to when reading
books, a boy expressed an intense inner push for emotional growth:

> I want to be moved, changed somehow. I seek change, metamorphosis.
> I want to grow (not just in relation to books, either).

Awareness of feelings and emotions gains importance. The same boy
wrote, in response to a question about being poetic:

> I find myself feeling more and more and thinking less and poetry is a
> means of expression for what I feel.

In reply to the question about who they were, several of the youngsters described themselves in distinctly emotional terms:

> [I am] A person who needs attention and a person that needs to be ac-
> cepted. He can't be turned away because he gets hurt easily. [male, age
> 16]

> I am a very misunderstood person. . . . People think that my life is
> easy because I am talented, but I have a lot of problems of my own just
> because of these talents. I often even get cut down for something good
> that I do. This is very hard to cope with. I am a very sensitive and
> emotional person. I get angered or saddened very easily. I can also get
> happy easily. I think I like this part of me. All these emotions some-
> how make me feel good about myself. . . . I am not a very confident
> person, though people think I am. [male, age 16]

> I am a person who has feelings . . . I have friends. I love life. I believe
> in Christ. Sometimes I forget who I am and lose my temper and get
> over angry, but doesn't *everyone!* NOTE: I HAVE FEELINGS. [female, age
> 12]

The note of insistence on feelings shows at once the frustration felt when
they are ignored by others and how important they are to these gifted children's self-definition.

Empathy and understanding of others can be quite conscious, as it was
for the girl just quoted:

> I can see myself in other people, I can see things I've done in what
> other people do. I *really* understand people's thoughts and actions be-
> cause I think of times I was in their place. [age 14]

Such expressions of understanding and caring for others are frequent in the
responses of these youngsters.

Although adolescence is developmentally a time when interest in one's
own and others' feelings comes to focus, the articulateness and insight of
these gifted youngsters is rather exceptional. The emotional maturity and
sensitivity that some proportion of adolescents achieve in late adolescence
appears in the gifted—those engaged in emotional growth—in early adolescence.

Periods of intense emotional growth can bring on such sudden inner
shifts as to produce moments of disequilibrium and estrangement in which
one feels at odds with the surroundings, as if suddenly alien to what was
familiar before. Such feelings of unreality are not a cause for concern, by
themselves. What calls for concern is the fact that great emotional intensity
and sensitivity combined with high intelligence make a youngster acutely
aware of the precariousness of human existence and, in fact, of our world.
Because of this, and because others have so little understanding of this, gifted
children can be extremely vulnerable and at risk (Leroux, 1986; Roedell,
1984).

Feelings of unreality are the inevitable product of great intensity of feeling, of feeling "different" and experiencing a rapid shift in perspective.

> Sometimes when I am just standing there I kind of go into a little daze
> and am sort of unaware of where I am. I look at the people and things
> around me and think it's all unreal. I wonder why I'm me, why God
> created an earth. Sometimes I just feel like everything around me in-
> cluding myself is just part of a dream. [female, age 14]

Sometimes I think I am going insane and I wish I had someone intelligent to talk to. [another female, age 16]

In the next excerpt, the feeling of unreality is combined with emotional experimentation in the form of thinking of the parents as strangers, which can be interpreted as a step toward individual autonomy.

When I ask myself who I am, sometimes I wonder if I'm *really* here.
Or, I'll look at mom and dad and ask myself, who are these people,
and I try to picture them as total strangers. [female, age 15]

Inner dialogue and self-judgment are an essential part of moral growth. Although in his cognitive theory of moral development Kohlberg minimized the importance of emotions, the penetrating genius of William James (1902) saw a definite and necessary link between the strength of one's emotions and moral character. For there to be congruence between beliefs and actions, a person must feel the issues with passion. For James, moral questions are real questions only to those who feel them so strongly that they feel called by them to an active response. They are not problems to reason out but problems the heart knows how to answer more quickly and more immediately. Self-judgment, then, is an evaluation of one's own self, and no personal process of evaluation is possible without the appraising mechanism of feeling (Bowlby, 1969). Without feeling, our subjective life would be just so many bits of data washed of color and meaning.

Here are some examples of how these youngsters monitor themselves. Their sensitive conscience is fitted with a spur to self-correction—the opposite of most adolescents, who, being highly self-conscious and greatly concerned about how they are noticed, tend to be lacking in self-judgment. The following inner dialogue was a response to the question, "Do you ever think about your own thinking? Describe."

I sometimes think of things I think are fun and others think otherwise.
That's when I think about *my* thinking. [male, age 15]

When I take a stand on something, I later wonder why I did that. I
think about how I came to that conclusion. I think about if I was right,
according to the norms of society. I think about my friends and other
people I know and wonder if I really feel the way I let on, and if I am
fooling myself by thinking things I really feel. [the same male at age
17]

The issues of right and wrong figure prominently here. This activity in itself is not unusual, but the process of sorting them out is already strongly autonomous. He examines the origin of his convictions and asks himself whether they are genuine or perhaps just self-deceptions. For contrast, here is another 17-year-old's response to the question, "In what manner do you observe and analyze others?"

> *Critically.* I have an unusual ability for finding people's faults and dis-
> covering their vulnerabilities. I use this knowledge, too—sometimes
> even unconsciously. . . . I am a manipulator, and it sometimes bothers
> me. I know how to handle friends, family, teachers, etc., which makes
> things comfortable for me but does sometimes bother my conscience.
> (Fleetingly, though.)

One might be inclined to wonder whether the future development of this boy will lead him to continue to muffle his conscience and become an even more skillful puppeteer, pulling the strings of others to his own advantage. This does not seem likely in his case, because, in answer to the question about what most attracts his attention in a book, he wrote that the characters were important and that he wanted "to be able to understand them and relate to them—to sympathize with them." He is the one who wrote, "I want to be moved, changed somehow." A person to whom such feelings are important is not likely to ignore them in others nor the impact of his actions on others. In another study Colangelo and Brower (1987), reported that their gifted subjects who were included in programs for the gifted worried about how it made their siblings feel who were not.

Searching, inquiring, and problem-finding are those special abilities (Getzels & Csikszentmihalyi, 1975) by which one discovers things that need discovering, questions that need to be asked, and problems that have yet to be conceived. Self-scrutiny, questioning, and the search for truth go together. Gifted youngsters often ask basic, philosophical, and existential questions. Somehow they develop not only a sense of objective truth but of inner truth as well.

> Lots of times I wish I wouldn't think so much. It makes me very con-
> fused about a lot of stuff in the world. And I always wish I could think
> up answers instead of just questions. . . . My parents and all my adult
> friends don't understand. I wish I could talk to somebody who would
> have the same questions I do, *and* the answers to them. Maybe instead
> of somebody intelligent, I need somebody insane. [female, age 16]

In Delisle's (1984) extensive collection of responses from younger children, one can find similar responses about arguing with teachers or persis-
tently asking questions. Moral concerns and evaluations, however, and issues

of personal responsibility, are more typical of adolescents. Here are two examples:

> I think about my morals and what I really think is right and wrong. I often find that how I feel is a contradiction of what society thinks. This makes me wonder if there is something wrong with me. I concentrate on why and how I became this way and if I will always be this way. [male, age 17]

> I live day to day like everyone else, but I am continually frustrated with the shallowness of how we live and relate to one another. Sometimes I hate myself because I am lazy and I feel unable to change. [female, age 16]

We see in these excerpts keen questioning and self-scrutiny. These youngsters are not only gifted in terms of their talents and abilities but in terms of character growth: They sincerely want to become morally responsible persons. Their self-knowledge is impressive for this age. Gardner (1983) proposed as a separate intelligence the knowledge of one's inner life, that is, the capacity to tell shades of feeling instantly, "to draw upon them as a means of understanding and guiding one's own behavior" (p. 239). He pointed out that certain cultures revere individuals who have access to their "real and direct feelings"; the Japanese call it *jikkan* and cherish the person attuned to his own *jikkan* (p. 273).

Awareness of one's real self appears early in those engaged in intense emotional growth. Gifted youngsters quickly realize that their self-knowledge, the way they know and understand themselves, differs from the way others see and know them. They thus realize that their real self is hidden from others and they can even be aware of keeping it that way.

> I'm somebody no one else knows. Some people see one part of me, others see other parts; it's like I'm acting. The real me is the one inside me. My real feelings, that I understand but can't explain. . . . My best friend is myself. [female, age 14]

The sense of an autonomous and individual self which develops in adolescence is sometimes expressed very strongly. This is perhaps especially so when it appears early, that is, in someone who is still perceived as a child:

> [I am] an individual! I'm me, and I can choose to do what I want, be what I want, make my own decisions, and just be me. I find it very

hard to respect someone who "follows the crowd" and refuses to be an individual. I was put on the earth as an individual and that's just what I intend to always be. [female, age 14]

The development of self-awareness and self-understanding of these gifted youngsters traces the general direction described for adolescents by Broughton (1980), Selman (1980), and others. What is distinctive in the gifted is an acceleration of development and a greater intensity of existential questioning. Of great importance is the value they place on their emotional side. It is not just awareness of having moods, feelings, and emotions that is noticeable; what stands out is also the realization that these are a distinct and essential part of one's self and for this are to be cherished.

CONCLUSION

With today's increased concern over lack of moral leadership, understanding the nature of emotional growth of the gifted needs our attention all the more. Two types of emotional growth were described in this chapter. The rational-altruistic type fits rather neatly into the socially favored model of hard-working sensible achievement and altruism. The other, the introspective-emotional type, demands understanding and considerable patience in regard to the extraordinary emotional sensitivity and intensity it presents. Because it seems so excessive, irrational, or immature, others often find it very difficult to live with. Here is a quote from a highly gifted young undergraduate, describing what it feels like to be different and to be living with an intensity incomprehensible to others:

> I am a "deviant." I am often considered "wild," "crazy," "out of control," "masochistic," "abnormal," "radical," "irrational," "a baby" . . . or simply too sensitive, too emotional, or too uptight. "Mellow out," . . . they say, to which I can only respond, "If I only could . . ." At birth I was crucified with this mind that has caused me considerable pain, and frustration with teachers, coaches, peers, my family, but most of all with myself. [Piechowski, 1987, p. 22]

Yet here we find the most deeply human potential. William James (1902), as noted earlier recognized how emotional intensity joins with superior intellect to create a genuinely moral person, someone for whom questions of personal responsibility engage both the emotions and the will. While a person like this may be difficult to understand and to deal with on a daily basis, she or he is nonetheless crucial in the greater scheme of the evolution of human potential (Feldman and Goldsmith, 1986).

REFERENCES

Baumrind, D. (1970). Socialization and instrumental competence in young children. *Young Children, 26,* 104–119.

Bloom, B. S. (1985). *Developing talent in young people.* New York: Ballantine.

Bowlby, J. (1969). *Attachment.* New York: Basic Books.

Broughton, J. (1980). The divided self in adolescence. *Human Development, 24,* 13–32.

Colangelo, N., & Brower, P. (1987). Labeling gifted youngsters: Long-term impact on families. *Gifted Child Quarterly, 31,* 75–78.

Colangelo, N., & Dettmann, D. F. (1985). Families of gifted children. In S. Ehly, J. Conoly, & D. Rosenthal (Eds.), *Working with parents of exceptional children* (pp. 233–255). St. Louis, MO: Mosby.

Cornell, D. G., & Grossberg, I. N. (1987). Family environment and personality adjustment in gifted program children. *Gifted Child Quarterly, 31,* 59–64.

Csikszentmihalyi, M., & Larson, R. (1984). *Being adolescent.* New York: Basic Books.

Dabrowski, K. (1967). *Personality shaping through positive disintegration.* Boston: Little, Brown.

Dabrowski, K. (1972). *Psychoneurosis is not an illness.* London: Gryf.

Damon, W. (1983). *Social and personality development.* New York: W. W. Norton.

Delisle, J. R. (1984). *Gifted children speak out.* New York: Walker.

Domino, G. (1979). Interactive effects of achievement orientation and teaching style on academic achievement. *Journal of Educational Psychology, 62,* 427–431.

Erikson, E. H. (1968). *Identity: Youth and crisis.* New York: W. W. Norton.

Feldman, D. H., with Goldsmith, L. T. (1986). *Nature's gambit: Child prodigies and the development of human potential.* New York: Basic Books.

Gardner, H. (1983). *Frames of mind.* New York: Basic Books.

Getzels. J. W., & Csikszentmihalyi, M. (1975). From problem-solving to problem-finding. In I. A. Taylor & J. W. Getzels (Eds.), *Perspectives in creativity* (pp. 82–112). Chicago: Aldine.

Getzels, J. W., & Jackson, P. W. (1962). *Creativity and intelligence.* New York: John Wiley.

Harter, S. (1983). Developmental perspectives on the self system. In P. H. Mussen (Ed.), *Handbook of child psychology,* (4th ed.) (pp. 275–385). New York: John Wiley.

James, W. (1902). *The varieties of religious experience.* New York: Modern Library.

Leroux, J. A. (1986). Suicidal behavior and gifted adolescents. *Roeper Review, 9,* 77–79.

Marcia, J. E. (1980). Identity in adolescence. In J. Adelson (Ed.), *Handbook of adolescent psychology.* New York: John Wiley.

Maslow, A. H. (1971). *The farther reaches of human nature.* New York: Viking.

Peck, R. F., with Havighurst, R. J. (1960). *The psychology of character development.* New York: John Wiley.

Piechowski, M. M. (1979). Developmental potential. In N. Colangelo & R. T. Zaffrann (Eds.), *New voices in counseling the gifted* (pp. 25–57). Dubuque, IA: Kendall/Hunt.

Piechowski, M. M. (1986). The concept of developmental potential. *Roeper Review, 8,* 190–197.

Piechowski, M. M. (1987). Family qualities and the emotional development of older gifted students. In T. M. Buescher (Ed.), *Understanding gifted and talented adolescents* (pp. 17–22). Evanston, IL: Northwestern University, Center for Talent Development.

Piechowski, M. M., Colangelo, N., Grant, B. A., & Walker, L. (1983, November). *Developmental potential of gifted adolescents.* Paper presented at the National Association for Gifted Children annual convention, Philadelphia, PA.

Piechowski, M. M., Silverman, L. K., & Falk, R. F. (1985). Comparison of intellectually and artistically gifted on five dimensions of mental functioning. *Perceptual and Motor Skills, 60,* 539–549.

Roe, A. (1975). Painters and painting. In I. A. Taylor & J. W. Getzels (Eds.), *Perspectives on creativity* (pp. 157–172). Chicago: Aldine.

Roedell, W. C. (1984). Vulnerabilities of highly gifted children. *Roeper Review, 6,* 127–130.

Sarton, M. (1970). *Journal of a solitude.* New York: W. W. Norton.

Selman, R. L. (1980). *The growth of interpersonal understanding.* New York: Academic Press.

CHAPTER 7

A Developmental Study of Adjustment Among Gifted Adolescents

Thomas M. Buescher and Sharon J. Higham

Examining the mechanisms of adolescent adjustment is difficult, not because the problems young people encounter at that age are unique, but rather due to the complex interactions underlying each individual and situation. Adjustment in adolescence encompasses several broad areas that have historically been noted by writers and clinicians. Adolescents are portrayed as adjusting to

- Biological maturation, sexual potency, and adult stature (Brooks-Gunn & Petersen, 1984; Lerner & Foch, 1986; Tanner, 1972)
- The uncertainty of adult and peer expectations, loss of intimacy with parents, and the fear of lingering isolation (Blos, 1979; Offer, Ostrov, & Howard, 1981; Sullivan, 1953)
- The momentary or long-term lack of clear identity and purpose (Elkind, 1984; Erikson, 1968)
- The personal reprioritizing of time, talents, and resources to prepare for the demands of adult life (Csikszentmihalyi & Larson, 1984).

While theorists have argued over *where* the emphasis for adjustment is centered, most agree that adolescent adjustment hinges on the tension created by competing desires to be independent of the family while becoming tightly woven into the adult world—the dilemma of "letting go while fitting in," of belonging (Buescher, 1985; Manaster & Powell, 1983). Young people between the ages of 11 and 15 in particular experience these pangs of adjustment when they seek to act independently and resourcefully, yet are constrained by the rules and demands of a less flexible peer group as well as the adult world. Konopka (1980) and others have pointed out that the tensions of adjustment revolve around the five key issues of hormonal imbalance, sexual awakening, unstable values, shifting self-image, and perceived changes within the network of family and friends.

CHALLENGES TO ADJUSTMENT FOR THE GIFTED

Like all adolescents, those young people recognized because of their outstanding academic and artistic abilities must cope with the myriad pressures of the adolescent passage. These adolescents experience an equally wide range of physiological, social, and emotional changes that mark the transition from child to adult in our culture. Yet being both gifted *and* adolescent means understanding and coping with a unique set of developmental circumstances that can reach beyond the normal dimensions of puberty and adolescence (Buescher, 1985).

Young gifted adolescents seem to be quite vulnerable to having their remarkable abilities misinterpreted by adults and peers. While their exceptional talents might lead to more recognition and stature than that afforded to more normal friends, these students do experience at the same time real distance and separation from their peers. As current research has documented, some bright adolescents, in the most extreme cases, become dissatisfied with their own accomplishments, abandon their recognized abilities, and struggle pointlessly through an anxious adolescence that is disappointingly resolved (Buescher, Olszewski, & Higham, 1987; Higham & Buescher, 1987).

Studying adjustment among these adolescents means underscoring several major characteristics about them at the outset. First, talented adolescents do not "know themselves" as well as we might believe. If anything, these students have prolonged doubts through adolescence about their own value and worth. Some researchers (Olszewski, Kulieke, & Willis, 1987) have identified patterns of disbelief, doubt, and lack of self-esteem among older students and adults: the so-called "impostor syndrome" described by many talented individuals after adolescence.

Second, gifted adolescents consistently report dramatic episodes of being pushed to the point of doubt and despair by insensitive teachers, peers, and even parents. Teachers in secondary schools are particularly singled out for trying to disprove the talents of individual students, saying, in effect, "Prove to me you are as gifted as you think you are." Coping with the vagaries of adolescence while also proving oneself again and again in the classroom or peer group significantly drains energy allocated for the normal tasks of adjustment and leads to frequent frustration and isolation.

Third, several dynamics of giftedness continually interfere with adjustment gains during adolescence. While the six issues described in the following paragraphs seldom interact all together at any one moment, they do represent potent obstacles, singly or in any combination, during the early years of adolescence.

Ownership. Talented adolescents simultaneously "own" and yet question the validity and reality of the abilities they possess. While talents have been recognized in many cases at an early age, doubts about the accuracy of identification and the objectivity of parents or favorite teachers linger (Delisle & Galbraith, 1987; Galbraith, 1983). The power of peer pressure toward conformity, coupled with any adolescent's wavering sense of being predictable or intact, can lead to the denial of even the most outstanding ability. The conflict that ensues, whether mild or acute, needs to be resolved by gaining a more mature "ownership" and responsibility for the identified talent.

Dissonance. By their own admission, talented adolescents are often perfectionists. They have learned to set their standards high, to expect to do more and be more than their abilities might allow. Childhood desires to do demanding tasks *perfectly* become compounded during adolescence. Strained by the shifting tides of physical maturation, self-image, and peer judgments, it is not uncommon for talented adolescents to experience real dissonance between what is actually done and how well they *expected* it to be accomplished. At the heart of this dynamic is a lack of awareness of their own growing talents as they strive to increase the quality and acceptability of their performances. Often the dissonance perceived by young people is far greater than most parents or teachers would actually realize.

Taking Risks. While risk taking has been used to characterize younger gifted and talented children, it ironically decreases with age, so that the bright adolescent is *much less likely* to take chances than a more typical peer. Why the shift in risk-taking behaviors? Gifted adolescents appear to be more aware of the repercussions of certain activities, whether these are positive or negative. They have learned to measure the decided advantages and disadvantages of numerous opportunities and to weigh alternatives. Yet their feigned agility at this too often leads them to rejecting even those acceptable activities that carry some risk (e.g., advanced placement courses, stiff competitions, public presentations), where high success is less predictable and lower standards of performance less acceptable in their eyes. One other possible cause for less risk taking could be the need to maintain control—to remain in spheres of influence where challenging relationships, demanding course work and teachers, or intense competition cannot enter without absolute personal control.

Competing Expectations. Adolescents are vulnerable to criticism, suggestions, and emotional appeals from others. Parents, friends, siblings, teachers are all eager to add their own expectations and observations to even the brightest students' intentions and goals. Often, others' expectations for talented young people compete with their own dreams and plans. Delisle (1985) in particular has pointed out that the "pull" of an adolescent's own expectations must swim against the strong current posed by the "push" of others' desires and demands. The dilemma is complicated by the numerous options within the reach of a highly talented student: The greater the talent, the greater the expectations and outside interference.

Impatience. Like most adolescents, gifted students can be impatient in many ways: eager to find solutions for difficult questions, anxious to develop satisfying friendships, and prone to selecting difficult but immediate alternatives for complex decisions. The predisposition for impulsive decision making, coupled with exceptional talent, can make young adolescents particularly intolerant of ambiguous, unresolved situations. Edward De Bono (1978) has characterized these youngsters as being victims of the so-called "intelligence trap": Their impatience with a lack of clear-cut answers, options, or decisions drives them to seek answers where none readily exist, relying on an informing, though immature, sense of wisdom. The anger and disappointment when hasty resolutions fail can be difficult to surmount, particularly when less capable peers gloat about these failures.

Premature Identity. As Erikson (1968) has particularly noted, one of the central goals of adolescence is the successful resolution of one's own ego identity. Elkind (1984) has focused on some adolescents' tendency to develop "patchwork selves," in their effort to reach a premature sense of identity as a way of coping with society's pressure to move quickly from childhood into adulthood. Clinical data from talented adolescents reveal a similar pattern. It appears that the weight of competing expectations, low tolerance for ambiguity, and the pressure of multiple potentials each feed very early attempts to achieve an adultlike identity, a stage normally achieved after the age of 21. This can create a serious problem for talented adolescents. They seem to reach out prematurely for career choices that will short-cut the normal identity-crisis-and-resolution process.

STUDYING HOW ADOLESCENTS ADJUST TO THEIR GIFTEDNESS

Using interview findings (Buescher & Higham, 1984) about how a small group of highly talented adolescents seemed to understand and adjust to situational stressors at ages 13 and 14, Buescher and Higham (1985) developed several measures that could probe specific areas of coping and adjustment. The threefold purpose of carrying out these earlier descriptive studies was (1) to clarify and codify a taxonomy of particular coping strategies; (2) to quantify a broad range of adjustment activities suggested by the research literature on adolescents; and (3) to plot the frequency and use of specific activities across age, sex, and program participation. These descriptive studies and their results laid the groundwork for the two studies whose results will be examined in this chapter.

Instrumentation

Using combinations of information from adolescents, counselors, parents, and earlier researchers, a four-part survey instrument for young adolescents was constructed (Buescher & Higham, 1985). The first section contained seven narrative vignettes (lettered A to G) that set the stage for each respondent's interpretation and reaction. A set of questions followed each of the vignettes, and respondents were asked to rate characters according to how much they were "like me." Age and sex of students portrayed in the vignettes matched the characteristics of the respondent groups.

The second portion of the instrument listed 11 coping strategies gifted adolescents might employ at school or among friends. Respondents were asked to note the frequency of their use of these behaviors. The 11 items reflected kernel aspects of the seven previous vignettes. The strategies and their associated vignettes are listed in Figure 7.1.

A third portion of the instrument probed how students would prioritize for themselves specific coping strategies already examined in the two previous sections. The forced-choice responses provided a clear focus for clusters of coping strategies used by adolescent boys and girls at various ages.

The final section asked respondents to consider how being talented affected particular aspects of their lives, namely, relationships with adults, friendship patterns, labeling, acceptance, and the optimal development of special abilities. A background sheet rounded out other pertinent demographic facts about the adolescents, including what kind of educational opportunities and programs were available in their schools and communities, school size, and years in special programs.

After conducting a pilot test with a smaller group of academically talented adolescents to determine instrumentation clarity and mechanics, we distributed the survey to 85 students who were between 12 and 15 years old and who participated in academic-year programs at Northwestern University. Results and analyses of that formative study provided a strong framework for mounting the more extensive studies described in this chapter.

Figure 7.1   Coping strategies suggested by gifted adolescents and arranged by their viewpoint as 'acceptable' to use

Strategies suggested by adolescents	Associated Vignette[a]	Weighted Ranking
VIEWED AS MOST ACCEPTABLE		
Accept and use abilities to help peers do better in classes (Strategy #11)[b]	G	10
Make friends with other students with exceptional talents (Strategy #6)	--	9
Select programs and classes designed for gifted/talented students (Strategy #9)	--	8
Build more relationships with adults (Strategy #2)	E	7
Achieve in areas at school outside the academics (Strategy #8)	B	6
Develop/excel in talent areas outside school setting (Strategy #3)	--	5
Be more active in community groups where age is no object (Strategy #4)	--	4
Avoid programs designed for gifted/talented (Strategy #1)	F	3
Adjust language and behavior to disguise true abilities from your peers (Strategy #10)	C	2
Act like a "brain" so peers leave you alone (Strategy #7)	D	1
Pretend not to know as much as you do (Strategy #5)	A	0
VIEWED AS LEAST ACCEPTABLE		

[a] While not every strategy suggested by adolescents was translated into a vignette, the seven vignettes included do reflect all aspects of the 11 major coping strategies used for the study.
[b] Strategy number as referred to in the text is given in parentheses after each strategy.

Methodology and Samples

The Young Adolescent Survey (Buescher & Higham, 1985) was administered to talented adolescents who participated in a variety of special programs during the summer of 1985. Respondents had agreed to participate in several developmental studies coordinated by the Center for Talent Development at Northwestern University. Adolescents completed the survey in one proctored session of 90 minutes. Other instruments completed at the same time included the young adolescent version Self-Perception Profile for Children (Harter, 1985) and an extensive background survey, developed at the center, for obtaining data about adolescents and their families.

In the first of the two studies, four groups of adolescents ($N = 604$) completed the three-instrument examination during 1985. All students had previously participated in one of the national academic talent searches, by taking the Scholastic Aptitude Test as a seventh or eighth grader. Programs participating included Rocky Mountain Talent Search Summer Institute, University of Denver; Northwestern University and Argonne National Laboratory Summer Institute; Northwestern University Summer Program for Academically Talented Adolescents; and 1985–86 LetterLinks Learning Program, Center for Talent Development. Students in this first sample ranged in age from 11 to 16, with the majority being 13 to 14. The breakdown by sex was 62% males and 38% females. They represented grades 6 through 11.

The second study was completed during the spring and summer of 1986 at Northwestern University. During this study, participating adolescents completed three instruments: The Young Adolescent Survey (Buescher & Higham, 1985), Harter's (1985) Self-Perception Profile for Children (young adolescent version), and an adapted version of Gouze, Keating, and Strauss' (1985) Adolescent Coping Strategies Questionnaire. A screened sample of 128 young adolescents participated in this study. Their ages were also from 11 to 16, in roughly the same proportion as the earlier sample. They represented grades 6 through 11.

The remainder of this chapter summarizes the results of these two studies and suggests avenues for interpreting the findings. The presentation is framed by our current understanding of the process of talent development and its role in adolescent adjustment for highly talented learners. Results from the studies of talented adolescents described here indicate some interplay among *owning* one's talent, seeking *opportunities* for developing that talent, and *adjusting* to the internal and external demands such a process makes during early adolescence. Our discussion weaves these three themes together.

INFLUENCE OF AGE AND SEX ON ADJUSTMENT

Age

Age is argued to be one of the strongest influences on behavior and adjustment during adolescence (Lerner & Foch, 1986). Younger adolescents lack the experiences, opportunities, and maturity of older adolescents; older students do not perform or behave as maturely as young adults. Since this strong effect for age had been demonstrated in a wide range of studies of adolescent development, including but not limited to adjustment (Petersen, 1988; Simmons, Blyth, & McKinney, 1984; Simmons, Blyth, Van Cleave, & Bush, 1979), it seemed likely that age would garner similar effects in the adolescent adjustment studies described here.

What was more important, however, was the general question posed often by developmental psychologists: Are the effects of age on such behavior irreversible? Does a young person's age have more predictive value than her or his opportunities and experiences, when one examines patterns of adjustment? The question is particularly keen in the field of education for the talented, where there is conflicting evidence about the more rapid mastery and maturity of highly talented students (Tannenbaum, 1983). If talented adolescents experience less influence of age during their development, then perhaps their adjustment problems and chosen solutions in adolescence are more similar to those of young adults. On the other hand, if talented adolescents cope with the everyday stressors of life like all others their age, what does that say about the impact of any recognized talent on their internal lives before adulthood?

The first area probed for age effects was that of coping with recognized talent. In this study the adolescents' *preferred* coping strategies were ranked for each age group from 12 to 15 years. Only the three top-ranked strategies were considered for each age group. Sex of the adolescents was not considered at this point.

The most interesting facet of these rankings across all age groups was the curvilinear movement of what had been hypothesized to be the most "positive" strategy: using one's talent to help others. Over the course of four years, this strategy moved from second place to first, by way of third. An opposite curvilinear transition was also shown by one of the flexible, independent strategies: achieving in school in areas *outside* academics (#8). It appears to *rise* in popularity until the age of 14 but then drops to third place again in the rankings by all participants.

The strategy of making friends with students with similar abilities (#6) appeared to be most important in the early years of adolescence but weakened as the apparent attractiveness of a broader peer group materialized at later ages.

The ranking of this group's vignette characterizations by age categories (13 and younger, 14 and older) yielded equally interesting results. The vignettes were ordered according to how much their principal characters "acted like" each respondent. Clearly, vignette G (using talents to help others) was most unanimously selected to be "like me," while vignette A (doing poor work so no one expects more) was seen to be "least like me" among most respondents. Age may solidify choices about how one must relate to known abilities. Most important, the vignettes' ordering closely approximated that of the coping strategies just presented, across the composite age groups.

All study participants had also completed the young adolescent version of Harter's (1985) instrument, and we looked to see if age effects were apparent there as well. Table 7.1 contains the study group's Harter scale scores, arranged by meaningful age blocks. For each question on the Harter instrument, students' scores can range from 1 to 4. A subscale score is the mean of the responses for the six questions that comprise a subscale and therefore also ranges from 1 to 4. We considered scores of 3 and above to represent more positive self-perceptions. The table shows the percentage of students with high mean scores on the subscales of academic competence, social acceptability, physical appearance, and global self-worth. Perfect scores on each subscale (i.e., mean scores of 4) are broken out from the rest of the scores of 3 and above in the table.

As can be seen, there are sharp contrasts at all ages between the total academic competence and global self-worth scores and the total social acceptability and physical appearance scores. A substantial majority of the students viewed themselves as being academically competent (80%) and generally worthy (71%) over the entire age span, yet only about half of the group

Table 7.1 Percentage of Mean Scores of 3 and 4 on Harter Subscales by Age

Harter Subscale	Mean Score	Percentage of Scores			
		Age: 12	13	14	15
Academic Competence	$\geq 3 < 4$	65	56	55	66
	4	19	17	17	26
Total		84	73	72	92
Social Acceptability	$\geq 3 < 4$	38	60	50	51
	4	3	5	8	
Total		41	65	58	51
Physical Appearance	$\geq 3 < 4$	52	40	37	46
	4		5	8	5
Total		52	45	45	51
Global Self-Worth	$\geq 3 < 4$	61	61	59	54
	4	6	15	15	14
Total		67	76	74	68

Figure 7.2   Graphic Representation of the Four Harter Subscale Totals, by Age

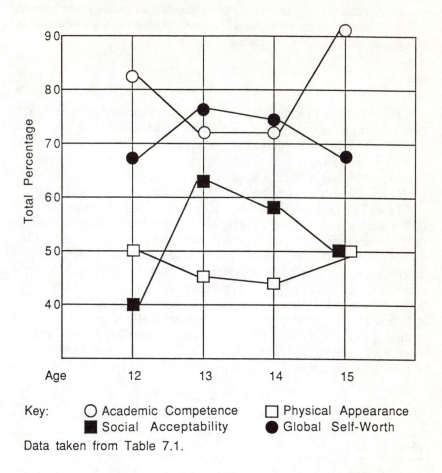

Key: ○ Academic Competence   □ Physical Appearance
        ■ Social Acceptability   ● Global Self-Worth
Data taken from Table 7.1.

members viewed themselves as competent in social acceptability (54%) and physical appearance (48%).

One way of interpreting these general findings is that talented students put more stock in their intellectual abilities as a measure of their worth and much less emphasis on how attractive they are to others (Olszewski, Kulieke, & Willis, 1987). What is interesting *across* the age groups, however, is the subtle curvilinear relationships in each of the four areas. Figure 7.2 projects the findings in Table 7.1 onto a graph showing these tendencies. When the percentages for the four subscales are plotted, an interesting pattern emerges: Ratings of academic competence and physical appearance fall be-

tween the ages of 13 and 14, while global self-worth and social acceptability
rise at that same age. The resulting image is that more widely disparate ratings are common at ages 12 and 15, while the estimations are closer together
at ages 13 and 14. Regardless of age, however, satisfaction with their appearance consistently received the lowest rating.

Sex

There had been earlier evidence to support the investigation of adjustment patterns by controlling for sex. Clinical data indicated that young adolescent boys and girls not only were dealing with somewhat different issues,
they were also using varied approaches to cope with them (Buescher &
Higham, 1984). As a result, the coping strategies and vignettes, as well as
the Harter scales, were reanalyzed while controlling for sex as well as age.

Table 7.2 compares the preferential rankings of some of the coping strategies when sex is considered. Only those that were ranked in the top four are
shown; hence, only 6 of the original 11 strategies appear in the table. Contrasts and similarities can be seen by examining some of the patterns in these
figures. First, the curvilinear appearance of what we considered to be the
most "positive" strategy (#11, using talents to help others) is identical for
both boys and girls. It is more frequently used at ages 12 and 15 and less so
at 13 and 14. The opposite curvilinear function is also shown for strategy 8
(achieving in areas *at school*, outside academics) regardless of sex of respondents, yet its rise and fall in usefulness seems swifter for girls than boys.

Another interesting finding is the relatively low ranking of strategy 9

Table 7.2   Preferential Rankings of Coping Strategies[1] by Age, and Sex

	Girls				Boys			
Rank	Age: 12	13	14	15	12	13	14	15
1st	6	8	8	11	6	6	8	11
2nd	11	6	3	3	11	8	6	6
3rd	8	11	11	5	8	11	11	8
4th	9	3	6	8	3	3	3	3

[1] Strategies identified by number, are defined as follows:
   #3=Excel in talent areas *outside* school
   #5=Pretend abilities are not present
   #6=Make friends with students with similar abilities
   #8=Achieve in areas *at school*, outside academics
   #9=Select programs/classes for talented students
   #11=Use talents to help peers do well in classes

(selecting programs/classes for talented students). It can be seen as the fourth choice for girls at age 12 but appears at no other point in any age or sex group. The same is true for strategy 5 (pretending one's abilities are not present); in this large sample it only appears once in the top-four rankings, as a third choice among 15-year-old girls. Its elevation to this level may simply reflect the subjects' having exhausted more positive strategies earlier, rather than a strong *desire* to mask true abilities. It is, however, a defense that has been at least anecdotally described in earlier research on older adolescents (Higham & Buescher, 1987).

Strategy 6 (making friends with other students with similar abilities) also demonstrates sharp contrasts. Both boys and girls rank this strategy as the one most used at the age of 12; but at 13 its frequency has slipped to second for girls while remaining first for boys. At age 14, girls rank this factor as their fourth priority. Boys, on the other hand, still view its utility favorably, ranking it second at age 14 and again at age 15. By age 15, girls do not even include this strategy in their top four choices.

Patterns of use of strategy 3 (excelling in talent areas *outside* school) also appear to be quite different when sex of the subjects is considered. Girls give it higher priority as they get older; boys consistently rank it as a fourth choice at every age.

Sex appears to have less influence in the ranking of the vignettes. While some differences are evident in the rank orderings for each group, the general pattern of responses ("like me" or "not like me") is quite similar to the results shown in Table 7.2. Vignettes B and G (depicting strategies 8 and 11) are consistently regarded as being "most like" the respondents, regardless of age or sex. Vignettes A (strategy 5) and D (strategy 7, acting like a brain so peers leave you alone) are viewed as being "least like" the study respondents. These results corroborate the earlier findings, namely, that talented young adolescents prefer to cope with their abilities by using them to help peers or by seeking new "labels" in the school community (strategy 8) as a means of diluting the negative aspects of being regarded as a gifted or talented student. Both girls and boys are least interested in overt *masking* of their abilities or acting out an obnoxious or withdrawn stereotype.

Age and Sex Combined

Does sex in combination with age influence talented adolescents' self-esteem in a particular way? To answer this, the study group's Harter scale scores were regrouped, controlling for the age and sex of the students and plotting scores at or above 3 in the same four subscales discussed earlier: academic competence, social acceptability, physical appearance, and global self-worth.

The results, when broken down by age and sex, were similar to the group's composite scores. Girls and boys at every age in adolescence generally feel somewhat better about their academic competence and global self-worth than they do about their appearance and sociability. An interesting curvilinear rise in social acceptance is evident among girls. In addition, physical appearance scores for girls decline steadily from age 12 onward, as do the global self-worth scores reported.

In summary, components of self-esteem seem to fluctuate more due to age than sex; but, in the case of global self-worth and physical appearance, the self-esteem of talented young women drops more as they approach age 15 than does that of young men.

INFLUENCE OF SPECIALIZED PROGRAM PARTICIPATION ON ADJUSTMENT

Historically, advocates for specialized educational opportunities for gifted and talented students have urged the creation of programs for young people that group them together. While various arguments are given for this organizational option, little research is provided to substantiate the claims made about its urgency and effectiveness. The problem becomes particularly acute during adolescence when the creation of specialized programs can separate young people from important earlier friendship circles. One benefit often cited is that selective grouping for academic purposes may support the development not only of talent but of each adolescent's personal growth and identity with a group of true peers.

In an effort to provide some empirical basis for this thinking, the largest study group, which contained over 600 talented adolescents, was grouped according to program participation as well as age and sex. This section describes the results of those analyses, based on student responses to the vignettes and the coping strategies questionnaire.

First, we sorted the subjects into three groups: (1) those who were in programs (IP), (2) those for whom programs were unavailable (NPA), and (3) those who had avoided available programs (AAP). Students "in programs" identified themselves as participating in at least one of several kinds of programs for gifted and talented students: honors/AP classes, self-contained programs for the gifted and talented, special classes within or beyond magnet programs, focused programs (Olympics of the Mind, Future Problem Solving), after-school or Saturday programs, fast-paced classes, and so forth. Sixty-five percent of the group were in the IP category. Students in the NPA category (17% of the sample) indicated that none of these options were available in their middle schools or high schools. Those respondents in the AAP

Table 7.3 Distribution of Mean SAT-M and SAT-V Scores by Age, Sex, and Program Participation

Age and Sex	In Programs	No Programs Available	Avoid Available Programs
Males, age ≤ 13			
SAT-M	551.724	570.000	535.000
SAT-V	453.824	473.913	478.333
Males, age ≥ 14			
SAT-M	592.055	468.621	508.667
SAT-V	502.431	550.690	447.333
Females, age ≤ 13			
SAT-M	515.152	497.778	446.667
SAT-V	476.212	434.444	468.333
Females, age ≥ 14			
SAT-M	497.083	492.500	421.000
SAT-V	476.170	436.667	480.000

category (18% of the sample) had chosen *not* to participate in one of the aforementioned kinds of program, even though they were clearly eligible and the options were available to them. Nearly equal numbers of girls and boys fell into each category, although it appears that more girls than boys avoid programs, particularly as they get older.

One initial interest was whether or not program participation was related to level of academic talent. Table 7.3 shows the distribution of SAT scores for the study subjects, according to their age, sex, and type of program participation. Scores shown are for both the verbal (SAT-V) and mathematics (SAT-M) tests. As can be seen, boys' mean SAT-M scores exceeded those of the girls, with the exception of the NPA group. This is a typical finding among the talent search participants. However, SAT scores do not appear to vary systematically by program participation.

We also wondered in what ways program participation might be related to selected coping strategies and patterns of adjustment. Tables 7.4 and 7.5 summarize, for boys and girls, respectively, the mean vignette/strategy ratings, ordered according to the positiveness of the implicit strategy and broken down by age group and type of program participation. That is, the various coping strategies were lined up with their counterpart vignettes; then each combination was rank-ordered according to its relative degree of positiveness, as shown in Figure 7.1. Finally, vignette/strategy mean scores were computed for each age group and program type.

Table 7.4   Relationship of Program Participation to Vignette/Strategy Mean Ratings, for Males, by Age

| Vignette/Strategy[1] | Vignette/Strategy Mean Rating[2] | | | | | |
| | Age $\leq$ 13 | | | Age $\geq$ 14 | | |
	IP	NPA	AAP	IP	NPA	AAP
G 11	1.821	1.483	3.500	1.810	1.676	2.063
B 8	3.009	2.966	3.625	2.929	2.973	3.563
E 2	4.189	4.621	4.125	4.583	4.351	5.125
F 7	4.208	4.207	4.000	4.417	3.947	2.250
C 10	3.670	3.483	3.625	3.619	2.947	2.375
D 7	4.538	4.759	5.375	4.976	5.081	5.250
A 5	5.075	5.276	5.250	5.106	4.816	4.815

[1] Vignettes, lettered A through G, are paired with their matching strategy numbers and rank ordered according to the "positiveness" of the strategy, with the most positive at the top of the list. Since there were 11 strategies and only 7 vignettes, not all of the strategies are represented here.

[2] The rating scale ranged from 0 to 6, with 0 representing the response, "exactly like me," and 6 representing the response, "not at all like me." Scores of 1 through 5 represented statements along a continuum between these two extremes.

Considering just the males (Table 7.4), certain discrepancies in mean ratings are apparent between students who either participate in programs (IP) or have no programs available to them (NPA) and those students who willingly choose *not* to participate (AAP). For example, in the younger of the two male groups, mean ratings for the very positive vignette-G/strategy-11 combination by the IP and NPA groups were twice as affirming as ratings by the AAP group. More surprising, G(11) was nevertheless the one the AAP group rated as most "like me"! A similar trend occurs for G(11) and B(8) in the 14-and-older groups. Yet mean ratings become somewhat more similar as the strategies implicit in the vignettes become more negative. There are two notable exceptions to this, however. The discrepancies are particularly pronounced for the older boys on F(1), which represents avoiding programs designed for the gifted, and C(10), which represents adjusting language and behavior to hide one's talents. In both cases use of these strategies is considerably higher among the AAP group members than among the other two groups.

The trend for the most positive strategies to receive the least affirmative scores from the AAP group also holds true among the older adolescent females (see Table 7.5). Among the younger females, however, the NPA group is least affirming in this regard. Also unlike the boys, the various groups of girls show rather wide discrepancies in their ratings for the less positive strategies. This is particularly pronounced for the older girls on C(10), where, like the boys, the greatest use of this strategy falls to the AAP group.

Looking at these adjustment patterns among the three program participation types in a different way, more evident shifts appear. Table 7.6 shows a breakdown by program participation of how boys' mean vignette ratings have rank-ordered the vignettes. While minor shifts occur among 12- and 13-year-old students, their rankings are fairly consistent across program types, even though those choosing not to be in programs have less positive feelings in general. The students age 14 and older show less consistency in this regard. The sinking ranking for vignette B (strategy 8, looking for a new label be-

Table 7.5   Relationship of Program Participation to Vignette/Strategy Mean Ratings, for Females, by Age

Vignette/ Strategy [1]	Vignette/Strategy Mean Rating [2]					
	Age $\leq$ 13			Age $\geq$ 14		
	IP	NPA	AAP	IP	NPA	AAP
G 11	1.542	1.818	1.714	1.714	1.500	2.750
B 8	3.222	3.727	3.286	2.768	3.071	3.250
E 2	4.085	4.818	4.571	4.393	5.000	5.250
F 1	4.873	4.818	4.208	4.518	3.947	4.250
C 10	3.764	3.818	2.429	3.393	3.286	2.750
D 7	5.222	5.455	4.857	5.446	5.643	5.500
A 5	5.556	5.455	5.571	5.571	5.643	5.500

[1] Vignettes, lettered A through G, are paired with their matching strategy numbers and rank ordered according to the "positiveness" of the strategy, with the most positive at the top of the list. Since there were 11 strategies and only 7 vignettes, not all of the strategies are represented here.

[2] The rating scale ranged from 0 to 6, with 0 representing the response, "exactly like me," and 6 representing the response, "not at all like me." Scores of 1 through 5 represented statements along a continuum between these two extremes.

Table 7.6   Relationship of Program Participation to Vignette Mean Ratings and Resulting Rank Order, for Males, by Age

Age ≤ 13			Age ≥ 14		
IP	NPA	AAP	IP	NPA	AAP
G	G	G	G	G	G
1.821	1.483	3.500	1.810	1.676	2.063
B	B	B	B	C	F
3.009	2.966	3.625	2.929	2.947	2.250
C	C	C	C	B	C
3.670	3.483	3.625	3.619	2.973	2.375
E	F	F	F	F	B
4.189	4.207	4.000	4.417	3.947	2.250
F	E	E	E	E	A
4.208	4.621	4.125	4.583	4.351	4.817
D	D	A	D	A	E
4.538	4.759	5.250	4.976	4.816	5.125
A	A	D	A	D	D
5.075	5.276	5.375	5.106	4.081	5.250

Note: Rating scale ranges from 0 ("exactly like me") to 6 ("not at all like me"); resulting rank order shown here positions the most "like me" vignettes at the top and the least "like me" vignettes at the bottom, for each category of respondent.

yond academics at school) and the progressively elevated position of vignette A (strategy 5, pretending not to know as much as one really does) suggest a general strategy of masking true abilities, as noted in the rise of vignette F (strategy 1, avoiding programs for the gifted/talented). In other words, the less these older boys participated in special educational opportunities, the more likely they were to employ less positive coping strategies to accommodate their recognized talents.

Unfortunately, even stronger trends in this regard are shown among adolescent girls who choose not to participate in special programs. Table 7.7 describes these trends, which again are more noticeable among the older adolescent group. For the girls, it is vignette E (strategy 2, building relationships with adults) that sinks in the rank ordering, while the most negative, vignette A (strategy 5, pretending not to know as much as one really does), rises to a higher position. The concurrent rise in vignette C (strategy 10, hiding true abilities from peers) signals a general trend toward more deliberate masking of known talents as one gets older, if there is no consistent program support available.

To summarize at this point, the positiveness and priority of strategies gifted adolescents use in coping with stresses related to their own recognized talents are influenced by the age and sex of the adolescents and the degree to which they participate in special programs designed for academically talented students. Those influences notwithstanding, however, there are some overarching patterns that demand closer attention and have important bearing on needed programs in education and counseling. Attention to these patterns would facilitate both adjustment and talent development for this age group. It is to these concerns we now turn.

Table 7.7   Relationship of Program Participation to Vignette Mean Ratings and Resulting Rank Order, for Females, by Age

Age ≤ 13			Age ≥ 14		
IP	NPA	AAP	IP	NPA	AAP
G	G	G	G	G	G
1.542	1.818	1.714	1.714	1.500	2.750
B	B	C	B	B	C
3.222	3.727	2.429	2.768	3.071	2.750
C	C	B	C	C	B
3.764	3.818	3.286	3.393	3.286	3.250
E	E	F	E	F	A
4.085	4.818	4.208	4.393	3.947	4.000
F	F	E	F	E	F
4.873	4.818	4.571	4.518	5.000	4.250
D	D	D	D	A	E
5.222	5.455	4.857	5.446	5.357	5.250
A	A	A	A	D	D
5.556	5.455	5.571	5.571	5.643	5.500

Note: Rating scale ranges from 0 ("exactly like me") to 6 ("not at all like me"); resulting rank order shown here positions the most "like me" vignettes at the top and the least "like me" vignettes at the bottom, for each category of respondent.

RISK PATTERNS IN ADJUSTMENT

Results of these two studies focusing on talented adolescents' adjustment raise several serious concerns that counselors, educators, and parents must try to resolve. The purpose of these studies has been not only to describe the course of the coping mechanisms used between ages 11 and 16, but also to focus on patterns that might identify significant risks to the development of promising talent and so suggest effective interventions during the adolescent years.

One pitfall has already been described, namely, the adverse effects of lack of "ownership" of one's own talents. Some of the ways that this carries over into other aspects of adolescent adjustment have become clearer. Common sense would dictate that not owning the reality of one's abilities would make the avoidance of programs and opportunities that much easier to consider and accomplish, and our results document this relationship. The pronounced use of more negative coping strategies (masking, lowering expectations, avoiding friends with equal abilities) also signals the presence and effects of lack of challenge and support in a talented adolescent's life.

A related risk factor that appears to operate is sagging self-esteem. When young talented adolescents cannot see themselves as having worth on the basis of their exceptional abilities, social skills, and self-control, they run the risk of seeking that affirmation through social acceptability and physical appearance alone. While both of these aspects of self-esteem assume disproportionate value in adolescence, they can create significant risk for a young person for whom the importance of his or her own talents to friends and family is in doubt. The critical role of parents and teachers in shaping a positive impression cannot be ignored. Clinical evidence underscores the major role that family structure and dynamics play in shaping self-esteem among talented adolescents (Buescher, 1986b; Piechowski, 1987). It also documents the compatibility of coping mechanisms with the level of self-esteem (Buescher et al., 1987).

The third risk factor is perhaps the most difficult to explicate, for it appears rooted in the socialization practices of our society. Simply stated, girls appear to be more at risk than boys for avoiding and walking away from their own outstanding talent in early adolescence. Some of the differences described earlier in this section about how boys and girls seek to accommodate exceptional talents into their own lives during adolescence are summarized in the following paragraphs.

Girls and boys approach the dilemma of talent and "belonging" with nearly identical strategies at the age of 12: They look for and find friends with similar abilities and build relationships with that small group. By age 13, however, girls and boys part company in their coping styles. Girls appear to respond in a more mature way to the tug of adolescence, seeking to widen the pool of friendships, while boys dig deeper into these earlier, more familiar friendship patterns. Thirteen-year-old girls begin to build new "labels" for themselves which can counteract the less desirable ones associated with being talented. These labels might include being in student council, performing in the chorus or band, or being touted as a dancer or athlete. It is important to note that these labels, while located in the school, do exist *outside* academic classrooms. Boys at 13, on the other hand, put their energies into solidifying skills and talents within their select circle of male and female friends.

By age 14, girls have taken another step with their special talents, but in this case it is often *outside the school doors*. Perhaps this is an effort to stretch abilities into a richer circle of friends in the broader community; or it could be an attempt to keep one's talents from becoming a barrier to friendships with other students, most commonly boys. Regardless of the intent, fewer girls with exceptional talent remain visible and active in that regard in the adolescent school community. Boys at age 14 pursue a different tack, reaching beyond the smaller accepting clique to a more visible stage at the school. Their intent is to identify and cultivate promising areas for second "labels" *within* school areas but parallel to academics. Choices often mentioned include music, drama, fine arts, athletics, debate, journalism, and photography. These second labels serve to dilute the effects of having attention called to their more primary academic abilities. As with girls at age 13, the desired effect is to broaden friendship opportunities, particularly in deference to girls.

Age 15 finds boys and girls continuing their divergent paths. Girls, responding perhaps to the tension of "belonging" in a richly different social grouping, use their recognized talents and abilities to aid less able peers and so gain wider acceptance in a heterogeneous group. Academic abilities are forged into assets for what seems to be one last attempt to make talents serve a useful purpose and not be a source of alienation. Yet, by 16, even these efforts are often abandoned. "Belonging" becomes an inescapable force, pulling young women from programs that might be ideally suited for their academic needs but desolate in terms of satisfying social ones. In the struggle to develop talent in highly specialized classes away from desired friendships, some exceptional young women sacrifice talent for acceptance.

Do boys fare any better? At age 15, talented high school boys appear to be most attracted to solidifying a new, comfortable label explored at age 14 and initially developed parallel to their academic talents. Sophomore boys invest seemingly inordinate amounts of time and energy in extracurricular interests; yet academic placements are rigidly maintained. By age 16, these young men have built a cohesive group of friendships that are richly mixed in interests yet very similar in levels of academic talent. This diversity/equity

amalgam is enhanced by the group's sharing of individual talents and resources to facilitate the prosperity and influence of the group: "Scholars tu-
toring scholars" could well be its purpose. When young women have nurtured their talents up to age 16, they often behave in a strikingly similar way
with each other.

In summary, talented adolescents seem to have accomplished very similar goals by age 16, particularly forging closer friendships with a small group
of desired peers. The striking difference is that often for girls the chosen
friends and opportunities lack any relationship to and support for strong
talent areas; for boys, that is seldom the case. Support services for talented
adolescents need to recognize the presence of this obviously conflictual dynamic and build strategies for addressing it.

CONCLUSION

Being gifted and talented as well as adolescent poses unique problems
for the evolution and refinement of coping techniques. Coleman (1985) attributes these difficulties to feelings of being *different*, which can interfere
with optimal social acceptance and even personal development. Feeling different can be magnified by the reactions of the peer group or the overt labeling inflicted by schools or special programs for the gifted.

The studies described here have put empirical weight behind anecdotal
and life-history reports attributed to gifted and talented students who have
felt different and have described the problems they faced and the strategies
they used to gain acceptance and support from others. The findings emphasize the complex effects of several key developmental challenges on the
growth of outstanding talent during adolescence:

1. The desire to belong or fit in rather than be separated from families
   or friends
2. The lengthy influence of an unstable body image on shifting self-
   esteem
3. The growing weakness of previously strong coping mechanisms
   honed during childhood
4. A general lack of satisfaction with relationships with others
5. An impatient quest for independence and identity that overlooks in-
   consistencies in personal beliefs and earlier concepts of self

Adjustment during adolescence is the serious attempt to restore equilib-
rium to a complicated psychosocial and biological system that is momentarily
out of balance. The normal ebb and flow of human development requires

continual adjustment processes to keep individuals on an even keel and ready to expand existing abilities and acquire new skills that enrich a variety of talents. Many questions remain to be answered about how gifted students weather the adolescent passage. Why do some flourish while others succumb to pressures that reach into their everyday lives? Are young people with certain personalities more at risk than others for ineffective coping strategies during adolescence? Further research will provide more clues as to how adults can better support gifted and talented students at home and at school during the adolescent years.

REFERENCES

Blos, P. (1979). *The adolescent passage.* New York: International Universities Press.

Brooks-Gunn, J., & Petersen, A. (Eds.). (1984). *Girls at puberty: Biological and psychosocial perspectives.* New York: Plenum Press.

Buescher, T. M. (1985). A framework for understanding the social and emotional development of gifted and talented adolescents. *Roeper Review, 8*(1), 10–15.

Buescher, T. M. (1986a, March). *Adolescents' responses to their own recognized talent: Issues affecting counseling and adjustment.* Paper presented at the 63rd annual meeting of the American Orthopsychiatric Association, Chicago.

Buescher, T. (1986b, November). *The effect of family structure and expectations on the performance and adjustment of highly talented adolescents: Selected case studies.* Paper presented at the annual meeting of the National Association for Gifted Children, Las Vegas.

Buescher, T., & Higham, S. (1984, March). *Young gifted adolescents: Coping with the strains of feeling different.* Paper presented at the 61st annual meeting of the American Orthopsychiatric Association, Toronto.

Buescher, T., & Higham, S. (1985). *Young adolescent survey: Coping skills among the gifted/talented.* Unpublished instrument, Northwestern University, Center for Talent Development.

Buescher, T., Olszewski, P., & Higham, S. (1987, April). *Influences on strategies gifted adolescents use to cope with their own recognized talent.* Paper presented at the 1987 biennial meeting of the Society for Research in Child Development, Baltimore.

Coleman, L. (1985). *Schooling the gifted.* Menlo Park, NJ: Addison-Wesley.

Csikszentmihalyi, M., & Larson, R. (1984). *Being adolescent: Conflict and growth in the teenage years.* New York: Basic Books.

De Bono, E. (1978). *Lateral thinking.* New York: Harper Books.

Delisle, J. (1985). Counseling gifted persons: A lifelong concern. *Roeper Review, 8*(1), 4–5.

Delisle, J., & Galbraith, J. (1987). *The gifted kids survival guide, II.* Minneapolis: Free Spirit.

Elkind, D. (1984). The patchwork self. In *All grown up and no place to go* (pp. 159–177). Reading, MA: Addison-Wesley.

Erikson, E. (1968). Identity, youth, and crisis. New York: W. W. Norton.

Galbraith, J. (1983). *The gifted kids survival guide, ages 11–18.* Minneapolis: Free Spirit.

Gouze, K., Keating, D., & Strauss, L. (1985). *Adolescent coping strategies in developmental steps.* Paper presented at the biennial meeting of the Society for Research in Child Development, Toronto.

Harter, S. (1985). *Self-perception profile for children* (rev.). Denver, CO: University of Denver.

Higham, S., & Buescher, T. (1987). What young gifted adolescents understand about feeling different. In T. Buescher (Ed.), *Understanding gifted adolescents* (pp. 26–30). Evanston, IL: Northwestern University, Center for Talent Development.

Konopka, G. (1980). Stresses and strains in adolescents and young adults. In L. Bond & J. Rosen (Eds.), *Competence and coping during adulthood.* Hanover, NH: University Press of New England.

Lerner, R. M. & Foch, T. T. (1986). *Biological-psychosocial interactions in early adolescence: Life span perspectives.* Hillsdale, NJ: Lawrence Erlbaum.

Manaster, G., & Powell, P. M. (1983). A framework for understanding gifted adolescents' psychological maladjustment. *Roeper Review, 6*(2), 70–73.

Offer, D., Ostrov, E., & Howard, R. (1981). *The adolescent: A psychological self-portrait.* New York: Basic Books.

Olszewski, P., Kulieke, M., & Willis, G. (1987). Changes in the self-concept of gifted students who participate in rigorous academic programs. *Journal for the Education of the Gifted, 10*(4), 287–304.

Petersen, A. (1988). Adolescent development. *Annual Review of Psychology, 39,* 583–607.

Piechowski, M. (1987). Family qualities and the emotional development of older gifted students. In T. Buescher (Ed.), *Understanding gifted and talented adolescents* (pp. 17–23). Evanston, IL: Northwestern University, Center for Talent Development.

Simmons, R. G., Blyth, D., & McKinney, K. (1984). The social and psychological effects of puberty on white females. In J. Brooks-Gunn & A. Petersen (Eds.), *Girls at puberty* (pp. 229–272). New York: Plenum Press.

Simmons, R. G., Blyth, D., Van Cleave, E., & Bush, D. (1979). Entry into early adolescence: The impact of school structure, puberty, and early dating on self-esteem. *American Sociological Review, 44,* 948–967.

Sullivan, H. S. (1953). *The interpersonal theory of psychiatry.* New York: W. W. Norton.

Tanner, J. M. (1972). Sequence, tempo, and individual variation in growth and development of boys and girls, 12 to 16. In J. Kagan & R. Coles (Eds.), *Twelve to sixteen: Early adolescence* (pp. 1–24). New York: W. W. Norton.

Tannenbaum, A. (1983). *Gifted children: Psychological and educational perspectives.* New York: Macmillan.

CHAPTER 8

Personality Dimensions of Gifted Adolescents

Paula Olszewski-Kubilius and Marilynn J. Kulieke

Within the literature on gifted individuals there are many studies that examine personality dimensions. These studies cover a variety of age groups and employ many different personality instruments, yet they can be categorized around several key issues. One broad area of research has to do with discerning personality differences between gifted and nongifted individuals. Within this area comparisons can be made between gifted students and non-gifted same-age peers and between gifted students and nongifted chronologically older students. Studies of the first type address the issue of whether gifted individuals have unique patterns of personality characteristics compared to nongifted agemates, while the second addresses the issue of early psychological maturity for the gifted.

Another broad area of research has to do with differences on personality dimensions within gifted populations. Comparisons between gifted females and males predominate. The literature within each of these three areas will be reviewed briefly as a prelude to a study that also addresses these issues.

REVIEW OF RESEARCH

Comparisons Between Gifted and Nongifted Individuals of the Same Age

Because there are so many studies that address this issue and because the personality constructs they examine are so varied, the studies will be grouped and presented by broad age ranges.

Elementary School Children. Several researchers studying anxiety in high IQ students have found that they have lower levels of anxiety than their more average counterparts. Scholwinski and Reynolds (1985) gave the Manifest Anxiety Scale to high-IQ elementary school children and found lower levels of anxiety among the gifted students, compared to norming groups of same-age children. Lower levels of anxiety about school were found by Davis and Connell (1985) for high-IQ fourth, fifth, and sixth graders, compared to nongifted students of the same age. Milgram and Milgram (1976) found that gifted fourth- through eighth-grade Israeli girls (high IQ) had lower scores on the Wallach and Kogan versions of the Sarason scales of anxiety, when compared to nongifted girls of the same age.

Several studies comparing gifted to nongifted students on self-esteem and self-concept have found that the gifted students obtain higher scores on these measures. High-IQ elementary-school-age children have been shown to have higher scores on the personal worth and self-esteem subscales of the California Test of Personality (Lehman & Erdwins, 1981). Maddux, Scheiber, and Bass (1982) obtained higher scores for the intellectually gifted sixth graders on the Piers-Harris self-concept instrument, compared to nongifted students. Ketcham and Snyder (1977) found that their sample of high-IQ children, grades 2 through 4, had higher self-concept scores than a same-age norming group in the same instrument.

Milgram and Milgram (1976) utilized the Tennessee Self-Concept Scale and found that their gifted fourth- through eighth-grade students had greater feelings of personal adequacy in the family, were less guarded and defensive, and gave fewer indications of psychological disturbance, compared to same-age nongifted students. On the other hand, the older nongifted students in this study had a more positive body image, described themselves more positively, and reported a greater sense of personal worth and self-confidence, compared to their gifted counterparts.

Several studies with elementary school children have found differences between gifted and nongifted students on measures of locus of control. Milgram and Milgram (1976) reported differences for their sample of fourth- through eighth-grade students; the gifted students had significantly greater internal locus of control and thus assumed more responsibility for past events and expressed greater feelings of competence to affect future desirable events. Davis and Connell (1985) similarly reported that gifted fourth, fifth, and sixth graders were higher than average on intrinsic motivation and autonomy of judgment, and lower on feeling that their behavior was controlled by unknown causes. Lucito (1964) found that high-IQ sixth graders were significantly less conforming than low-IQ children of the same age. Thus, gifted elementary school students appear to be more internally focused, at least regarding their own achievement.

Finally, one study found differences on aspects of sociability for gifted and nongifted students. Lehman and Erdwins (1981) compared gifted high-

IQ elementary-school-age children to average IQ students and found their high-IQ third graders had higher scores on several of the social subscales on the California Test of Personality, notably social skills and cooperation.

Adolescents. There are several studies that focus on the personality dimensions of gifted adolescents. The Milgram and Milgram (1976) report previously mentioned indicates that among fourth- through eighth-grade gifted students, the older gifted students had less positive self-perceptions, compared to their same-age, nongifted counterparts. Killian (1983) found no differences between gifted and nongifted seventh through twelfth graders on the High School Personality Questionnaire, which assesses dimensions such as extroversion, anxiety, independence, school achievement, creativity, neuroticism, and leadership.

The California Psychological Inventory (CPI) is probably the most frequently used personality instrument for adolescent populations and includes dimensions such as dominance, capacity for status, sociability, social presence, self-acceptance, sense of well-being, responsibility, social maturity, self-control, tolerance, good impression, achievement via conformity and independence, intellectual efficiency, psychological mindedness, flexibility, and femininity. Lessinger and Martinson (1961) report that eighth-grade gifted boys show favorable differences (i.e., higher average scores) on every scale of the CPI, compared to a random group of eighth-grade boys. The gifted girls in their study were also higher on every CPI subscale, except for femininity, than a random sample of same-age girls.

Bachtold (1969) used the Survey of Interpersonal Values with seventh-, eighth-, and ninth-grade gifted students and found that gifted males placed less value on recognition than nongifted males, while gifted females placed more value on independence compared to nongifted females.

Several studies of gifted adolescents have looked specifically at the personality dimensions of individuals gifted in mathematics. Kennedy (1962) found that these students had profiles on the Minnesota Multiphasic Personality Inventory that were within normal limits. Dagget-Pollins (1983) found that eighth graders gifted in mathematics were higher on the CPI subscales of flexibility and psychological mindedness, and lower on their general sense of well-being and need to make a good impression, when compared to a random group of eighth graders. Haier and Denham (1976) found that eighth-grade males gifted in math were generally dissimilar to a random group of eighth-grade males on the CPI subscales. The greatest differences were found on achievement via independence and degree of flexibility and adaptability, with the gifted males scoring higher than the other student group.

Eighth-grade girls gifted in math were also found to be dissimilar to a random sample of same-age females on subscales of the CPI and were particularly low on femininity, achievement via conformity, and socialization (degree of social maturity and integrity), compared to the control group (Haier & Denham, 1976). These gifted girls were higher on achievement via independence than the nongifted girls.

Both girls and boys gifted in math were found by Dagget-Pollins (1983) and Haier and Denham (1976) to place higher value on theoretical and political interests/motives and lower value on religion on the Allport Study of Values, compared to nongifted students of the same age, but these differences were not statistically significant.

A study of older adolescents using the CPI (Purkey, 1966) found that gifted high school students generally were better adjusted and possessed more "favorable" personality characteristics, when compared to average high school students. In this study, gifted students scored significantly higher on almost all of the 18 scales of the CPI, compared to nongifted students, except for socialization and femininity for males and socialization, self-control, and femininity for females. Bonsall and Stefflre (1955), however, found few differences between gifted and nongifted high school seniors on aspects of temperament such as general activity, restraint, sociability, emotional stability, friendliness, thoughtfulness, and cooperation, when socioeconomic status (SES) was controlled. This latter study suggested that in many personality studies, particularly those comparing samples where SES may be unknown and/or confounded with group membership, differences on personality dimensions may not be reliable.

In summary, research that has focused on discerning differences between gifted students and their same-age, nongifted counterparts has tended to find that differences do exist and that they generally favor gifted students. Gifted students appear to be more independent, intrinsically motivated, flexible, self-accepting, and psychologically well adjusted than their nongifted peers. There is also some limited evidence to suggest that young adolescent gifted students are somewhat lower on measures of general well-being than their same-age peers.

Comparisons Between Gifted Students and Nongifted, Chronologically Older Individuals

There are several studies that address the issue of early psychological maturity for gifted students by comparing their scores or profiles on personality instruments to those of nongifted individuals who are older in age. The studies attempt to discern whether gifted students show developmental advancement in their personality functioning that is similar to their developmental advancement in intellectual functioning. Lehman and Erdwins (1981) compared high-IQ third graders, average third graders, and average sixth graders on the California Test of Personality. The gifted children differed significantly from both average groups on various subscales. They were higher than the average third graders on sense of personal worth, social skills, antisocial tendencies, and sense of personal freedom. They were also higher than the average sixth graders on personal freedom, cooperation, and self-esteem. However, the authors note that there was no consistent pattern to the differences obtained, and thus it is not clear whether or not the gifted students evidenced early psychological maturity.

Ritchie, Bernard, and Shertzer (1982) gave their academically talented 10-year-olds a test of interpersonal sensitivity and found that they performed slightly better than average 10-year-olds but not as well as academically average 12-year-olds. These authors concluded that sensitivity in interpersonal situations does not show the kind of developmental advancement that cognitive tasks or cognitively laden personality attributes (e.g., achievement orientation) do for gifted children.

On the CPI, Lessinger and Martinson (1961) found that gifted eighth-grade girls were similar to gifted high school girls on 11 of the 18 scales. The high school females were higher on capacity for status, social presence, self-acceptance, achievement via independence, dominance, and intellectual efficiency, while the eighth-grade girls were higher on sociability. For the males in the study, Lessinger and Martinson also found that "the maturity of the gifted eighth graders (boys) was much more closely related to that of the gifted high school boys" (p. 573). Similarly, Davids (1966) found that gifted high school girls and boys obtain scores on the CPI that are closer to norms for college-age girls and boys than to the norms for same-age children.

Thus, there is limited research evidence that gifted children may evidence personality functioning for certain variables that is more mature than expected for their age.

Comparisons Between Gifted Females and Gifted Males

There are a few studies that examine differences between gifted females and males, all dealing with students who are of junior high age or older.

Bachtold (1969) found that 12- to 14-year-old gifted males gave less value to support and benevolence and higher value to leadership, compared to gifted girls, but the groups did not differ on dimensions such as conformity, need for recognition, or independence. Haier and Denham (1976) found that eighth-grade girls and boys gifted in math had very similar profiles on the CPI, and Davids (1966) found no differences between high-achieving high school boys and girls, using the same instrument.

Killian (1983) found no differences between gifted girls and boys from grades 7 through 12, on the High School Personality Questionnaire (HSPQ). Karnes, Chauvin, and Trent (1984), however, did find some differences between gifted high school boys and girls on the HSPQ: Gifted males were more tenderminded, sensitive, and overprotected than gifted females. Gifted females were more excitable, impatient, and unrestrained, compared to gifted males. Fox (1976) found that junior-high-age females who had high SAT scores (talent search participants) had significantly higher scores on the aesthetic, social, and religious scales of the Allport-Lindzey Study of Values, compared to talent search males; while males had higher scores on the theoretical, economic, and political scales, compared to females.

Finally, for college students, Tomlinson-Keasey and Smith-Winberry (1983) reported that gifted college males, based on scores on the CPI, could be characterized as more active, ambitious, forceful, insightful, resourceful, versatile, clever, imaginative, outgoing, and rebellious, compared to gifted females. Gifted females, on the other hand, were more honest, industrious, obliging, sincere, modest, steady, conscientious, appreciative, patient, helpful, gentle, respectful, and accepting of others, compared to gifted males.

Thus, most studies comparing gifted males and females do not find substantial differences. Among those that do obtain differences, the variations are consistent with expectations along sex-stereotypical lines.

Summary

In summary, the research literature on personality dimensions of gifted individuals reveals that

1. Gifted students do differentiate themselves from nongifted same-age peers on personality dimensions, and these differences tend to be favorable to gifted students, at least until adolescence.
2. There is limited research evidence to suggest that the personality profiles of gifted students, with regard to maturity, resemble or even exceed those of chronologically older, nongifted individuals. Thus there is some support for a hypothesis of early psychological maturity for gifted children.
3. Gifted females and gifted males are more similar than different on personality profiles, and those differences that exist generally are consistent with sex stereotypes.

METHODOLOGY FOR STUDY OF PERSONALITY DIMENSIONS

The research reported in this chapter examines the personality dimensions, values, needs, and self-concept of a select group of intellectually talented adolescents who participated in a summer program. The study employed a variety of instruments. The purposes of the research were to provide a detailed, comprehensive profile of gifted male and female adolescents, to address the issue of psychological maturity with our sample of students by comparing them to older students, and to determine to what extent gifted female and male adolescents differ from one another.

Subjects

The subjects for this study were drawn from the 306 students who attended the 1985 Midwest Talent Search (MTS) summer program for academically talented students, at Northwestern University. All of the students completed the self-concept assessment, while a smaller sample ($n = 111$) completed the other personality instruments. Sample sizes vary slightly due to missing data. The students had SAT scores of 430 or greater on the verbal subtest or 500 or greater on the mathematics subtest. The sample was approximately 60% male and 40% female. The students' ages ranged from 11 to 16, although the majority (62.1%) were 13 or 14 years old. The sample was 69.4% Caucasian, 27% Oriental, and 3.6% of other racial background. Sixty-two percent came from families with an income of over $50,000 per year.

Instrumentation

The factor structures obtained by the authors of each instrument were used with our sample of subjects. Each instrument used a paper-and-pencil format.

The Allport-Lindzey Study of Values. The purpose of the Allport-Lindzey Study of Values (SOV) is to measure the relative prominence of six basic interests or motives in personality (Allport, Vernon, & Lindzey, 1970). The six scales and their corresponding interests are:

1. *Theoretical*—interest in discovery of truth
2. *Economic*—interest in what is useful
3. *Aesthetic*—highest value on form and harmony
4. *Social*—highest value on love of people
5. *Political*—interest in power
6. *Religious*—highest value on unity

The test is constructed so that 40 is the average score for any scale.

High School Personality Questionnaire. The High School Personality Questionnaire (HSPQ) is a self-report inventory that measures 14 personality characteristics (Cattell, Cattell, & Johns, 1984). It is intended for use with

12- through 18-year-olds. The scales are (1) warmth, (2) intelligence, (3) emotional stability, (4) excitability, (5) dominance, (6) cheerfulness, (7) conformity, (8) boldness, (9) sensitivity, (10) withdrawal, (11) apprehension, (12) self-sufficiency, (13) self-discipline, and (14) tension.

School Motivation Analysis Test. The School Motivation Analysis Test (SMAT) (Krug, Sweeney, & Cattell, 1976) is an objective paper-and-pencil instrument of 10 predictive and meaningful dynamic primary traits. These are (1) assertiveness, (2) mating/sex (heterosexual drive), (3) fear, (4) narcissism (sensual satisfaction), (5) pugnacity/sadism (need to compete against and defeat others), (6) protectiveness/pity (maternalistic or paternalistic feelings), (7) self-sentiment (security of the self), (8) superego, (9) sentiment to school, and (10) sentiment to home. The first six traits are considered to be primary drives, while the last four are acquired interest patterns.

Myers-Briggs Type Indicator. The Myers-Briggs Type Indicator (Briggs-Myers, 1962) attempts to implement Jung's theory regarding basic differences in the way people prefer to use perception and judgment. The four basic pairs of preferences and the ways they structure the individual's personality are as follows: (1) extroversion or introversion—general orientation to the outer versus inner world, (2) sensing or intuitive perception based on the senses or intuition, (3) thinking or feeling—judgments based on true or false versus valued and not valued, and (4) judgment or perception—dealing with the external world using either judgment or perception.

Harter Self-Perception Profile for Children. The Self-Perception Profile for Children (Harter, 1985) consists of five separate subscales of children's perceptions of themselves in different domains, as well as a global measure of self-worth. These six subscales are (1) scholastic competence, (2) social acceptance, (3) athletic competence, (4) physical appearance, (5) behavioral conduct, and (6) global self-worth.

RESULTS

Study of Values

Comparison of Gifted and Norming Groups. The first set of results is related to differences in mean scores, for both sexes combined, in our sample of gifted junior-high-age MTS students and a high-school-age norming sample provided in the handbook from the Allport-Lindzey SOV. Table 8.1 shows that there are significant differences between these groups on four of the six basic values. The MTS group is significantly higher on theoretical, aesthetic, and political interests and significantly lower on religious interest compared to the norming group.

The second set of results also can be found in Table 8.1, which breaks down the same data according to sex. Both male and female MTS students show significantly higher scores on theoretical interest and significantly lower scores on religious interest than their respective norming groups. MTS males show significantly higher political interest than the male norming group, and MTS females show significantly higher aesthetic interest than the female norming group.

In order to determine whether the MTS sample had means similar to an older cohort, they were compared to a norming sample of college students (see Table 8.2). The MTS sample (both sexes combined) still scores significantly higher on theoretical and political interests and significantly lower on religious interests, when compared to the older cohort of students. These findings hold when males and females are examined separately. Thus, gifted males and females differentiate themselves from older students in the same way as they differentiate themselves from nongifted students of the same age.

Comparisons Within the Gifted Group. Table 8.1 shows the means and significance levels for comparisons between MTS males and females. This table shows that there are significant within-group differences for five of the six interests. Males have significantly higher scores than females on theoretical, economic, and political interests. Females have significantly higher scores than males on aesthetic and social interests. Males and females do not differ on religious interests.

High School Personality Questionnaire

Comparison of Gifted and Norming Groups. Of the 14 personality characteristics measured by the HSPQ, significant differences were obtained between the MTS students and the same-aged norming group (both sexes combined) on 10 (see Table 8.3). The MTS sample has significantly higher scores than the norming group on warmth, intelligence, emotional stability, dominance, cheerfulness, conformity, boldness, and self-sufficiency. They have significantly lower scores on apprehension and tension. There are no significant differences between the groups on excitability, sensitivity, withdrawal, and self-discipline.

Table 8.3 also breaks down these differences according to sex. The MTS male and female samples both have significantly higher scores than their respective norming groups on intelligence, emotional stability, dominance, and boldness and significantly lower scores on apprehension and tension. In ad-

(*text continues on p. 136*)

Table 8.1 High School Norming Group and MTS Student Mean Scores on the Allport-Lindzey SOV

Interests	Mean Scores: Both			Mean Scores: Male			Mean Scores: Females			t for MTS Males vs. MTS Females
	H.S. Norming Group¹ (N=12,616)	MTS Students (N=90)	t	H.S. Norming Group¹ (N=5,320)	MTS Students (N=48)	t	H.S. Norming Group¹ (N=7,296)	MTS Students (N=42)	t	
Theoretical	40.2	44.8	-5.9**	43.3	46.6	-3.6**	37.0	42.6	-5.3	2.2**
Economic	40.5	41.5	-1.4	42.8	44.2	-1.4	38.2	38.5	-0.3	2.9**
Aesthetic	36.7	38.8	-2.7**	35.1	34.2	0.8**	38.2	44.1	-5.3	-6.6**
Social	40.2	39.0	1.6	37.1	36.5	0.6	43.3	41.7	1.5	-3.4**
Political	41.1	43.6	-3.8**	43.2	46.5	-3.9**	39.1	40.4	-1.5	3.9**
Religious	40.8	31.8	9.8**	37.9	30.9	5.8**	43.8	32.8	8.7	-0.8

** p < .01   ¹The norming sample consisted of 10th to 12th graders.

Table 8.2 College Sample and MTS Student Mean Scores on the Allport-Lindzey SOV

Interests	Mean Scores: Both			Mean Scores: Males			Mean Scores: Females		
	College (N=3,778)	MTS (N=90)	t	College (N=2,489)	MTS (N=48)	t	College (N=1,289)	MTS (N=42)	t
Theoretical	39.8	44.8	-6.4**	43.8	46.6	-2.7**	35.8	42.6	-6.1**
Economic	40.3	41.5	-1.5	42.8	44.2	-1.2	37.9	38.5	-0.5
Aesthetic	38.9	38.8	0.1	35.1	34.2	0.7	42.7	44.1	-1.1
Social	39.6	39.0	0.8	37.1	36.5	0.5	42.0	41.7	0.3
Political	40.4	43.6	-4.7**	42.9	46.5	-3.7**	37.8	40.4	-2.6**
Religious	41.0	31.8	9.2**	38.2	30.9	5.3**	43.8	32.8	7.4**

** p < .01

Table 8.3 Norming Groups and MTS Student Mean Scores on the High School Personality Questionnaire

Characteristic	Mean Scores: Both Sexes			Mean Scores: Males			Mean Scores: Females			t for MTS Males vs MTS Females
	Norming[1] Group (N=7,519)	MTS Students (N=106)	t	Norming[1] Group (N=3,736)	MTS Students (N=62)	t	Norming[1] Group (N=3,584)	MTS Students (N=44)	t	
Warmth	10.9	11.8	−2.4*	10.0	11.7	−4.0**	11.9	11.8	.1	−.1
Intelligence	6.8	8.5	−9.2**	6.5	8.5	−7.7**	7.1	8.6	−5.6**	−.4
Emotional stability	8.8	10.5	−5.3**	9.4	11.0	−3.8**	8.1	9.8	−3.3**	1.8
Excitability	10.6	10.1	1.4	10.6	10.1	1.0	10.5	10.0	1.0	.2
Dominance	8.7	10.3	−5.0**	10.3	11.4	−2.9**	7.1	8.9	−4.1**	4.1**
Cheerfulness	9.7	10.3	−2.0*	10.1	11.0	−1.9	9.2	9.5	.5	1.9
Conformity	11.1	11.9	−2.4*	10.6	11.4	−1.9	11.5	12.5	−1.9	−1.6
Boldness	9.9	11.3	−4.2**	10.6	12.0	−3.3**	9.2	10.4	−2.2*	1.7
Sensitivity	10.4	10.3	.2	7.0	8.0	−2.1*	13.8	13.5	.5	−6.7**
Withdrawal	8.6	9.0	−1.6	9.1	9.2	−.2	8.0	8.9	−1.8	.5
Apprehension	9.4	7.0	7.2**	9.0	6.5	5.9**	9.7	7.7	3.9**	−1.6
Self-sufficiency	8.8	10.0	−3.6**	9.7	10.2	−1.3	7.9	9.6	−3.5**	.8
Self-discipline	10.2	10.7	−1.8	10.3	10.8	−1.3	10.0	10.6	−1.2	.3
Tension	10.4	9.0	4.1**	10.1	8.6	3.3**	10.7	9.5	2.2*	−1.2

[1] The data for the norming sample are based on adolescents of age 14 1/2.

* p < .05
** p < .01

dition, MTS males score significantly higher on warmth and sensitivity, compared to the male norming sample; and MTS females score significantly higher than the female norming group on self-sufficiency.

Comparisons Within the Gifted Group. The data comparing MTS males with MTS females on the HSPQ are also shown in Table 8.3. MTS males score significantly higher than females on dominance, while MTS females are significantly higher than males on sensitivity. There were no other major differences within the gifted group.

School Motivation Analysis Test

Comparison of Gifted and Norming Groups. Table 8.4 shows the SMAT data for the MTS males and females compared to their respective same-sex norming sample of nongifted junior-high-age students. (Data for a norm-

Table 8.4 Norming Group and MTS Student Mean Scores on the School Motivation Analysis Test

Trait	Mean Scores: Males			Mean Scores: Females			t for MTS Males vs MTS Females
	Norming[1,2] Group (N=1,188)	MTS Students (N=62)	t	Norming[2] Group (N=1,241)	MTS Students (N=44)	t	
Assertiveness	7.2	6.9	1.0	6.7	6.8	− .3	.3
Mating/sex	8.2	5.1	9.9**	8.8	4.5	13.4**	1.3
Fear	6.2	4.9	4.9**	6.3	5.5	2.9**	−1.5
Narcissism	8.3	5.5	9.0**	9.5	5.8	11.6**	− .7
Pugnacity/sadism	7.8	5.5	7.1**	7.6	4.7	8.5**	2.0
Protectiveness/ pity	6.7	5.6	3.9**	7.6	5.8	6.4**	− .3
Self-sentiment	7.6	6.2	4.8**	8.1	5.6	8.0**	1.9
Superego	7.1	6.9	.7	7.1	6.9	.4	− .1
Sentiment to school	8.0	5.9	7.5**	8.1	6.1	6.4**	− .6
Sentiment to home	6.3	5.0	4.8**	6.8	4.9	5.9**	.2

[1] Only integrated scores are reported.
[2] The data for the norming sample is based on students aged 14 1/2.

** $p < .05$

ing group of males and females combined was not available in the manual.) MTS males are significantly lower than the male norming sample on traits of mating/sex, fear, narcissism, pugnacity/sadism, protectiveness/pity, self-sentiment, sentiment to school, and sentiment to home. MTS females show the same pattern of results when compared to their norming group.

Comparisons Within the Gifted Group. There are no significant differences between MTS females and males on any of the SMAT scales (refer to Table 8.4).

Myers-Briggs Type Indicator

Comparison of Gifted and Norming Groups. Several different norming groups were available for comparison on the Myers-Briggs Type Indicator (see Table 8.5). Two same-age norming groups were used, a junior high school sample and a gifted group of seventh-to-ninth graders; as were two older norming samples, a group of male National Merit Scholarship finalists and a group of college liberal arts students.

When males in the MTS group are compared to the two same-age norming groups, we see the several trends. MTS and junior high school males are more frequently classified as extroverts than introverts, whereas males in the gifted seventh-to-ninth-grade sample are evenly split on this pair. On the sensing-versus-intuitive dimension, MTS and gifted seventh-to-ninth-grade males are predominantly intuitive. This is dramatically reversed for the junior high male sample, which is predominantly sensing. Males were predominantly thinking rather than feeling across all three samples, although this is more pronounced for the MTS students. All three groups suggest that males tend toward perceiving rather than judging, although both the MTS and junior high groups are more evenly split between the two than are the gifted seventh-to-ninth graders.

The MTS female sample is fairly evenly split between extroversion and introversion, while students in both the junior high school and gifted seventh-to-ninth-grade samples are predominantly extroverts. On the sensing-versus-intuitive dimension, both the MTS and gifted seventh-to-ninth-grade females lean heavily toward the intuitive side, while the junior high school females are predominantly sensing. All three groups are predominantly feeling rather than thinking. The final indicator, judging versus perceiving, shows that all three female groups are predominantly perceiving, although this trend is strongest for the MTS and gifted seventh-to-ninth-grade sample.

When the MTS sample is compared to the older students, the results for males show that the older gifted sample of National Merit Scholarship final-

Table 8.5 Frequency of Preference for MTS Students and Comparison Groups on Meyers-Briggs Type Indicator

Preference Pairs	MTS		Jr. High School[1]		Gifted 7th-9th Graders[2]		Nat'l Merit[3]	College Students[4]	
	Males (N=62)	Females (N=44)	Males (N=100)	Females (N=121)	Males (N=34)	Females (N=25)	Males only (N=100)	Males (N=2,177)	Females (N=241)
Extroversion	56	48	68	75	50	58	42	54	58
Introversion	44	52	32	25	50	42	58	46	42
Sensing	40	26	72	70	21	12	17	38	30
Intuitive	60	74	28	30	79	88	83	62	70
Thinking	72	45	56	41	56	42	66	54	34
Feeling	28	55	44	59	44	58	34	46	66
Judging	46	31	49	47	38	35	43	43	45
Perceiving	54	69	51	53	62	65	57	57	55

1 Pre-college prep 7th and 8th graders from Swarthmore High School, mean IQ =114 (Myers, 1970).
2 High IQ's and rank of 95th percentile or better on all achievement tests taken (Myers, 1970).
3 Random sample drawn from larger sample of 671 (Myers, 1970).
4 College liberal arts majors (Myers, 1970).

ists leans toward introversion, while the MTS and college males lean toward extroversion. With regard to the other three dimensions, all three samples are predominantly intuitive, thinking, and perceiving. The MTS males closely resemble the college liberal arts males except on the thinking/feeling dimension, where the MTS males show a much stronger preference for thinking.

The MTS females and the college females share a similarly strong preference for intuition over sensing. MTS females tend toward introversion, while the college sample leans toward extroversion. On the other two scales, both groups tend to be feeling more than thinking and perceiving more than judging, although the former is more pronounced for the college females, while the latter is very strong only for the MTS females. There were no comparisons between the MTS female sample and the National Merit Scholarship sample because the latter sample was males only.

Comparisons Within the Gifted Group. For each of the four pairs of indicators on the Myers-Briggs scale, continuous scores were created (not shown in the table). When females and males in the MTS sample are compared to each other on each of these dimensions, there is a statistically significant difference on only one of the indicators: Females have significantly higher means on the feeling-versus-thinking indicator. (Female mean is 100.9; male is 82.1.) This means that MTS females use feeling significantly more than their male counterparts.

Harter Self-Perception Profile for Children

Comparison of Gifted and Norming Groups. Comparisons between the MTS sample and an eighth-grade norming sample could only be made for males and females separately. Table 8.6 shows these data. The MTS males have significantly higher means for scholastic competence, behavioral conduct, and global self-worth, compared to the norming males. Athletic competence is significantly lower for the MTS males, compared to the norming sample.

The MTS females have significantly higher scores on the same subscales as the males (i.e., scholastic competence, behavioral conduct, and global self-worth), when compared to the norming sample of eighth-grade females. Notably, there are no significant differences for females on social acceptance, athletic competence, or physical appearance.

Comparisons Within the Gifted Group. When males in the MTS sample are compared to females, Table 8.6 shows that there are differences on only two scales; that is, males have significantly higher scores on athletic competence while females have significantly higher scores on behavioral conduct.

Table 8.6 Norming Sample and MTS Student Mean Scores on the
Harter Self-Perception Profile for Children

| | Mean Scores: Males | | | Mean Scores: Females | | | t for MTS Males vs. MTS Females |
	Norming Group (N=72)	MTS Students (N=196)	t	Norming Group (N=70)	MTS Students (N=108)	t	
Scholastic competence	2.8	3.3	-7.0**	2.7	3.2	-5.3**	1.6
Social acceptance	3.1	3.0	.5	3.1	3.0	1.3	- .2
Athletic competence	3.2	2.8	4.0**	2.6	2.5	.3	3.6**
Physical appearance	2.9	2.9	-.1	2.6	2.8	-1.8	.7
Behavioral conduct	2.9	3.1	-3.2**	3.0	3.3	-3.6**	-2.2*
Global self-worth	3.0	3.2	-3.0**	2.9	3.2	-3.2**	-.1

*p < .05
**p < .01

DISCUSSION

Synthesis of This Study with Prior Research

The Allport-Lindzey Study of Values has been used with several other samples of gifted students. Both Haier and Denham (1976) and Daggett-Pollins (1983) found, as we did, that the theoretical and political interests were those for which academically gifted students had the highest means. In addition, our findings replicate those of Daggett-Pollins, who found that their sample scored the lowest on religious interest.

The results for the High School Personality Questionnaire yielded some findings that are confirmed in the literature, notably those of Davis and Connell (1985), Milgram and Milgram (1976), Scholwinski and Reynolds (1985), and Purkey (1966). These results show more positive psychological profiles, better adjustment, and lower levels of anxiety for gifted students. The finding of greater self-sufficiency and boldness for gifted students in this study also has some support in previous work (Milgram & Milgram, 1976; Davis & Connell, 1985). This study found that the MTS students were more conforming than their same-age nongifted counterparts, which is consistent with Ringness (1967) but inconsistent with the work of Lucito (1964).

Our data on the Myers-Briggs scale show no differences in the level of extroversion between gifted and nongifted males, which is consistent with the results of Wrenn, Ferguson, and Kennedy (1962). However, MTS females tended to be more introverted compared to nongifted groups, which is inconsistent with Wrenn et al. (1962). The findings of this study on the Harter scale show high levels of global self-worth and a generally positive self-concept for MTS students, which is consistent with previous research (Ketcham & Snyder, 1977; Lehman & Erdwins, 1981; Maddox et al., 1982; Milgram & Milgram, 1976).

Regarding sex differences, our results for males versus females on the SOV are consistent with the findings of Bachtold (1969). We also found significant sex differences on two subscales of the HSPQ: Females had higher sensitivity scores and males had higher dominance scores. These results are consistent with previous work by Karnes et al. (1984) that found higher scores for females on sensitivity as well as excitability, but they are at variance with the work of Killian (1983), who found no sex differences on the HSPQ.

The sex difference obtained on the thinking/feeling dimension of the Myers-Briggs scale confirms the findings of McGinn (1976) for verbally talented students participating in a summer talent search program. In addition, the sex differences obtained in this study on the Harter subscale of behavioral conduct (higher scores for females) are consistent with the findings of Hultgren and Marquardt (1986), although these authors did not test for statistically significant differences.

Few studies that we reviewed compared gifted students to older students on the dimensions we studied. Our results for the SOV indicate that gifted males and females differentiate themselves from college-age students on the same values and to a similar degree as they differentiate themselves from nongifted students of the same age.

For the Myers-Briggs Type Indicator, the MTS females evidenced early psychological maturity only on the sensing/intuitive dimension. The MTS males evidenced psychological maturity on the introversion/extroversion, sensing/intuitive, and judging/perceiving dimensions.

Profiles of Gifted Adolescents

Our results show that gifted males take a more cognitive approach to life, being more critical, rational, and intellectual than their nongifted male agemates. They have a greater desire for the direct expression of personal power and influence, which may result in their seeking leadership positions. They also tend to be less religious and mystical in their approach to life, compared to nongifted males. Gifted males are mentally and emotionally healthy and not troubled by undue levels of apprehension and tension.

The gifted adolescent male is more sensitive than the nongifted adolescent male, as well as more dominant and bold. The gifted male, relative to the norming-group male, behaviorally expresses significantly lower levels of need for personal security, to be competitive with and to defeat others, to be paternalistic, to satisfy egocentric sensual needs, and to be interested in school or home. He is more likely to rely on intuition rather than his five senses, and on thinking rather than feeling in dealing with the external environment. In relation to his sense of self, the gifted male is more likely than a nongifted male to feel that he is competent in the area of academics, behaves well, and possesses an overall positive feeling of self-worth. Gifted males, however, do not perceive themselves to be as competent athletically as do nongifted males.

The gifted female, like her male counterpart, takes a more cognitive, empirical, and rational approach to life, relative to nongifted females. She also places a high value on aesthetics, with form and harmony and artistic episodes being important to her. Her desire for the direct expression of personal power and influence tends to be higher, too, compared to the nongifted female. She places less value on religion and mysticism than her nongifted counterpart, and she has a higher mental capacity and ability to handle abstract problems. The gifted female adolescent tends to be emotionally stable and free of debilitating anxiety and fear. There is also a greater tendency for dominance, assertiveness, aggressiveness, stubbornness, and bossy behavior on the part of the gifted female, compared to her nongifted counterpart.

The gifted female appears to be more venturesome and uninhibited while feeling more free from guilt and more self-satisfied than the nongifted girl. She is more self-sufficient and resourceful than her nongifted agemate, preferring to make her own decisions.

The gifted female expresses lower levels of need, relative to the nongifted female, in the areas of mating, personal security (fear), self-centered sensual satisfaction, competition with and defeat of others, maternalistic tendencies, and involvement and connectedness to school and home.

The gifted female is more likely to be an introvert than her nongifted agemates and is also much more likely to rely on intuition than on her five senses as a means of making decisions. She is decidedly internally oriented, giving weight to her own internal perceptions, stirrings, and feelings. Her perceptions of self-worth, conduct, and scholastic competence are positive and higher than the nongifted female.

Gifted males and gifted females differentiate themselves in several ways. The gifted male places more value on a cognitive approach to life and exhibits a greater desire for personal power than the gifted female. Form and harmony and social relations are of greater value to the gifted female, compared to the gifted male. Gifted males are more dominant, while gifted females are more sensitive. Gifted males give much less weight to their feelings in making judgments than do gifted females. The gifted male has a greater sense of athletic competence than the gifted female, although his perception of his conduct is not as positive as hers.

SUMMARY

In general, gifted junior-high-age girls resembled gifted junior-high-age boys in values, personality characteristics, expressed needs, preferences for ways of perceiving and judging, and perceptions of competence and self-worth. Many more differences were obtained between the MTS students and same-age nongifted students. Gifted girls, however, are not just like gifted boys; each has a unique set of characteristics, which has implications for the choices gifted males and females make for their future, especially in regard to selecting careers, jobs, and roles. Gifted males need to be directed toward careers that respond to their value for the analytical and intellectual and their leadership chracteristics. Gifted females need to be encouraged toward careers that give weight to both their intellectual values as well as their aesthetic values. Females also have leadership characteristics but, due to their internal and intrapsychic focus, may experience conflicts related to career situations that demand and emphasize relationships with people and external events. Gifted females need assistance in integrating those aspects of their personalities to maximize their leadership potential.

REFERENCES

Allport, G. W., Vernon, P. E., & Lindzey, G. (1970). *Manual for the study of values: A scale for measuring the dominant interest in personality.* Boston: Houghton-Mifflin.

Bachtold, L. M. (1969). Personality differences among high ability underachievers. *The Journal of Educational Research, 63*(1), 16–68.

Bonsall, M. R., & Stefflre, B. (1955). The temperament of gifted children. *California Journal of Educational Research, 6*(4), 162–165.

Briggs-Myers, I. (1962). *The Myers-Briggs type indicator.* Palo Alto, CA: Consulting Psychologists Press, Inc.

Cattell, R. B., Cattell, M. D., & Johns, E. (1984). *Manual and norms for the High School Personality Questionnaire.* Champaign, IL: Institute for Personality and Ability Testing.

Dagget-Pollins, L. (1983). The effects of acceleration on the social and emotional development of gifted students. In C. P. Benbow & J. C. Stanley (Eds.), *Academic precocity: Aspects of its development* (pp. 160–178). Baltimore: Johns Hopkins University Press.

Davids, A. (1966). Psychological characteristics of high school male and female potential scientists in comparison with academic underachievers. *Psychology in the Schools, 3,* 79–87.

Davis, H. B., & Connell, J. P. (1985). The effect of aptitude and achievement status on the self-system. *Gifted Child Quarterly, 29*(3), 131–135.

Fox, L. H. (1976). Sex differences in mathematical precocity: Bridging the gap. In D. P. Keating (Ed.), *Intellectual talent research and development* (pp. 183–214). Baltimore: Johns Hopkins University Press.

Haier, R. J., & Denham, S. A. (1976). A summary profile of the nonintellectual correlates of mathematical precocity in boys and girls. In D. P. Keating (Ed.),
Intellectual talent research and development (pp. 225–241). Baltimore: Johns Hopkins University Press.

Harter, S. (1985). *Manual for the Self-Perception Profile for Children*. Denver, CO:
University of Denver.

Hultgren, H., & Marquandt, M. (1986, April). *A self-perception profile of Rocky
Mountain Talent Search Summer Institute participants*. Paper presented at the annual meeting of the American Orthopsychiatric Association, Chicago.

Karnes, F. A., Chauvin, J. C., & Trent, T. J. (1984). Leadership profiles as determined by the HSPQ of students identified as intellectually gifted. *Roeper Review, 7*(1), 46–48.

Kennedy, W. A. (1962). MMPI profiles of gifted adolescents. *Journal of Clinical Psychology, 18,* 148–149.

Ketcham, R., & Snyder, R. T. (1977). Self-attitudes of the intellectually and socially
advantaged student: Normative study of the Piers-Harris children's self-concept
scale. *Psychological Reports, 40,* 111–116.

Killian, J. (1983). Personality characteristics of intellectually gifted secondary students. *Roeper Review, 6*(1) 39–42.

Krug, S. E., Sweeney, A. B., & Cattell, R. B. (1976). *Handbook for the School Motivation Analysis Test (SMAT)*. Champaign, IL: Institute for Personality and
Ability Testing.

Lehman, E. B., & Erdwins, C. J. (1981). The social and emotional adjustment of
young, intellectually gifted children. *Gifted Child Quarterly, 25*(3), 134–137.

Lessinger, L. M., & Martinson, R. A. (1961, March). The use of the California Psychological Inventory with gifted pupils. *Personnel and Guidance Journal*, 572–
575.

Lucito, L. J. (1964, September). Independence-conformity behavior as a function of
intellect: Bright and dull children. *Exceptional Children, 31,* 5–13.

McGinn, P. V. (1976). Verbally gifted youth: Selection and description. In D. P.
Keating, (Ed.), *Intellectual talent: Research and development*. Baltimore: Johns
Hopkins University Press.

Maddux, C. D., Scheiber, L. M., & Bass, J. E. (1982). Self-concept and social distance in gifted children. *Gifted Child Quarterly, 26*(2), 77–81.

Milgram, R. M., & Milgram, N. A. (1976). Personality characteristics of gifted Israeli children. *The Journal of Genetic Psychology, 129,* 185–194.

Myers, I. B. (1970). *The Myers-Briggs Type Indicator*. Palo Alto, CA: Consulting Psychologist Press.

Purkey, W. W. (1966). Measured and professed personality characteristics of gifted
high school students and an analysis of their congruence. *The Journal of Educational Research, 60*(3), 99–103.

Ringness, T. A. (1967). Identification patterns, motivation, and school achievement
of bright junior high school boys. *Journal of Educational Psychology, 59*(2), 93–
102.

Ritchie, A. C., Bernard, J. M., & Shertzer, B. E. (1982). A comparison of academically talented children and academically average children on interpersonal sensitivity. *Gifted Child Quarterly, 26*(3), 105–109.

Scholwinski, E., & Reynolds, C. R. (1985). Dimensions of anxiety among high IQ children. *Gifted Child Quarterly, 29*(3), 125–130.

Tomlinson-Keasey, C., & Smith-Winberry, C. (1983). Educational strategies and personality outcomes of gifted and nongifted college students. *Gifted Child Quarterly, 27*(1), 35–41.

Wrenn, C. G., Ferguson, L. W., & Kennedy, J. L. (1962). Intelligence level and personality. *Journal of Social Psychology, 7*, 301–308.

CHAPTER 9

Characteristics of the Developmental Path of Eminent and Gifted Adults

Joyce L. VanTassel-Baska

In the lives of eminent persons and gifted individuals, there exist important variables that may account for the perception of "success," in the view of society and of the individual. Society's highest standard is eminence—high-level achievement and societal recognition, usually marked by a contribution that has historical significance in a given field or across several fields. The individual's highest standard may be life satisfaction—how positive one feels about one's achievements in a career area and in relationships. For educators of the gifted, both perceptions are important considerations when formulating and promoting programs for gifted and talented learners. What are reasonable expectations for such programs? Can they provide an important form of nurturance for gifted individuals? Can they foster eminence? These questions can perhaps best be addressed by an investigation of the available literature exploring the variables that account for success among eminent individuals in society.

What is it that makes a Picasso? Is it superior intellect, carefully nurtured by home and society? Is it *zeitgeist*, with eminence being more a matter of luck, of being the right person to fit the mood of the era? Is it a set of sociological factors related to family background, child-rearing practices, education, and peer relationships? The intent of this chapter is twofold: first, to seek answers to these questions by studying the lives of eminent persons, and second, to discuss the interactive nature of key variables that may best account for eminence. Within this chapter, eminence is adjudged on the basis of important contributions to society, as assessed by citations in biographical dictionaries.

Childhood giftedness is usually viewed as advanced development in intellectual areas or as exemplary performance in a specific area (as in the case of prodigies). Adult giftedness, on the other hand, is judged as outstanding performance or sustained effort resulting typically in a significant contribution to society. At the adult level, advanced development is usually a necessary but not sufficient condition for eminence. Factors such as timing, location, and opportunity may unduly influence whether eminence is likely. Furthermore, we may think of eminence as a relative concept, as we do giftedness. One may be "eminent" within one's community, making a significant impact in that sphere. Moving out from that sphere, we find the term *eminence* applicable to outstanding individuals in various areas of public and private life at regional, state, national, and international levels. Thus the view that none of Terman's subjects were "eminent" appears inappropriate if we are willing to entertain a less rigorous criterion than international renown for a particular contribution. Certainly the professional esteem and regard with which many of his subjects were held, as evidenced by entry into prestigious associations like the American Academy of Sciences, attests to a degree and level of eminence.

Another necessary-but-not-sufficient condition for eminence is being well known at the national and international level. Unfortunately, in our present society we have a tendency to confuse "eminence" with "fame." The distinction between them lies in the quality and nature of one's contribution: Eminence is related to the furthering of knowledge and, as such, possesses substantiation beyond the phenomenon of name recognition.

While we need to acknowledge that eminence cannot be reliably predicted from childhood giftedness (Howley, 1987; McClelland, 1973), it is important to focus on key elements in the lives of eminent people that may represent necessary (although not sufficient) conditions for attaining such high levels of achievement, as well as to consider the extent to which these characteristics might be nurtured by societal institutions like the home and the school. We must keep in mind, however, that eminence is culture-bound, and the factors that give rise to eminence shift from one age to the next (Bull, 1985); an Eisenhower or a Patton, for example, would probably not have achieved eminence without the context of World War II. We must also remember that widespread awareness of an individual's contributions may not occur during that person's lifetime; Emily Dickinson, for example, lived and worked in relative obscurity, and only posthumously was she recognized as a major American poet. In such cases—and there are many like hers—the societal recognition that defines *eminence* eluded the individual in life and obviously was not a factor in the individual's level of achievement. Conversely, societal recognition during one's lifetime may be viewed as having a negative effect on subsequent creative production, as is the case of Ernest Hemingway, whose lionization seems to have led to diminished expression of his literary talent.

RELATIONSHIP BETWEEN INTELLIGENCE AND EMINENCE

Although eminence and intelligence have been thought by many to have a high correlation, researchers have tended to focus more on one phenomenon or the other, even while acknowledging the relationship between them. Both Galton (1869) and Terman (1925) were profoundly interested in biography as a means of sorting out the connection of early experience to adult eminence and outstanding contributions. Unfortunately, many biographies do not provide sufficient data for such an investigation; since there is no unifying theme or purpose underlying the myriad biographies available, they do not all present all of the salient information on all subjects. Nevertheless, Galton (1869) argued that eminence was an appropriate index for natural ability, since the truly exceptional individual could not be held back by societal obstacles. He further noted that social advantage did not give rise to eminence unless natural ability was also present. To prove his assertions, he examined the lives of statesmen, English judges, literary people, military commanders, scientists, poets, musicians, painters, and divines. His conclusions support his argument that eminence emerges from families of both social advantage and ability.

The Roe study (1953) examined 64 male scientists who were considered eminent in their fields. The study found that these men typically were the eldest children in middle-class families and sons of professional men. Most had experienced either illness or a severe disruption in family life—death of a parent or divorce—at an early age. In boyhood they did a great deal of reading; they tended to be shy, even aloof, and showed little interest in girls. In general, they married late and had a stable home life. Although most did not choose a career until their junior or senior year of college, driving absorption in their work was found to be common among all of them—they worked long hours, frequently with no vacations.

Cox (1926), in her extensive study, found that children who grew up to attain eminence generally came from a privileged family situation and had "superior advantages"—stimulating social contacts and excellent educational opportunities—in early childhood. Cox found that, while many of the eminent evinced "high-IQ behavior" early in childhood, intelligence was not the major hallmark of future achievement; in youth, most subjects in her study also displayed personality traits associated with success: persistence, confidence in their abilities, and great strength of character.

In the Goertzels' (1962) study, the predominant family constellation included a passive father and a dominant mother who promoted the child's welfare above all else. Furthermore, adversity was found to be a critical factor; many of the eminent Americans in this study experienced handicaps of some type early in life. From such challenges they learned to cope with and transcend adverse circumstances.

Numerous retrospective studies have sought to uncover predictors and correlates of adult eminence. In the Walberg et al. (1981) study of childhood traits and environmental conditions of eminent adults, intelligence was found to be the most distinguishing childhood characteristic. Simonton (1978) stressed the importance of early access to role models in the lives of eminent individuals. In a study of Nobel laureates, Zuckerman (1979) found that the process of self-selection into an elite network of scientists through apprenticeships was a key pattern in their lives.

Thus it appears that a convergence of three factors—birth into a family that values learning, early precocity in a particular area, and well-focused self-direction—forms an important nexus from which eminence may arise. However, these three factors overlap the sociological, intellectual, and psychological domains, and the resulting tangle of variables makes eminence a difficult phenomenon to predict using childhood characteristics alone.

The Terman study (1925) and follow-up work (Terman & Oden, 1959; Sears & Barbee, 1977) are unique among the research in this area because they focus on a group selected on the basis of a single criterion—intelligence as measured by the Stanford-Binet—and because the researchers collected as much other data on the life factors as possibly could be gathered from a questionnaire. The 75% return from the 1977 survey, more than 50 years after the initial selection process, says much about the group's cooperation, acceptance, and willingness to participate well beyond what would normally be expected from a research sample.

The underrepresentation of minorities and the geographical limitations of the sample are somewhat problematic. Beyond these caveats, however, the systematic longitudinal data collection has allowed for comparisons within the group that are very informative. While the group included a few millionaires and many more academics, professionals, and "achievers" than one would expect from an average sample, extraordinary accomplishments, such as a Nobel Prize or an outstanding artistic work, were not much in evidence. Sears and Sears (1980) reported on important within-group differences at midlife. The highest achievers in the sample tended to come from families in which the parents had a higher level of education, a lower divorce rate, better home libraries, and attitudes that fostered ambition. The 1959 data (Terman & Oden, 1959) showed that these higher achievers differed significantly from the rest of the sample in a number of ways: They were engaged in a wider range of occupations, which appeared related to parental encouragement of initiative and independence, and they were far more likely to participate in hobbies, sports, and professional societies. The personality characteristics that separated them from the rest of the group centered on behaviors that supported early ambition and career choice.

Given the differential career opportunities available to men and women during the historical period of this study, it is not surprising that "life satisfaction" goals and achievements differ between the sexes. Both the men and the women in the study rated pleasure in family life highly, but men derived more of their rewards from job satisfaction, while women were more likely to value friendships and cultural activities. Women who worked outside the home displayed an independence and competence that set them apart from their peers but very much parallel the characteristics of women in our current cultural milieu, especially the younger ones.

Overall, the Terman study demonstrates that, even when a group is selected and studied solely on the basis of intelligence, a cluster of sociological and psychological factors—namely, family background, achievement, and drive—can exert sufficient influence to divide the subjects into two distinct groups with markedly different outcomes on relative success and life satisfaction measures at later ages.

Bloom (1985) perceived a constellation of factors influencing talent development in his study of eminent adults in a variety of fields: The nurturance of the talent area in the home, the right teacher/tutor at the right time, opportunity for self-evaluation through competition, and the individual's commitment to the talent area at the critical time all coalesced as important factors in his study. Bloom found the influence of K–12 schooling to be minimal; indeed, many of his subjects saw school as either an impediment to or an inconsequential part of their development as talented individuals, and this was particularly true for those whose gifts were in the arts and athletics.

Piechowski (1978, 1982) intensively studied the lives of Antoine de Saint Exupéry and Eleanor Roosevelt. In examining key influences, he found that the internal worlds of these two individuals in childhood and beyond constituted the most salient feature that might have accounted for their expressed talent. Both created elaborate fantasies, partially as an escape from rejection, but over time as a preferred style for filtering reality. Piechowski infers that the richness and depth of their inner emotional lives distinguished them and undergirded the talent for which each was eventually to gain renown.

Gruber (1982) focused on the life of Darwin in an effort to understand adult eminence. He saw Darwin as a man with an accumulating passion for and involvement in his chosen area of study, and he attributed Darwin's success to that factor rather than to sheer brilliance. DeGroot's (1965) study of chess players also supports this perspective. Thus greater focus in an area of intense interest over time may be as indicative of the eminence process as any other factor, given a reasonably high level of intelligence.

SOCIOLOGICAL CONDITIONS

Home Environment

Clark (1983) examined the lives of successful black Americans and traced the roots of such success back to the nature of the home environment. He cited a number of home and family factors that contribute to black students' success in school. Primary among these are substantial parental involvement in the child's schooling, a fundamentally positive parent/child relationship, and clear parental expectations for behaviors and performance in all areas of the child's life.

In the Goertzels' (1962) study, the evidence strongly suggests that eminence arises from a home environment in which learning and achievement are respected, and particularly from one in which both parents have a strong drive toward intellectual or creative achievement. These parents often have nonconformist attitudes toward traditional schooling, however, as is reflected in the fact that many eminent people were tutored at home by one or both parents. For example, General Patton's father, who believed that an appropriate education entailed reliving the history of humanity experientially, tutored his son in a style intended to duplicate the passage of primitive humans through the evolutionary stages in a compressed way. Norbert Wiener was pushed somewhat unmercifully by his father, who felt that traditional schooling did not begin to tap into the actual potential of children.

The Roe (1953) study of eminent scientists also substantiated the importance of a learning-centered home where parents had extensive libraries and encouraged their children to pursue individual interests and talents. Witty (1930) found that parents of gifted children were themselves fascinated with and involved in mathematics, music, reading, invention, and other similar pursuits. Brandwein (1955) found that Westinghouse scholars came from homes where intellectual nurturance was available and promoted.

It is interesting to note that many eminent individuals have come from families where the parents were extremely opinionated, usually in the arenas of politics and religion. The influence of such parents often appeared to give rise to the child's development of an early passion for causes, particularly altruistic ones, and a desire to realize the dream put forth by the parents. According to Goertzel and Goertzel (1962), Susan B. Anthony's involvement in women's rights was predicated on her parents' devotion to political action; Jane Addams and Margaret Sanger also both began to develop their reformer tendencies as young children, through their fathers' inspiration. Education and science tended to be valued more heavily than religion in the majority of families producing eminent persons. While some variance was evident, nonsectarianism and agnosticism predominated as "religious approaches" in these families. Work was seen as the grand passion, and the children were encouraged to follow suit.

Profiles of the parents of eminent men tend to focus on a passive, failure-prone father and a dominant, even smothering, mother who wills the child's success by persistent attention to the nurturance of his talent. Pablo Casals' mother, for example, broke up the family and sank into poverty in order to accompany Pablo to Barcelona for special schooling in the cello (Casals, 1970). Frank Lloyd Wright's mother had wooden replicas of Gothic cathedrals placed in his nursery to stimulate his interest in architecture—she had determined before he was born that he would become a famous architect (Wright, 1966). A surprising number of eminent men had fathers who were alcoholic; in fact, alcoholic fathers predominate among humorists of eminence. Stephen Leacock, for example, became so angered by his father's drunken behavior that he exiled him from the family, threatening to kill him should he ever return.

Whatever the liabilities of growing up in such circumstances, there seems to be a salutary effect—a release from conservatism and fear of innovation, which leads in turn to a greater likelihood of producing something novel, particularly in the case of artists. Goertzel and Goertzel (1962) found that 64% of eminent military men, adventurers, and dictators came from homes that were mother-dominated or mother-smothered, as did 54% of eminent poets. Not surprisingly, many of these men had lifelong difficulties in areas such as sex-role identity, developing a satisfactory relationship with a female other than the mother, and acquiring friends among male contemporaries.

Goertzel and Goertzel (1962) also investigated the stability of the families in which their subjects grew up, paying special attention to such factors as marital discord, separation or divorce, job dissatisfaction of the parents (especially if accompanied by high aspirations), and lack of adjustment to the family situation. They found that only 58 homes among the 400 they investigated could be considered untroubled, and in many of these 58 the child who was to become eminent suffered in some way. Poverty or loss of fortune or status was a frequent form of trouble in the homes of these eminent persons. Those who were wealthy tended to pursue political action as a creative outlet. Troubled homes were in the backgrounds of 90% of eminent actors, authoritarian politicians, novelists, and playwrights studied.

Albert (1980) reported a high incidence of parental loss among eminent individuals, but he noted that these tragedies often resulted in the child's being accorded a special role in the family. Albert then compared this to the similar high rate of parental loss among criminals and depressed mental patients, suggesting that the healthier responses to adversity among the eminent attested to the importance of individual perception and interpretation of traumatic events. MacKinnon (1962), in a study of top-flight architects, also found many subjects who came from homes that were not conducive to sound psychological development.

These data suggest that the presence of traumatic events can be either beneficial or detrimental to creative productivity in adulthood. Indeed, it would seem that for some individuals, the more troubling the nature of the home, the more the child's imagination is fired in ways that eventually result in an outstandingly productive life in which ability, motivation, and personality need have been successfully merged.

Facing life's problems—whether family traumas or idiosyncratic fears—with strength and determination is often a characteristic of the eminent. The death of his brother became a driving force for Salvador Dali, who felt he had to live up to the expectations of his parents for their "perfect" dead child (Goertzel & Goertzel, 1962). Charles Lindbergh had a strong fear of failing, and therefore spent most of his time fighting the fear by challenging it directly, first by motorcycle and later by airplane (Goertzel & Goertzel, 1962). The gifted seem to be more vulnerable to suicide and depression than to psychosis, albeit to a lesser degree than the general population, according to the follow-up Terman studies (Terman & Oden, 1959). The intensity of their striving toward a particular goal may keep the gifted from being too preoccupied with an anxiety state, thereby contributing to better mental health.

Peer Relationships

Typically the gifted have few close friends and the highly gifted tend to experience difficulty in forming meaningful relationships with agemates. Many are especially close to one sibling or other children in the extended family. Difficulties in peer relationships often occur because the gifted child is unwilling to conform to what might be considered normal societal pressure, and his agemates view his behavior as aberrant and unacceptable. Terman (1925) reported that many gifted children found it easier to have a close friend who was 1 or 2 years older or who had similar intellectual abilities or interests.

In some cases eminent individuals exist in almost total isolation, with only a family member, often the mother or father, to serve as "friend." For Emily Dickinson, always a rather solitary figure, her brother's wife fulfilled the role of opening up a new world for Emily outside the austerity of her Amherst home (Ward, 1961).

A high degree of intelligence may heighten the difficulty of conforming to societal norms around the institution of marriage. Terman and Oden (1959) found that the brightest subjects in their study, as defined by scores on the Concept Mastery Test, never married.

Schooling

Parents of gifted students have tended to disregard conventional schooling, preferring instead to arrange for a tutor or to instruct their children at home themselves. Students have also expressed a dislike of conventional schooling. Secondary schools, in particular, are unpopular among the gifted. As one Westinghouse scholar put it, "The best thing they did for me was leave me alone." College work, however, was frequently seen as more challenging.

Many of the eminent, approximately 60%, had serious school problems (Goertzel & Goertzel, 1962). They were bored with the curriculum, misunderstood by their teachers, taunted by their peers, and subject to failure in the system. After a teacher yelled at him for completing his Opus 1 in class, Edvard Grieg soaked himself under a rainspout so that he would be sent home. Einstein was considered dull by his teachers, and school authorities found Edison so impossible to work with that he was ultimately removed from school and tutored at home.

Despite the difficulty with school, the vast majority of the eminent displayed an exceptional talent or ability at an early age. At age 4, Marie Curie could identify all the equipment in her father's laboratory. Yehudi Menuhin began to study violin seriously when he was 3½ years old. Enrico Fermi designed working electric motors while he was in elementary school. Many of those who went on to become eminent moved through their schooling at an accelerated pace; Norbert Wiener, for example, graduated from Harvard with his doctorate at 18, and Mary Ellen Chase was placed in a fifth-grade reading group on her first day of school.

Sometimes a child's passion for a particular area inhibits his or her ability to perform in a traditional schooling situation. Pablo Picasso was one such example: By the time he was 10 years old, art had become so important to him that he steadfastly refused to read and write, preferring to use his time painting instead. Even after his father removed him from school and provided him with a tutor, the situation did not improve. Sent to Madrid for art lessons, he chose instead to roam the city, observing its people and absorbing its culture. He returned home, unschooled but ready to put on his first one-man show before his 15th birthday.

PERSONAL PERCEPTIONS

As one examines the body of literature just cited, it becomes clear that adult success, whether judged by internal or external standards, is not arrived at in a linear path from the cradle on, and intelligence is but one of several important variables that influence life outcomes. As individuals become older, more educated, and more established in a career, ability appears to become less of a factor in distinguishing the gifted from their colleagues. This occurs largely because of a skewing of the norm reference group rather than because of the insignificance of ability: The filtering effect of college and early career involvement tend to match on ability factors, thus creating a more homogeneous group of individuals. Self-perception—both past and present—stands out as a critical variable, one that can either propel an individual toward productivity and success or enervate and immobilize her or him. While the data on home backgrounds may seem contradictory (i.e., Bloom and Terman et al. cited the positive nurturing influences, while Roe and the Goertzels noted the adversity theme), the seeming dichotomy resolves itself when the perception of the individual is taken into account.

Favorable and unfavorable home environments may be viewed by individuals as reasons to achieve or to fail. In the final analysis, it may be the individual's perception of past and present events that shapes behavior patterns. Eccles (1984) developed a model for understanding this phenomenon as it relates to women's achievement behaviors. She noted that a woman's perception of her achievement affects the decisions she makes about future directions much more than evidence of achievement itself does. This model is fairly consistent with the findings from studies of the eminent and the gifted, particularly those focusing on gifted girls and women. As Kulieke and Olszewski-Kubilius (chapter 4 in this volume) have found, there are significant gender differences with respect to the importance of aspects of family climate and family values. Gilligan (1982) and Belenky, Clinchy, Goldberg, and Tarule (1986) have found profound gender differences in ways of perceiving and understanding; women are far more likely to see the "connectedness" of reality, to seek to integrate past and present experience, and to strive to balance inner feelings with outer behaviors.

Achieving eminence in any domain represents pattern breaking at a very fundamental level. We have come to believe that the creative personality is risk taking, independent, and often unconventional. These qualities may be an outgrowth of an individual's perception of family life. For those who were raised in positive, nurturing environments, the perception of the environment may coincide with reality and produce stable performance at a remarkable level. For those raised in less positive circumstances, the adversity may fuel an ambition and desire to succeed that can at least begin to explain the disparity in the research on the family backgrounds of eminent individuals.

The personal characteristics that nurture eminence are perhaps as crucial as family variables. The traits of creativity, commitment, and curiosity (Klemm, 1977) found among eminent scientists, for example, develop over time within the individual. Most people we regard as eminent have lived a major period of their lives in the context of the career that has brought them honor and recognition. Eminence is thus incremental, the result of a life's work rather than a single invention or performance. The characteristics that separate the eminent from the merely competent are a driving desire to succeed and an ability to break out of old patterns. Within eminent individuals there exists an urge not to settle, conform, or become complacent; a zeal to continue the effort; and a willingness to recognize how short of the mark they may have fallen. Amabile's (1983) view that external evaluation plays a negative role in creative production is supported by the absence of such evaluation from the consciousness of the eminent. Only their work matters, and only *their* opinion of it (and that of a few significant others) is relevant.

A review of the literature on eminence presents a view of individual characteristics and resources central to our understanding of the relationship of giftedness and eminence. Figure 9.1 lists the individual characteristics cited as relevant in various studies of the lives of gifted persons, along with two of the circumstantial characteristics that have been reported to influence development of talented individuals. The individual characteristics are associated with behaviors, listed in the column on the right, that are necessary to activate them in a given context. The missing link, however, is how one nurtures the characteristics and then provides a context for their activation. Clearly, a rich home and school environment can help develop many of them. However, without the right context at a propitious moment, it is likely that activation of these characteristics to a given area of pursuit will not occur. Thus some gifted individuals may never achieve eminence, because of a failure in the linkage system. It is in this interface that a model for the development of eminence may have the greatest impact.

A MODEL FOR THE DEVELOPMENT OF EMINENCE

Figure 9.2 presents a conceptual model for the development of eminence. In the first circle are the factors that have to do with the development of the child within the social context of family, school, and community, where basic skills, knowledge, and attitudes are acquired. Prospective eminent individuals have all of these systems affecting their perception in potentially positive and negative ways. For example, in the case of adversity in the environment, such as poverty or parental loss, children may be driven all the more to achieve in the fundamental areas of learning.

The next circle shows the constellation of variables that relate to nurturance of key characteristics and behaviors, those powerful issues clearly associated with eminent behavior. The element of positive effect is generally inherent in the active nurturance of talent, at least in theory. Although the age

Figure 9.1 Behavioral Correlates of Circumstantial and Individual Characteristics of Eminent Individuals

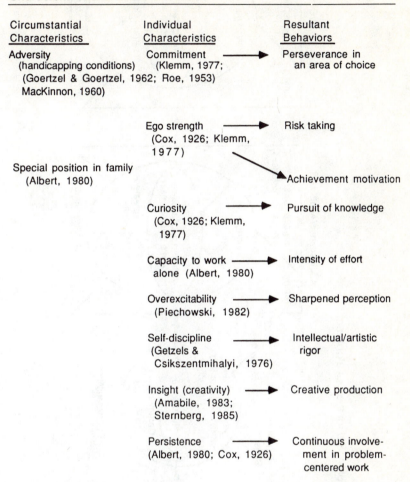

Circumstantial Characteristics	Individual Characteristics	Resultant Behaviors
Adversity (handicapping conditions) (Goertzel & Goertzel, 1962; Roe, 1953) MacKinnon, 1960)	Commitment (Klemm, 1977; ——▶	Perseverance in an area of choice
	Ego strength (Cox, 1926; Klemm, 1977) ——▶	Risk taking
Special position in family (Albert, 1980)		Achievement motivation
	Curiosity (Cox, 1926; Klemm, 1977) ——▶	Pursuit of knowledge
	Capacity to work alone (Albert, 1980) ——▶	Intensity of effort
	Overexcitability (Piechowski, 1982) ——▶	Sharpened perception
	Self-discipline (Getzels & Csikszentmihalyi, 1976) ——▶	Intellectual/artistic rigor
	Insight (creativity) (Amabile, 1983; Sternberg, 1985) ——▶	Creative production
	Persistence (Albert, 1980; Cox, 1926) ——▶	Continuous involvement in problem-centered work

at which this critical stage of development is reached may vary, there is little doubt that it must be responded to. For pure talent areas, such as mathematics, music, or art, nurturance must have taken shape by about age 10 (Bloom, 1985); often it begins even earlier. In the case of fields where knowledge is synthesized later on, such as acting or teaching, the timing of the nurturance of that specific gift could be extended. The right context for the nurturance process appears to be as critical at this stage as are key individuals. Individual family members, appropriate teachers, and other significant

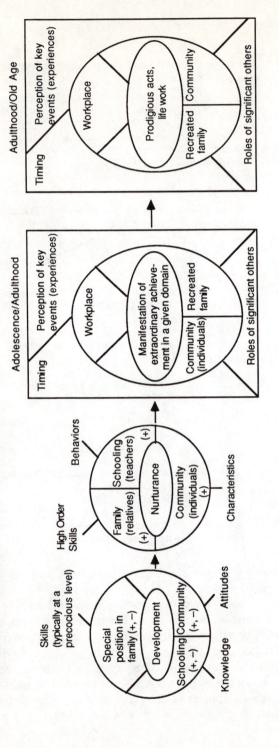

Figure 9.2   A Conceptual Model for the Development of Eminence

people can have a strong impact, as can the situations in which these people exert their influence. Many eminent people have cited the importance of someone else who believed strongly in what they were doing and nurtured them in the process.

The third stage of the model—adolescence/adulthood—contains several critical shifts. One of them relates to the activation of high-level skills and extraordinary achievement in a given talent domain, now in the context of the workplace rather than the school. A second shift that occurs at this level is the phenomenon of the recreated family unit, where individuals seek out, in a formal or informal way, a new support system to replace the old. A third shift at this stage of the development of eminence is in the realm of individual context. Experiences and their timing and interpretation, and the roles that others assume in one's life, take on critical importance in either facilitating or impeding the full development of potential eminence.

At the last stage—adulthood/old age—prodigious acts and a body of life's work represent the centerpiece of the full display of eminence, carried out in a social and individual context. Two important factors contribute to shaping this stage of development. The first is lifespan: If an individual does not produce creative work when his or her intellectual and/or artistic powers are at their height, he or she may never be able to do so at an older age. Or, as is the case with many eminent individuals, he or she may die in early or middle adulthood. A second factor is timing: There is a propitious time for a particular contribution to be made in any given field or cultural milieu. This aspect of eminence depends on chance (Tannenbaum, 1983), on being in the right place at the right time with the "right stuff." It is also important to note that, in many fields, peak contributions frequently have occurred within a relatively narrow band of years, thus raising the question of the likelihood of significant contribution beyond those stages (Gallagher, 1985).

IMPLICATIONS FOR EDUCATION

What implications might be made for educating gifted learners in ways that nurture their growth toward eminence, or at least toward the characteristics and behaviors associated with eminence? Is it possible to use education to compensate for those environmental factors that may inhibit certain gifted individuals from achieving eminence? Should disadvantaged students receive the bulk of special education intervention, since they represent the greater discrepancy between potential and actualization of that potential? What kind of program would suffice? Should the students at different stages in their development of key characteristics and behaviors associated with eminence receive different treatments? If the answer to these questions is affirmative, then the focus on the effort at the educational level should be on carefully diagnosing the needs of gifted learners and providing them with an appropriate context that would encourage them to use their abilities more fully. For some, this would imply knowledge and skill development; for others, it might imply more opportunity to practice key behaviors.

While educators may not wish to assume the responsibility of creating eminent persons in the sense of a Dickinson or an Einstein, they are in the business of promoting the pursuit of excellence through constant utilization of potential. If eminence is an outcome of such pursuit, and not merely the natural consequence of giftedness, it should be treated as such. Expectations for the gifted should be high, but judgment of levels of attainment should be construed primarily within each person's level of self-actualization. Thus it is sufficient that gifted children, as a result of special programmatic opportunities provided to them, exhibit the following behaviors: (1) awareness and integration of self, (2) working at and in a field of inquiry with a high degree of proficiency, (3) dedication and commitment in professional and personal pursuits, and (4) display of creative productivity (VanTassel-Baska, 1981). These, then, can be viewed as reasonable goals for the education of the gifted.

Yet, if the important differences among intellectually gifted individuals regarding creative output lie primarily in the nature of the home environment, personality factors, and motivational preoccupations, it would appear to be difficult for the school as a single institution of society to meet the needs of such individuals. Consequently, a resource model of support to gifted students needs to be created within geographical areas and across a span of years. The collaboration of parents, schools, and specialized individuals and institutions needs to occur in a context that focuses on the development and nurturance not just of talent but of attitudes and behaviors that support that talent.

CONCLUSION

Gifted children can be nurtured and encouraged to be open to new experiences, to experiment with new forms, and to develop new ideas and products. But we should not mistake the development of those qualities for eminence. If today's gifted students become eminent, it will be because of a unique blend of factors, some personal, some social, some educational, and some culturally developmental. Individualization, not eminence, should be the goal of the schooling process, so that all gifted children can experience opportunities that point them toward productive and purposeful lives.

REFERENCES

Albert, R. (1980). Family positions and the attachment of eminence: A study of special family positions and special family experiences. *Gifted Child Quarterly, 24*(2), 87–95.

Amabile, T. (1983). *The social psychology of creativity.* New York: Springer-Verlag.

Belenky, M. F., Clinchy, B. M., Goldberg, N. R., & Tarule, J. M. (1986). *Women's ways of knowing.* New York: Basic Books.

Bloom, B. (1985). *Developing talent in young people.* New York: Ballantine Books.

Brandwein, P. F. (1955). *The gifted student as future scientist.* New York: Harcourt, Brace.

Bull, B. L. (1985). Eminence and precocity: An examination of the justification of education for the gifted and talented. *Teachers College Record, 87*(1), 1–19.

Casals, P. (1970). *Joys and sorrows.* New York: Simon and Schuster.

Clark, R. (1983). *Family life and school achievement: Why poor black children succeed or fail.* Chicago: University of Chicago Press.

Cox, C. M. (1926). *The early mental traits of three hundred geniuses* (Genetic Studies of Genius, Vol. 2, ed. Lewis Terman). Stanford: Stanford University Press.

DeGroot, A. D. (1965). *Thought and choice in class.* The Hague: Mouton.

Eccles, J. (1984). Sex differences in mathematics participation. In M. Steinkamp & M. Maehr (Eds.), *Advances in motivation and achievement* (vol. 2, pp. 93–137). Greenwich, CT: Jai Press.

Gallagher, J. (1985). *Teaching the gifted child.* Boston: Allyn and Bacon.

Galton, F. (1869). *Hereditary genius: An inquiry into its laws and consequences.* London: Macmillan.

Getzels, J., & Csikszentmihalyi, M. (1976). *The creative vision: A longitudinal study of problem-finding in art.* New York: John Wiley.

Gilligan, C. (1982). *In a different voice.* Cambridge, MA: Harvard Educational Press.

Goertzel, V., & Goertzel, M. G. (1962). *Cradles of eminence.* Boston: Little, Brown.

Gruber, H. E. (1982). On the hypothesized relation between giftedness and creativity. In D. H. Feldman (Ed.), *Developmental approaches to giftedness and creativity* (pp. 7–29). San Francisco: Jossey-Bass.

Howley, A. (1987). The symbolic role of eminence in the education of gifted students. *Journal for the Education of the Gifted, 2,* 115–124.

Klemm, W. R. (1977). (Ed.). *Discovery processes in modern biology.* Huntington, NY: Robert E. Krieger.

McClelland, D. (1973). Testing for competence rather than for "intelligence." *American Psychologist, 28,* 1–14.

MacKinnon, D. W. (1962). The personality correlates of creativity: A study of American architects. In G. G. Nielson (Ed.), *Proceedings of the Fourteenth International Congress of Applied Psychology,* (vol. 2, pp. 11–39). Copenhagen: Munksguard.

Piechowski, M. M. (1978). Self-actualization as a developmental structure: A profile of Antoine de Saint Exupéry. *Genetic Psychology Monographs, 97,* 181–242.

Piechowski, M. (1982). Self-actualization profile of Eleanor Roosevelt, a presumed non-transcendent. *Genetic Psychology Monographs, 105,* 95–153.

Roe, A. (1953). *Making of a scientist.* New York: Dodd, Mead.

Sears, P., & Barbee, A. (1977). Career and life satisfactions among Terman's gifted women. In J. Stanley, W. George, & C. Solano (Eds.), *The gifted and the creative, a Fifty Year Perspective,* Baltimore, MD: The Johns Hopkins University Press.

Sears, P., & Sears, R. (1980, February). 1528 little geniuses and how they grew. *Psychology Today,* pp. 28–43.

Simonton, D. K. (1978). Multiple discovery and invention: Zeitgeist, genius or chance. *Journal of Personality and Social Psychology, 37,* 1603–1616.

Sternberg, R. (1985). *Beyond IQ.* New York: Cambridge University Press.

Tannenbaum, A. (1983). *Gifted children.* New York: Macmillan.

Terman, L. (1925). *Genetic studies of genius* (Vol. 1). Stanford, CA: Stanford University Press.

Terman, L. & Oden, M. (1959). *The gifted group at mid-life: Thirty-five years' follow-up of the superior child* (Genetic Studies of Genius, vol. 5). Stanford, CA: Stanford University Press.

VanTassel-Baska, J. (1981). A model of career education for the gifted. *Journal of Career Education, 1,* 325–331.

Walberg, H., Tsai, S., Weinstein, T., Gabriel, C., Rasher, S., Rosencrans, T., Rovai, E., Ide, J., Trujillo, M., & Vukosavia, P. (1981). Childhood traits and environmental conditions of highly eminent adults. *Gifted Child Quarterly, 25*(3), 103–107.

Ward, T. (1961). *The capsule of the mind: Chapters in the life of Emily Dickinson.* Cambridge, MA: Belknap Press.

Witty, P. (1930). *One hundred gifted children.* Kansas City: Kansas University Publications.

Wright, O. (1966). *Frank Lloyd Wright.* New York: Horizon Press.

Zuckerman, H. (1979). *Scientific elite: Nobel laureates in the United States.* New York: The Free Press.

PART III

INFLUENCE OF THE SCHOOL

This section of the book focuses on key issues that schools must face as they attempt to nurture the development of talent. Although research on the school's importance and effectiveness in talent development is fairly limited, educators of the gifted have nearly always supported school-based special interventions for such students. Evaluations of early programs like Cleveland Major Work (Barbe, 1955) point to the importance that former students assign to these programs in their lives. The case studies of Hauck and Freehill (1972) provide individual testimony that school programs have influenced student lives in profound ways. The longitudinal research on the Study of Mathematically Precocious Youth (SMPY) also reveals the impact of specific educational intervention—in this case, content acceleration—on the nature and type of educational progress made by its subjects (Benbow & Stanley, 1983). In her study of MacArthur Fellows, Cox found that school-based experiences that were linked to a specific individual—typically a teacher who provided encouragement and resource assistance in an area of talent—were viewed by her subjects as critical to their development (Cox, Daniel, & Boston, 1985). The Richardson Study, the most current and comprehensive effort to study gifted programs, identified broad aspects of local school programs that appeared to be most facilitative for gifted students: (1) inclusive identification strategies, (2) comprehensiveness, (3) curriculum flexibility, and (4) effective administrative operation (Cox et al., 1985). Approximately 35 other studies on the positive effects of school-based programs may be found in the literature (for a review, see Weiss & Gallagher, 1982).

On the other hand, there is some evidence that schools and their programs exert only minimal influence. Bloom's (1985) study of high-level talent found that schools played at best a secondary role in helping or hindering the development of talent, and similar findings have emerged from studies of eminent professionals (MacKinnon, 1965; Roe, 1953). These conflicting results make it impossible—at least for now—to arrive at a definitive assessment of the importance of schools in the total talent development process. Whatever light future research may shed on this issue, however, creating a supportive environment for gifted students will remain a wise and worthwhile goal. To that end, the contributors to Part III of this book lay out ideas for making schools more responsive to the needs of talented learners, in order to insure that schools are nurturant rather than neglectful.

In chapter 10 Harry Passow delineates important questions that must be asked about any proposed curriculum that is based on the various reform-oriented educational reports. He cautions that careful consideration must be given to the implications these reports hold for the education of the gifted. His perspective on trends within general education provides an important point of departure for considering curriculum deviations for the gifted. His questions probe the fundamental issues associated with differentiating programs and services for gifted learners.

James Gallagher in chapter 11 further elucidates the curriculum question by focusing on what constitutes an effective curriculum design for gifted learners. He provides a framework for evaluating curriculum effectiveness and discusses the problems associated with effective curriculum development in schools. He stresses the need to control for key variables in the teaching/learning process, in order to eliminate obstacles that may impede optimal curriculum implementation.

In chapter 12 Julian Stanley examines the importance of guiding gifted learners in their decision making regarding academic planning, particularly at the crucial junior high stage. He puts forth 10 suggestions that allow students to move through the school curriculum at a more rapid rate while accessing advanced work at an appropriate level. His treatment of the issue of curriculum flexibility expands on Passow's earlier questions.

Chapter 13 resounds with a call for helping gifted students with career planning and making life choices. Linda Silverman focuses much attention on gifted girls, who traditionally have more difficulty than boys in resolving career issues, because of their impact on family considerations. Silverman also looks at the importance of providing historical and current role models from the world of work, parent education, and opportunities for students to test their perceived interests and desires for the future through internships and other real-life experiences.

Although summer programs for gifted learners have proliferated over the last 10 years, the professionals involved in providing them have not systematically assessed their impact. In chapter 14 Paula Olszewski-Kubilius focuses on the effects of summer programs for the gifted and thus offers an important data-based perspective in this area. The chapter provides some basis for making judgments about the efficacy of such programs, the various purposes they serve, and the relationship they have to academic-year programs for gifted learners. The conclusions of the study reported on in the chapter point the way toward policy considerations for the field.

The capstone of this section is the fine essay by Richard Ronvik (chapter

15), which chronicles the major problems in administering effective school-based programs for gifted learners. A veteran director of such programs, Ronvik asserts that the field has failed to unify around sound program and curriculum methodologies, but rather has dilettantishly sought to pursue each new model, gimmick, or idea that crossed the educational landscape. While his tone may seem harsh, his message is an important one for the field to hear, as it represents a thoughtful perspective from the ranks of practicing educators of the gifted.

Although the role of the school in the talent development process remains somewhat beclouded, the authors in this section all contribute provocative and forceful ideas about what they believe schools need to be engaged in to promote the self-actualization of promising students. It is our hope that American education can find a way to catalyze such ideas into action.

Student Perspective: Female, 19 years old

Being classified as "gifted and talented" was always the one factor that was overwhelmingly responsible for defining my education. Apart from my actual teachers and their individual impact, being considered gifted has been the most significant determinant of what I learned, how I learned, and even where it would be taught. Many of the g/t programs which I was placed in involved removing kids from the classroom for some part of the day to participate in special activities. This was important, since it was definitely a mark of being "special" if you got to miss the afternoon reading group to learn more about American Indians. Up until fourth grade, my "enrichment" was limited to being placed in the high reading group or being allowed to work ahead when the class was in an open-classroom situation. Then in the fourth grade I began a program where I, along with about seven other students, was taken out of my regular class for the afternoon. We were encouraged to work on projects and reports, with an emphasis on creating artistically or discovering things ourselves through individual research. I remember little "teaching"; it was pretty much understood that we could do whatever we wanted, as long as it could be considered a "learning" experience. The woman who worked with us was also the school guidance counselor, and great emphasis was placed on having a close personal relationship with her and the other students. That was the first time I can remember having a social value attached to my academic placement. The group of students was very closely knit, and while we were in no way exclusive we were separate from the rest of the regular class in many ways. This continued into high school, where fourth-level students were considered smarter by other students, even when we were covering the same material. It is one thing when teachers place you apart because of academics, but when other students do the same, it is a different matter.

When I moved to another school before sixth grade, my "special" education took on the character which it would follow through high school. The emphasis was definitely one of acceleration rather than enrichment. For the next 7 years, being gifted would mean that I got to learn the same material as the rest of the students, only faster. I was never isolated in a small group again, probably because my new school was both larger and more traditional and so it scaled its programs for larger groups. My acceleration in grade school was designed primarily so that I would be prepared to be tracked into New Trier High School's highest level classes and the extra math which my junior high organized was to allow me to start geometry in high school with a year of algebra behind me. Throughout high school, I stayed in fourth-level courses and took advanced-placement courses during my senior year.

In looking back, I realize there were many factors that worked to form the manner in which I approached my education. Certain teachers stand out clearly in my memory. Many of my junior high English teachers were wonderful when it came to developing interesting projects that allowed you to use your own creativity. My seventh-grade social studies teacher in particular was a remarkable man who had a personal relationship with every student in the class. This, along with his energetic and upbeat method of teaching, encouraged everyone to be attentive and to do their best in his class.

In high school, I had two English teachers who were superior in terms of both the material they covered and the character of their classes. One was a woman who had me trying to impress her from the first day of class. Her determination to avoid trivial class discussions, the obvious care which she put into preparing for the class, her ability to be both stern and friendly, and her concern for her students inside and out of the class made her an exceptional teacher. When she assigned a paper, it was always in the form of a challenge to convince her of your opinion, rather than a glorified book report.

The other English teacher was a man whose method was much the same, but it was his personality that gave his class such an edge. He was harsh, sarcastic, blunt, and haughty, but never dull. His challenge was for us to become as sharp and quick to debate as he was. Not everyone took to his class because of his caustic manner, but I thought he was funny and loved it. I remember two of my high school science teachers as being good, but primarily for their success in feeding us large amounts of information at an accelerated pace. The level of creativity that the English teachers had put to use was missing here, but perhaps that was only due to the more technical subject matter.

Mostly I found disappointments in my high school teachers. I expected that if the district was making the effort to locate and place together the better students, that they would also make the effort to supply us with teachers who would keep us at least interested, if not challenged. This was often not the case. Rather, the "gift" of teaching a fourth-level class was given to older teachers with seniority, many of whom were truly at the bottom in terms of being challenging. For the most part my teachers were uninspired, boring, and bored. They taught the same sequence of the same readings in the same manner year after year, and all of the students sensed this. I think that many of the teachers interpreted brighter students as students who needed *less* teaching and stimulation rather than more. Their attitudes were almost an invitation to underachieve, to perform in terms of what they would accept rather than what you were capable of. If the majority of my teachers influenced me in any way, it was in learning how to deliver the most results with the least effort.

By far the most important influences on me were those of my family and peers. Because none of my close friends were in fourth-level classes with me, I wanted to identify less with the "brain" stereotype that they had of some students. Because I spent most of my time with these people rather than people in my classes, I adopted many of their opinions rather than those of the students I was with during school. At the same time that the attitudes of my friends influenced me against taking school too seriously, they were very much involved in using ranking as a standard of intelligence. According to them, I was considered smart no matter what my grades were, solely because I had been placed in all fourth-level classes. This was ridiculous, because many of the classes taught the same material to all different levels, but the "mystique" of the fourth-level class was deeply ingrained.

My parents were by far the most significant influence on me, both in the example which they set and in my desire to live up to their expectations. It was very important for me to believe that I was successful and bright, and this came primarily as a result of my parents' encouragement. Because of their support, I felt confident enough of my academic abilities to spend a lot of my time doing things besides concentrating on homework. Because I didn't feel the pressure to prove myself continually, I spent more of my effort on extracurricular activities. This was both good and bad, because I tended to care less about grades and heavily played down the ability of others to rank me. If I didn't do very well on a test, I could easily justify it to myself because I had been working in the orchestra for the school play that week or planning publicity for a speaker who was coming later in the month. Many students I know run into problems because they work under a tremendous pressure to get 100% on every test because they feel that this is the only way to prove their ability continually. For me, the situation was almost reversed. Though I wish that I had taken my school work a little more seriously, I'm very grateful for the chances I had to spend my time learning in other ways.

REFERENCES

Barbe, W. (1955). Evaluation of special classes for gifted children. *Exceptional Children, 22,* 60–62.

Benbow, C., & Stanley, J. (1983). *Academic precocity.* Baltimore, MD: Johns Hopkins University Press.

Bloom, B. (1985). *Developing talent in young people.* New York: Ballantine Books.

Cox, J., Daniel, N., & Boston, B. (1985). *Educating able learners.* Austin: University of Texas Press.

Hauck, B., & Freehill, M. (1972). *Gifted case studies.* Dubuque, IA: William Brown.

MacKinnon, D. (1965). Personality and the realization of creative potential. *American Psychologist, 20*(4); 273–281.

Roe, A. (1953). *Making of a scientist.* New York: Dodd Mead.

Weiss, P., & Gallagher, J. (1982). *Program effectiveness, education of gifted and talented students: A review.* Chapel Hill, NC: University of North Carolina.

CHAPTER 10

Critical Issues in Curriculum for the Gifted: Implications of the National Reports

A. Harry Passow

In examining the critical issues of curriculum for the gifted in terms of the implications of the national reports, it is useful to focus on what the reports do or do not say about the gifted and their education. If there is one term that all the reports use, almost to excess, it is *excellence*. One would have expected the National Commission on Excellence in Education (NCEE) to dwell on excellence and how it could be achieved, but excellence and its attainment is the theme of many other reports as well. At first blush, then, one would expect that the reports have a great deal to say about the gifted, since clearly the attainment of excellence is what education for the gifted is all about. In *A Nation at Risk,* the NCEE's 1983 report, excellence is defined at three levels:

> At the level of the *individual learner,* it means performing on the boundary of individual ability in ways that test and push back personal limits, in school and in the workplace. Excellence characterizes a *school or college* that sets high expectations and goals for all its learners, then tries in every way possible to help students reach them. Excellence characterizes a *society* that has adopted these policies, for it will then be prepared through the education and skill of its people to respond to the challenges of a rapidly changing world. [p. 12]

"Performing on the boundary of individual ability in ways that test and push back personal limits" is a reasonable statement of what should be at least one goal of education for the gifted. In the same section, the NCEE (1983) states:

Our goal must be to develop the talents of all to their fullest. Attaining that goal requires that we expect and assist all students to work to the limits of their capabilities. We should expect schools to have genuinely high standards rather than minimum ones, and parents to support and encourage their children to make the most of their talents and abilities. [p. 13]

"To develop the talents of all to their fullest" includes, one would expect, the gifted as well, and so one might view *A Nation at Risk* and perhaps the other national reports to be "good for the gifted." After all, if we are to have high expectations, high standards, tough requirements, more mathematics, more science, more foreign languages, that should upgrade education for the gifted, since that population would not be permitted to slide into "the mediocre educational performance that exists today" (p. 5) or to continue to squander "the gains in student achievement made in the wake of the Sputnik challenge" (p. 5), as the NCEE (1983) put it. Renewing "the Nation's commitment to schools and colleges of high quality throughout the length and breadth of our land" (p. 6) ought to have serious implications for education for the gifted as well. But there is little reason to be sanguine about this being the consequence of the national reports, for several reasons.

Feldman (1983) contrasted the concepts of excellence used by John W. Gardner in his 1961 book titled *Excellence* with that of David Gardner, who chaired the committee which produced *A Nation at Risk* (NCEE, 1983). Using John Gardner's *Excellence* (1961) as his jumping-off point, Feldman (1983) raised three issues by which to guide his discussion of a reconceptualization of the notion of excellence. These are

the importance of actual achievement as contrasted with predicted potentials, the need to recognize that differential value must be placed on some fields over others, and the need to encourage excellence in a wide variety of domains. [p. 3]

Feldman asserts that, despite the strong rhetoric of *A Nation at Risk*,

one is left with the impression that no real reforms have been recommended at all. Longer school days, more requirements, computers, technology, better teachers, etc. are essentially echoes of the *back to basics* reactions to the sixties. These bromides, mixed with some high-sounding rhetoric that anyone would warm to, are the *fundamental reforms* called for in the opening paragraphs of the report. . . . John Gardner tried nearly a quarter of a century ago to rouse the citizenry to confront issues of excellence head on. . . . One can only hope that another quarter century will not pass before the call [for fundamental changes in the ways that excellence is identified and encouraged] is heeded. [p. 4]

What do the national reports say specifically about the gifted and talented? There is some direct reference, but much of what is said is done so indirectly, mostly in connection with the discussion of tracking. Adler (1982), in his *Paideia Proposal*, argues that the revolutionary message of John Dewey's *Democracy and Education* (1916) "was that a democratic society must provide equal educational opportunity not only by giving to all its children the same quantity of public education—the same number of years in school—but also by making sure to give all of them, with no exceptions, the same quality of education" (Adler, 1982, p. 4). Adler advocates the *same objectives for all, without exception.* He argues, "The best education for the best is the best education for all" (p. 7). With the same objectives for all, he would also have the same course of study for all, kindergarten through grade 13, with no electives and no specialization and the only exception being the choice of a second language. Adler specifically recommends the abandonment of special programs for the gifted:

> The greatly improved quality of the Paideia curriculum makes special programs for the specially gifted totally unnecessary. Such programs are doubtless needed now because existing courses of study, instruction, and standards are so poor in quality and so deficient in content that the specially gifted suffer deprivation. But the Paideia program will give the specially gifted every opportunity to use their talents to the fullest measure. There is no need to retain special programs for them.
>
> If the specially gifted have surplus energy and avidity for learning after they have done their best in the required studies, this surplus can be used by having them learn more by teaching their less able classmates. [pp. 34–35]

In *High School,* Boyer (1983) observes that "gifted and talented students are often overlooked" because "teachers and administrators just assume they'll 'make it'" (p. 236). What gifted students want, he asserts, "is flexibility: to be allowed to go at their own pace, to satisfy course requirements as quickly as possible, and to move to new areas of learning" (p. 236). To enable and to encourage gifted students to "move on," Boyer recommends independent study, credit by examination, the International Baccalaureate program, separate academic high schools, residential schools such as the North Carolina School of Science and Mathematics, and special study with universities. He concludes that "every high school should have special arrangements for gifted students," but, "since it is impossible for all high schools to provide the top teachers and the sophisticated equipment needed to offer advanced study" (pp. 238–239), he also proposes magnet schools in the arts or science in urban areas and residential academies in less densely populated districts. Boyer notes that, "while the emphasis here is on science and mathematics, there is also a need to serve exceptional students in other fields, especially foreign languages and the arts" (p. 239).

Boyer (1983) also gives attention to the idea of accelerating students, arguing that "secondary schools and colleges have a special obligation to break the bureaucratic barriers and develop flexible arrangements for students" (p. 255), including such arrangements as "advanced placement, credit by examinations, early college admission, and 'university in the school' programs, to name just a few" (p. 255).

Two topics that figure prominently in a number of reports are *excellence and equity* and *grouping/tracking*. Both of these have implications for education of the gifted. The NCEE (1983) asserts strongly that "the twin goals of equity and high quality schooling have profound and practical meaning for our economy and our society, and we cannot permit one to yield to the other either in principle or practice" (p. 13). Adler (1982) argues just as strongly:

> Equality of educational opportunity is not, in fact, provided if it means no more than taking all children into the public schools for the same number of hours, days, and years. If once there they are divided into the sheep and the goats, into those destined for economic and political leadership and for a quality of life to which all should have access, then the democratic purpose has been undermined by an inadequate system of public schooling. [p. 5]

In *A Place Called School*, Goodlad (1983) argues that school tracking practices preclude equal access to knowledge. Increasingly, he believes, "the issue will be whether students as a consequence of the schools they happen to attend and the classes to which they are assigned, have equality of access to knowledge" (p. 131). In Goodlad's view, grouping and tracking practices create the myth that there are basically two kinds of people: those who are "head oriented" and those who are "hand oriented."

Other reports are equally critical of tracking practices that divide students along academic, general, and vocational lines. The solution proposed in several reports is to construct a common core curriculum for all. Goodlad (1983), for instance, recommends that at the secondary school level there should be "a common core of studies from which students cannot escape through electives, even though the proposed elective purports to be in the same domain of knowledge" (p. 297); elimination of grouping of students in separate classes on the basis of past performance; and random assignment of students to heterogeneous classes. All of these efforts would be aimed at offering "the most equity with respect to gaining access to knowledge while still preserving the more advantageous content and teaching practices of the upper tracks" (p. 298). What is needed, Goodlad concludes, is improved pedagogy, not differentiated, inequitable tracks and curricula.

Similarly, Adler (1982), as indicated earlier, advocates the same educational objectives for all, the same course of study for all, and the completion of "this required course of study with a satisfactory standard of accomplishment, regardless of native ability, temperamental bent, or conscious preferences" (p. 41). Adler's means for adjusting for individual differences, which he admits do exist, is to administer the program "sensitively and flexibly in ways that accord with whatever differences must be taken into account" (p. 44). He makes no specification, however, of what these differences are. He would provide some remedial assistance for those children who need help, but, as noted previously, Adler asserts quite flatly that the quality of the Paideia curriculum is such that special programs for the gifted are unnecessary.

A Nation at Risk (NCEE, 1983) contains recommendations for what are called the "five new basics," which all students seeking a diploma would be required to take: 4 years of English, 3 years of mathematics, 3 years of science, 3 years of social science, and one-half year of computer science. For the college bound (one can assume that the gifted are in this category), 2 years of foreign language are strongly recommended. Moreover, the high school curriculum should also include "programs requiring rigorous effort in subjects that advance students' personal, educational, and occupational goals, such as fine and performing arts and vocational education" (p. 26). In one of the few references to the elementary school, the report recommends that the curriculum there be designed to provide a sound base for studying the "five new basics" and that it should foster "an enthusiasm for learning and the development of the individual's gifts and talents" (p. 27). The five new basics are, of course, the same package of courses that every good high school has recommended in the past for college-bound students, with the exception of the half-year of computer science.

Both Boyer (1983) and Goodlad (1983) advocate a common curriculum which would constitute a common set of concepts, principles, skills, and ways of knowing aimed at providing a good general education for all. In Goodlad's view, the best preparation for work is a sound general education. Similarly, Boyer's (1983) priority is the mastery of English plus a "core of common learnings—a program of required courses in literature, the arts, foreign language, history, civics, science, mathematics, technology, health"—the traditional academic subjects, but for all students, not just the college bound. He would add a carefully planned program of "elective clusters," consisting of five or six courses that would enable the student to engage in advanced study in selected academic subjects or explore career options, or a combination of both. Boyer would also add what he calls the "new Carnegie unit"—a minimum of 30 hours a year of voluntary service in the community or at school.

The College Board's Educational Equality Project is based on the belief that many college entrants in recent years have not had the knowledge and skills needed for higher education, and the report (1983) aims at informing students about what they need to know and be able to do in six basic academic subjects and with respect to six basic academic competencies, plus computer competency, which is seen as an emerging need.

In *Horace's Compromise: The Dilemma of the American High School*, Sizer (1986) sees "education's job today [as] less in purveying information than in helping people to use it—that is, in the exercise of their minds" (p. 84). He would reorganize the high school into four areas or large departments: (a) inquiry and expression, (b) mathematics and science, (c) literature and the arts, and (d) philosophy and history. He would eliminate years of attendance and collection of credits as the basis for a diploma and would substitute an agreed-upon level of mastery, thus providing for flexibility and acceleration.

There are several more national reports on education and literally hundreds of state reports, as governors, legislators, and state education departments have joined the stream of those who see a crisis in American education and a need for drastic reform. Unlike the reforms proposed after Sputnik in 1957, when there was a focus on the education of the gifted and on developing America's resources of scientific talent, the current reports give little specific attention to the gifted, although they have implications for their education. The discussion thus far, however terse, provides a basis for examining some of the critical curriculum issues for the gifted which are implied in the reform reports. Some of these issues follow, with no particular order of priority intended.

- What concept(s) of *excellence* can be seen to guide the recommendations found in the various reports, all of which propose reform to restore educational excellence? Is the narrow concept of "greater rigor" in the traditional academic subject areas adequate? Is the press to "raise standards" appropriate if standards are defined in terms of test achievement in these subject areas? Is John Gardner's (1961) or David Gardner's (NCEE, 1983) concept guiding our idea of educational excellence? There are many dilemmas raised in the equity-versus-excellence debates; how do these impinge on educating gifted students?
- Do the various common general education curricula proposed in several reports, consisting essentially of the traditional college-preparatory subjects, constitute adequate and appropriate curricula for the gifted population, with its diverse characteristics and needs? Will the content of such curricula provide opportunities for the gifted to deal with more elaborate, more complex, and more in-depth study of major ideas, problems, and themes in ways that enable them to integrate knowledge with and across systems of thought? Put another way, will the common curricula limit students to acquisition of the knowledge that is tested by standardized exams, or can they provide opportunities for differential interactions with major

systems of thought that incorporate many concepts, generalizations, principles, and theories related to significant issues and problems? Is it correct to assume that the subjects that constitute a college-preparatory curriculum provide a rich enough and accelerated enough program for the gifted? Is Adler (1982) right when he states that the quality of his Paideia curriculum makes any differentiation for the gifted unnecessary?

- Which individual gifts and talents are appropriate bases on which to differentiate curriculum? Educators of the gifted have long argued the need to differentiate instruction in at least three ways; in *breadth* and/or *depth*, in *tempo* or *pace*, and in *kind* or *nature*. Do these kinds of differentiation constitute differential access to knowledge and thus contribute to educational inequity, as some reports suggest?

- What should be the balance between the general/common curriculum and the specialized curriculum, the one in which the individual pursues the development of her or his own talents, interests, or career options? To what extent should an individual be permitted and even encouraged to engage in intensive, specialized, accelerated, and enriched learning experiences, possibly impacting on her or his general education? Should educators be concerned that in-depth study or concentration in an area in which an individual has particular aptitude, interests, and potential will adversely affect the individual's general education? Should specialized study therefore be delayed until the tertiary level, as several reports suggest?

- As states follow the suggestions of some of the national reports and raise the requirements for high school graduation, students are being permitted fewer choices and electives. Meeting the requirements for graduation in some states makes it impossible for students to have experiences in the areas of aesthetics, let alone in their own areas of specialization, unless an overload is carried. How should gifted students be counseled in terms of curriculum choices? What bases may be used for such counseling?

- The national reports recommend that all students "take more"—more mathematics, more science, more foreign languages. Such a recommendation raises a number of issues concerning curricular balance between, on the one hand, science and mathematics and, on the other, aesthetic areas, languages, the humanities, and the social sciences. Are there different balances for different individuals, or should all students have the same exposure to these areas? If a youngster is gifted and highly motivated in, say, creative writing, should he or she be required to take advanced work in mathematics and science as well?

- To what extent will the general/common curriculum permit and encourage differentiated experiences that stress critical and creative thinking skills and other aspects of cognitive development that constitute the qualitative difference in the education of the gifted?

- The national reports almost completely ignore the affective development of students, as do most programs for the gifted. The "curriculum models" or "enrichment paradigms" suggested for the gifted—such as the Bloom Taxonomy (Bloom et al., 1956) and the *Structure of the Intellect* (Meeker, 1969)—focus on cognitive development, stimulation of problem-solving skills, and similar aspects of "thinking" and intellectual growth, sometimes narrowly and sometimes more broadly. Far less attention is given to the affective development of the gifted—to feelings, values, interests, morality, self-esteem, and the like. How much attention can we expect will be given to affective development, when excellence and outstanding performance are conceived of in terms of academic achievement?

• What should be the balance between independent, individual study and group or class activities? Although one or two of the national reports talk about developing independent learners, little is said about the role of independent study or individual activities as the means for such development. When is it important for gifted students to pursue their own interests, concerns, and problems on their own, and when should they be involved in settings in which they share, communicate, critique, and evaluate their own products and performances with their peers?

• The national reports seem to be in agreement that grouping and tracking constitute bad practices. Are there no circumstances when special groups are appropriate for educating gifted and talented students? If there are any, what are they, and what are the criteria for forming such groups?

• The national reports urge greater accountability and more frequent testing of students. They recommend the use of standardized tests without commenting on their basic limitations. Evaluation of the development of the gifted should also use critiquing, analyzing, and assessing products and performances. Will the emphasis on standardized testing restrict the broader and more appropriate concept of evaluation of the gifted?

• The national reports talk about "raising the standards" and speak of these standards in terms of academic achievement as measured by tests. For the gifted, the self-set standards by which they judge their own achievements are often much tougher than are those set by the school or society at large. What standards should be set for the gifted in respect to performance, and how might they be most effectively applied?

These are just a few of the critical issues regarding curriculum, to which teachers and other curriculum planners should give consideration in designing and implementing programs for the gifted. Complicating these considerations is the plethora of reports—national, state, and local—advocating what are purported to be "drastic reforms." Many such proposals are neither drastic nor reformatory. The analyses, the recommendations, and the policies are deserving of careful study, but their acceptance and implementation should not be automatic. While the reports cite many urgent issues, they must be examined in terms of one's own context, one's own philosophy, one's own population, and one's own resources. Thus, educators of the gifted must be thoughtful about interpreting the reports too directly as supportive of their efforts. In many respects, they may find the opposite to be true.

REFERENCES

Adler, M. (1982), *The Paideia proposal: An educational manifesto*. New York: Macmillan.

Boyer, E. (1983). *High school*. New York: Harper & Row.

Bloom, B., Englehart, M. D., Juret, E. J., Hill, W. H., & Kratwohl, D. R. (1956). *Taxonomy of educational objectives: Handbook I: Cognitive domains*. New York: David McKay.

College Board Educational Equality Project. (1983). *Academic preparation for college: What students need to learn*. New York: The College Board.

Dewey, J. (1916). *Democracy and education*. New York: Macmillan.

Feldman, D. H. (1983). Reconceptualizing excellence: Still a national priority. *Roeper Review*, 6(1), 2–4.

Gardner, J. W. (1961). *Excellence*. New York: Harper & Row.

Goodlad, J. (1983). *A place called school*. New York: McGraw-Hill.

Meeker, M. N. (1969). *The structure of intellect: Its integration and uses*. Columbus, OH: Charles E. Merrill.

National Commission on Excellence in Education. (1983). *A nation at risk*. Washington, DC: U.S. Department of Education.

Sizer, T. (1986). *Horace's compromise: The dilemma of the American high school*. New York: Basic Books.

CHAPTER 11

Curriculum Development and Evaluation in School Programs for Gifted Students

James J. Gallagher

There is little disagreement in the field of gifted education over the need for a differentiated curriculum for gifted children (Clark, 1985; Gallagher, 1985; Maker, 1982; Tannenbaum, 1983). The areas of disagreement emerge only when one discusses the specifics of the general idea. What sort of different curriculum? Who will decide? How can you demonstrate the merit of your particular position on this issue? This chapter will address the process of curriculum development and implementation and the role played by evaluation in addressing these questions.

The evaluation of programs for gifted students faces some peculiar problems because of the unique nature of this population. In some ways they are the mirror image of problems faced while attempting to evaluate programs for learners who have mental retardation. While it is difficult for educators to report sizable improvements with children who have retardation, it is hard *not* to find positive results for the gifted. One can hardly do anything in an educational sense so badly that gifted students will not look good anyway.

Why do we get a good response for any curriculum attempt for the gifted? We can start with the disappointment and boredom of the gifted student in the regular program. Almost anything different would be perceived by the student as an improvement. Second, we also have the gratitude of the family, who recognize that we are trying, at least, for something better. Finally, we have students of excellent potential who will hardly do less than "above average," no matter what we do. This positive aura has reduced the pressure to demonstrate or evaluate the quality of our programs. But the increased costs of our programs (Gallagher, Weiss, Oglesby, & Thomas, 1983) and our own standards should push us to a more responsible position so that we can feel comfortable with such special programs.

Gifted students in our schools are often 2 or more years advanced in

178

achievement over other students, and consequently are able to deal with more complex ideas and concepts than their age-mates. They also have greater ability to learn skills of problem solving and creative thinking, which enable them to use to best advantage their considerable talents by doing more effective information processing, problem solving, and problem finding.

The following are the general areas of curriculum modification that have widespread acceptance in the field of education for the gifted (Gallagher, 1985):

1. Gifted children should master important conceptual systems that are at the level of their abilities in various content fields.
2. Gifted children should develop skills and strategies that enable them to become more independent, creative, and self-sufficient searchers after knowledge.
3. Gifted children should develop a joy and excitement about learning that will carry them through the drudgery and routine that are inevitable parts of learning. [p. 80]

These seem to be in striking concordance with the curriculum goals for gifted programs operative in school districts across the country.

Such general principles, however, need a good deal of translation into operational forms before we can judge whether different content or special skills instruction is appropriate. One clear indicator from these suggestions, however, is that "more of the same" from the general curriculum (do 20 problems instead of 5) is clearly inappropriate as an intervention strategy for these children.

A number of observers have tried to categorize various types of curriculum differentiation for gifted students. I (Gallagher, 1985) have identified four different types, as follows:

1. *Content acceleration.* This represents the introduction of material from a later grade to an earlier grade level, as in the early teaching of algebra to gifted elementary students.
2. *Content enrichment.* A variety of experiences and activities are provided that elaborate on the basic concepts taught in the regular program. The additional material is based upon established curriculum goals for this age group, rather than different goals.
3. *Content sophistication.* Material that focuses on larger and more abstract systems of ideas and concepts is taught. This would raise the complexity of the material presented to match the advanced abilities of these students.
4. *Content novelty.* Completely new and different material especially use-

ful for gifted students is introduced such as symbolic logic, the effect of biomedical advances on family life, and so forth. The idea is to provide material of particular interest or usefulness to those who will be community leaders, planners, and scholars.

Part of the responsibility of designing curriculum is to suggest strategies by which the material may be introduced, extended, and concluded (Maker, 1986; VanTassel-Baska, 1986). Sisk (1986) displays an impressive array of instructional strategies that can be utilized to begin and to extend a particular curriculum topic. These include simulations, role playing, visualization, futuristics, journal writing, creative problem solving, group dynamics, independent study, synectics, and bibliotherapy. The effective teacher knows, intuitively or explicitly, how to use such strategies to interest and excite students so that they become personally involved in the ideas that are being presented or are to be discovered along the way. The choice of which of these approaches and strategies would be used would depend upon the students, the particular educational setting in which they are placed, and the objectives and preferences of the teacher.

WHO DECIDES WHICH CONTENT?

The question of who makes the final decision on which differential content would be pursued is by no means an easy one. Should it be a scholar with special knowledge of the complexities of a particular content field? Should it be the teacher or a committee of teachers who will choose? At least one author has suggested that gifted students themselves should be a part of the decision (Renzulli, 1977).

The field of education for the gifted has been beset by an apparent contradiction between two alternative ideas for the desirable development of a differentiated curriculum for gifted students. The first of these ideas is that gifted students often have very creative ideas of their own and like to determine their own directions rather than having them imposed by authorities such as teachers. Therefore, there has been a tendency to say that gifted children should have the opportunity to choose for themselves the nature of their curriculum.

The second idea, however, is that gifted students should be presented with the most sophisticated systems of ideas in given content areas that they are capable of mastering. This means that the important systems of ideas, theories, generalizations, and so on, that lie at the heart of individual disciplines should be presented to them. Obviously, if gifted students use their own interests as the basis for their differentiated study, they are not likely to "stumble" upon these major or key systems of ideas as their desired topic. Yet both of these goals have obvious merit. Is there a way of combining them?

The concept that would seem most relevant to resolving this dilemma is that of "freedom within structure." This would mean that the teacher would choose, as the curriculum objective, some area of significant thought in the discipline involved but would allow the students a great deal of freedom in exploring the domain represented by that system of ideas. For example, if the idea to be mastered is that "Environment shapes humanity's behavior, but humanity also shapes the environment," then students can be allowed a wide variety of projects or investigations from which to choose that would illustrate that concept. One student can choose to analyze houses developed under a wide variety of environmental and climatic conditions, looking for similarities and differences. Another could be charting readings on air quality in the area, and a third could be designing clothes that would be suited to different sets of environmental conditions.

In this fashion, the students can each be doing their own preferred activities, but those activities all would focus around a given major idea chosen by the teacher and together would serve to define the concept more thoroughly through the use of a variety of examples illustrating the idea.

CURRICULUM EVALUATION

The need for more systematic review of programs for gifted students is addressed by Horowitz and O'Brien (1986), who call for "a significant increase in research on effective educational programs for children who are identified as gifted and talented. . . . It is worthwhile to develop and maintain these programs only if we have some evidence that they make a real difference" (p. 1151).

As I have pointed out elsewhere (Gallagher, 1985), the teacher of gifted students may have anywhere from 200 hours (resource room) to 900 hours (self-contained, all-day class) in a year to provide special instruction. From all of the available sets of knowledge and skills, one chooses a particular set for these children. The fundamental question is, Why *this* set rather than another? How does one judge the adequacy of choice, organization, and implementation of curriculum? The process is a complex one requiring a varied set of approaches.

Given even the most positive of intentions, how would we propose to demonstrate to others the effectiveness of our good works? The hard choices that must be made among a myriad of alternative possibilities for instruction was faced in 1950 by Tyler. He proposed four fundamental questions that should determine the criteria for any choice:

1. What educational purposes should the school seek to attain?
2. What educational experiences can be provided that are likely to attain these purposes?
3. How can these educational experiences be effectively organized?
4. How can we determine whether these purposes are being attained?

One typical view of educational evaluation is that we should be concerned with the way in which the educator answers question 4. But if our program review is to be definitive, we really have to determine an evaluation strategy that will address each of the four questions, and a few more besides.

Stages of Curriculum Evaluation

I have identified in Figure 11.1 seven separate stages of curriculum evaluation, described as follows.

1. *Selection of curriculum.* One of the first decisions is whether the proposed differentiated curriculum is important enough to be worth the valuable time of the teacher and students. Some independent estimate of the value of the proposed curriculum seems called for. This involves a number of levels of analysis, each with its own unique measurement issues and problems. One can look at the educational purposes or the curriculum objectives, for example. These objectives would be the sets of knowledge or skills that one is intending to impart to the students. In this case, some way needs to be found to judge not only the appropriateness of the specific sets of knowledge or skills chosen, but also whether one can defend the choice of these particular objectives, given the limited amount of instructional time available.

If the materials have little significance or importance in the first place, beyond being of some interest to the student and the teacher (i.e., teaching in some detail, for 3 weeks, the battle of Gettysburg, hour by hour, day by day), then the efficacy of the curriculum is essentially defeated before any of the other stages come into play. That is, even though such mundane material could be presented by the teacher with consummate skill and with admirable strategies, resulting in a high level of student interest, it would still fail to accomplish anything truly significant because it lacks importance in the larger arena of knowledge value.

2. *Teacher preparation for curriculum delivery.* There surely will need to be some attempt to acquaint the teacher with the major objectives of the curriculum, whether these be content or process, or both. Consequently, some test or indication of teacher mastery of working with these objectives

Figure 11.1   Curriculum Evaluation Questions

EVALUATION STAGE	ANALYTIC QUESTION	STRATEGY
1. Selection of curriculum	Is the choice of the curriculum materials and objectives worthy?	Use of expert judges to validate the choice
2. Teacher preparation	Has the teacher mastered the content and process necessary to curriculum presentation?	Test of factual information and/or observation under pilot conditions
3. Organization and lesson plan	Do the lesson plans match with the objectives for the curriculum?	Review by "experts"
4. Classroom presentation	Did the presentation follow the objectives and lesson plans?	Analyses of audiotape or videotape and/or observation of class sessions
5. Teacher/student interaction	Did the students appear to be motivated or curious? Did they respond appropriately in the class sessions?	Analyses of tapes or transcripts and/or class observations
6. Teacher perception of impact	Did the teacher feel positively about the lessons? Were there shortcomings in the presentations or student response?	Survey of teachers and/or interviewed or diary
7. Student impact	Have the students been measurably changed by the experience? knowledge? attitudes? motivation, or more?	Students change in knowledge or other factors in pre-post analysis

is required. This phase of the evaluation could be satisfied with a written test, if the teacher is required to have some specific knowledge of the content. A demonstration by the teacher of a sample lesson would be even more convincing. At any rate, there should be some way of insuring that the teacher has the necessary skills and knowledge to carry out the program.

3. *Organization and lesson plan.* Having ascertained that teacher mastery is sufficient, the next question is, How does the teacher plan to implement it? Being able to reproduce knowledge of the curriculum content is not the same as being able to plan a sequence by which the content is presented, extended, and concluded. One aspect of evaluation, for example, is a review of the teacher's plans for presentation in respect to appropriateness. A trained teacher can judge and rate the organization and planned strategies. Is one to use the discovery method? Are the teachers asked to give "advanced organizers" as aids to student conceptualization? Does the teacher make an outrageous statement to stir the students' interest or action? Does the teacher present an especially difficult problem so as to follow up with teaching the skills that will allow the student to attack that problem? How appropriate is the choice of strategies to the material and the particular students involved?

A clear plan of action in terms of suggested questions and a sequence of activities can provide a base for evaluation of the second stage teacher lesson plan. Let us take one specific example illustrating the seminar method proposed by Adler (1982). An example of the teacher's plans for the seminar lesson based on readings from Machiavelli's *The Prince*, is shown in Figure 11.2. Here are listed the anticipated questions for: a) introducing the topic, b) examining central points, and c) closing the discussion. Again matching this plan against the reality of what actually happened can reveal how close to the original intentions the teacher came.

Under the section Core Examining Central Points in Figure 11.2 Adler plans to pose the key question as to which of four positions the students will choose and defend. In this example these four positions would be determined by their answer to two questions, whether Machiavelli was right or wrong about mankind being mainly evil and whether Machiavellian strategies would or would not work in the modern world? The student might decide that men were mainly evil and that Machiavellian strategies would not work in today's world. That would be one of the four positions that they would then have to defend.

If there are serious problems with stages 1 through 3 listed above, then little can be expected from the rest of the sequence. It is as though the student was supposed to have taken a powerful drug and instead took a sugar pill or a placebo. The lack of student response in such an instance would not be a criticism of the effectiveness of the drug (or the curriculum). In fact, we would not know anything about its effectiveness. Similarly, a failure to present a curriculum concept effectively does not really speak against the instructional strategies employed even if the students don't respond well to their tests or other impact indices.

4. Classroom presentation. Planning is one thing but implementation is another. We are all aware of how our careful plans often evaporate under the stress of unexpected events in the classroom or as a result of distractibility as we wander off on our own tangents or respond to student reactions. So

Figure 11.2 Great Books Teacher Training Project Question Frame Based on Machiavelli's *The Prince*

QUESTIONS	FOLLOW-UP QUESTIONS

Opening--Introducing the Topic

1. Propose a better title for the book, eliminating reference to princes and making it of interest to the largest possible contemporary audience. (Round-robin question)

1. What is your title?

2. To what occupations, careers, professions, activities is this book, thus entitled, applicable? To what, not applicable at all?

2. Why do you think so?

3. Have you ever used the term "Machiavellian"?

3. Was it used as a term of praise o dispraise? Why?

4. Would Aristotle or Rousseau have approved of Machiavelli's Prince? Would Jefferson?

4. Why/Why not?

5. What kind of book is this: like Plato; like Aristotle; like Rousseau?

5. What makes you think so?

6. Can you name some Machiavellians in history or in the contemporary world?
   a. What public figures?
   b. What American presidents?

6. How are they similar to/different from one another?

Core--Examining Central Points

1. According to Machiavelli, it is better to be: (Y=yes; N=no)
   a. hated or feared? (Y)
   b. hated or loved? (N)
   c. a person that keeps your promises? (N)
   d. a person who has people behind you? (Y)
   e. a person who has friends/followers? (Y)

1. Where in the text do you find it?

2. Write the following words and rank order in terms of their importance to Machiavelli's theory:
   force of number
   force of arms
   cunning/guile
   friends/adherents
   reputation for being virtuous
   being virtuous
   a. Which did you rank first?
   b. Which did you rank last?

2. a. Why?
   b. Why?

3. Let me explain the chart's four positions.
   a. What line are you on?

3. a. Why did you take that position?

Closing--Relationship to the World

1. If most men are for the most part good, are they thus by nature or nurture? (Vote)

1. Why do you say so?

2. In which of the following communities--the family, the state, the corporation, or the world--do you think Machiavelli's roles are most applicable?
   a. In the family?
   b. Of the other three, in which is it desirable to be Machiavellian?

2. a. Why/why not?
   b. Why?

3. Which of the two superpowers--the United States or the USSR--is the more Machiavellian in its relation with the other?

3. Why?

some measure of what actually happened in the classroom would seem to be the next step on the trail from idea to student outcome.

Weiss (1988) presents sample lessons, based on Adler's (1982) model, designed to illustrate the seminar method of instruction. One can test how well each sample lesson in fact demonstrates the seminar method by matching the actual classroom activity against the general rules for seminar leaders and against the lesson plan devised. Some of the seminar leader behaviors are as follows:

Asking a series of questions that give direction to the discussion
Being sure the questions are understood or rephrasing them until they are
Raising issues that lead to further questions
Asking questions that allow for a range of answers deserving consideration and demanding judgment
Allowing for discussion of conflict or differences
Examining the answers and drawing out implications or reasons

One can review a videotape or a transcription of an audiotape, to see if these basic requirements were carried out. Classroom observers, alerted to these six points, could rate the classroom activities on the spot. In these ways, a clear measure could be made of the match between desired seminar principles and actual outcomes.

5. *Teacher/student interaction.* Did the students behave as they were supposed to or respond the way that we anticipated? If student response or interaction was one of the intended outcomes, then how do we demonstrate that it happened in the way anticipated? Classroom observations or audio/video recordings would be needed to analyze the effectiveness of this component.

The curriculum materials could be conceptually important and the teaching strategies could be admirably prepared in advance, only to have the whole thing come apart in some unfortunate type of teacher/student interaction. If the teacher pretends to be the only authority and refuses to be challenged on the material at hand, or insists on proceeding with the material even in the face of the clear observation that the students are drifting away or are actively antagonized by the lesson, then the results will be less than salutary. It is important to note how well the teacher is able to carry out the intentions of the lesson while simultaneously making appropriate adaptations to the always unpredictable student response and maintaining student interest and motivation. An audiotape or videotape of a class session or sessions can provide the answer to questions such as, How many students participated in the discussion? How many appeared to have grasped the basic points of the discussion? Were they able to defend their position? These are all elements of the teacher/student interaction, as is teacher willingness to tolerate differences of opinion, an aspect of teacher style.

   6. Teacher perception of impact. How did the teacher feel about the entire episode? Was she or he happy with how it went? Were there weak spots in the presentation or in the student response that could point to better ways of accomplishing the goals than the ones that form the basis for this curriculum implementation effort? Some form of interview or rating scale is needed to assess teacher perception. Such feedback can be valuable for the teacher in question as well as for other teachers viewing the class. It is important to remember that if the teacher is unhappy with her or his performance or with the student response, then the curriculum, regardless of its other virtues, will not be used in that classroom.

   7. Student impact. In the end, some indication should be available that the students were affected in some fashion, or we can hardly extol the virtues of our particular curriculum effort. Examples include students knowing more about a topic, changing their attitudes about an idea, mastering a particular skill, and so forth. Teacher-made tests have traditionally been employed for this purpose, but student reports or products can also be clear indicators of mastery. Student feelings cannot be ignored, either. If the students dislike the content or process, they will not likely pursue the topic beyond the requirements of the classroom.

   Student impact can be measured in the Machiavellian lesson, for example, by reviewing with them at a later date the Machiavellian principles to see how they remember the basic idea of the class sessions. Student products such as essays, poems, or dramas based on these principles could give an indication of another level of mastery, when reviewed by competent judges.

Focus of Evaluation

   The purpose of outlining these seven stages of curriculum evaluation is to illustrate the multiplicity of choices available to the program evaluator. Stress can be placed at whatever stage the evaluator feels is most important. This is particularly the case in a *formative evaluation* model, where an attempt is being made to improve the effectiveness of the presentation (House, 1980). In many evaluation studies, a *summative evaluation* decision may be reached on the overall usefulness of the curriculum without testing to see if the curriculum has been presented as originally intended. Any serious flaw in any part of the seven-stage sequence just discussed can spell trouble for summative results (i.e., student impact or product). Thus, even when things do not go completely right, we can find out a lot of useful information through a formative evaluation by discovering at which stage, or at what combination of stages, things went off the track. Consideration of these stages also gives us some insight into the myriad factors that combine to produce a satisfactory outcome.

Measurement

The seven stages can be adequately evaluated only if we take a rather unconventional attitude toward measurement and measuring instruments. One of the problems in many program or curriculum evaluation studies has been the excessive and inappropriate use of standard measuring instruments. In many cases, educational administrators who have learned in their college courses of the virtues of standardized tests are eager to use instruments that will not be criticized. When that fact is put together with the easy availability of group IQ tests or standard achievement batteries, then there is the real possibility that some substantial error can be made in the choice of instruments in the evaluation effort.

Callahan and Caldwell (1983) delineated the following major problems in the use of standard instruments of intelligence and achievement in evaluating a program for the gifted:

1. The goals and objectives measured by these tests are the goals and objectives of the basic curriculum. If these are not the goals of the program, then these tests are invalid for assessing the program.
2. Such tests assume all gifted students are studying or learning the same thing, i.e., the standard curriculum.
3. Such tests emphasize particular content skills not often taught as part of the gifted/talented program.

Fortunately, other types of measurement are available that are more appropriate to the task. The issue comes down to the relative merits of *qualitative* versus *quantitative* measurement. Qualitative measurement places the emphasis on studying the perceptions, feelings, and attitudes of the subject being researched, while quantitative measurement focuses upon objective assessment of quantities under controlled conditions. The administration of an intelligence test would be an example of quantitative measurement, whereas interviewing parents and children, or observing them in a naturalistic setting such as the classroom, would be an example of a qualitative approach (Edgerton, 1984).

In the field of evaluation research, there is considerable room for both approaches. Since the desired end product of a curriculum evaluation effort is the ability to make some type of decision, the qualitative approach is clearly appropriate, since it stresses values and opinions, which are often keys to decision making.

Doing qualitative research, however, does not mean abandoning careful planning or systematic procedures. As Stainback and Stainback (1988) point out,

> Researchers in education engaging in qualitative research must, like those engaging in quantitative research, make decisions regarding procedural strategies in a logical and systematic fashion and clearly articulate the strategies chosen in order to provide a framework from which the data collected can be understandable and perceived in proper perspective by others.

Figure 11.3 shows the distinctions these authors make between the quantitative and qualitative approaches. It is important to realize that both approaches can be appropriate for evaluation, depending upon the question being posed and the target group under study. As the qualitative approach becomes more professionally accepted, we are likely to see more instrumentation and models developed in this area. This will be especially helpful for the evaluation of programs for the education of gifted students.

CONCLUSION

The larger question posed here is, how do we propose to improve systematically our curriculum content and instructional strategies for gifted children? The answer suggested is that we must collect feedback from a variety of sources on the various stages of program and curriculum as they develop.

By accentuating and enhancing the elements that generate positive feedback and by amending those that engender negative feedback, we can continue the process of strengthening our program interventions. The alternative to this procedure is to become complacent with our current curricula or to use new and untested curriculum offerings that do little to inform us about accomplishing our goals.

REFERENCES

Adler, M. (1982). *The Paideia proposal: An educational manifesto*. New York: Macmillan.

Figure 11.3 Summary of Differences Between Quantitative and Qualitative Research

Dimensions	Quantitative Paradigm	Qualitative Paradigm
Purpose	Prediction and Control-Seeks causes and effects of human behavior.	Understanding-Seeks to understand people's interpretations and perceptions.
Reality	Stable-Reality is made up of facts that do not change.	Dynamic-Reality changes with changes in people's perceptions.
Viewpoint	Outsider-Reality is what quantifiable data indicate it to be.	Insider-Reality is what people perceive it to be.
Values	Value-free-Values can be controlled with appropriate methodological procedures.	Value-bound-Values will have an impact and should be understood and taken into account when conducting and reporting research.
Focus	Particularistic-Selected, predefined variables are studied.	Holistic-A total or complete picture is sought.
Orientation	Verification-Predetermined hypotheses are investigated	Discovery-Theories and hypotheses are evolved from data as collected.
Data	Objective-Data are independent of people's perceptions.	Subjective-Data are perceptions of the people in the environment.
Instrumentation	Nonhuman-Preconstructed tests, observational records, questionnaires and rating scales are employed.	Human-The human person is the primary data collection instrument.
Conditions	Controlled-Investigations are conducted under controlled conditions.	Naturalistic-Investigations are conducted under natural conditions.
Results	Reliable-The focus is on design and procedures to gain "hard" and replicable data.	Valid-The focus is on design and procedures to gain "real," "rich," and "deep" data.

Source: Stainback, S. & Stainback, W. 1988. *Understanding and conducting qualitative research.* Reston, VA: Council for Exceptional Children.

Callahan, C., & Caldwell, M. (1983). Using evaluation results to improve programs for the gifted and talented. *Journal for the Education of the Gifted,* 7(1), 60–74.

Clark, B. (1985). *Growing up gifted* (3d ed.). Columbus, OH: Charles E. Merrill.

Edgerton, R. (Ed.). (1984). *Lives in progress: Mildly retarded adults in a large city* (AAMD Monograph No. 6). Washington, DC: American Association on Mental Deficiency.

Gallagher, J. J. (1985). The evolution of education for the gifted in differing cultures. In J. Freeman (Ed.), *The psychology of gifted children* (pp. 335–350). Chichester, England: John Wiley.

Gallagher, J., Weiss, P., Oglesby, K., & Thomas, T. (1983). *The status of gifted/talented education: United States survey of needs, practices, and policies.* Los Angeles: National/State Leadership Training Institute.

Horowitz, F., & O'Brien, M. (1986). Gifted and talented children: State of knowledge and directions for research. *American Psychologist, 41,* 1147–1152.

House, E. (1980). *Evaluating with validity.* Beverly Hills, CA: Sage.

Maker, C. J. (1982). *Curriculum development for the gifted.* Rockville, MD: Aspen Systems Corporation.

Maker, C. J. (1986). Developing scope and sequences in curriculum. *Gifted Child Quarterly, 4,* 151–158.

Renzulli, J. S. (1977). *The enrichment triad model: A guide for developing defensible programs for the gifted and talented.* Wethersfield, CT: Creative Learning Press.

Sisk, D. (1986). Social studies for the future: The use of video for developing leadership. *Gifted Child Quarterly, 4,* 182–185.

Stainback, S., & Stainback, W. (1988). *Understanding and conducting qualtitative research.* Reston, VA: Council for Exceptional Children.

Tannenbaum, R. (1983). *Gifted children.* New York: Macmillan.

Tyler, R. (1950). Basic principles of curriculum and instruction. Chicago: University of Chicago Press.

VanTassel-Baska, J. (1986). Effective curriculum and instructional models for talented students. *Gifted Child Quarterly, 4,* 164–173.

Weiss, P. (1988). *Great ideas: A seminar approach to teaching and learning* (program guide). Chicago: Encyclopedia Britannica.

Wickless, J. (Ed.). (1983). *Criteria for excellence: Gifted and talented program guidelines.* Baltimore, MD: Maryland State Department of Education.

CHAPTER 12

Guiding Gifted Students in Their Academic Planning

Julian C. Stanley

Many years ago, in "The Ballad of East and West," Rudyard Kipling somewhat chauvinistically stressed the common bond unifying the intellectually talented:

Oh, East is East, and West is West,
    and never the twain shall meet,
Till Earth and Sky stand presently
    at God's great Judgment Seat;
But there is neither East nor West,
    Border, nor Breed, nor Birth,
When two strong men stand face to face,
    though they come from the ends of the earth!

If we consider Kipling's "two strong men" to be "intellectually talented youths," we have a summing up of the rationale for the current talent searches across the land. Intellectual talent transcends sex (Kipling's view notwithstanding), circumstance, and nationality. It requires special educational opportunities for highly able young students with respect to their area(s) of great talent. Such students are joined together all over the world by a common bond of promise and educational need.

More than 200 years ago the poet Thomas Gray set forth his immortal "Elegy Written in a Country Churchyard," in which we also may find justification for talent searches:

Full many a gem of purest ray serene
    The dark unfathomed caves of ocean bear;
Full many a flower is born to blush unseen,
    And waste its sweetness on the desert air.

There is also a story in the oral tradition that reveals a similar theme: A man died and went to heaven. He was met at the pearly gates by St. Peter, who greeted him cordially and offered to introduce him to anyone in heaven. The man asked to meet the greatest general who had ever lived. St. Peter immediately summoned an unimpressive old man. The new entrant to heaven stared disbelievingly and said to St. Peter, "This man is a fraud. In my own home town he was only a lowly janitor." "Yes," said St. Peter, "I know that. But if he had been a general, he would have been the best the world has ever known."

It is a society's responsibility, and should also be its privilege, to help prevent potential O'Keefes, Einsteins, Gandhis, and Dickinsons from coming to the "mute inglorious" ends about which Gray mused in that country churchyard long ago. The problem has changed little, but the prospects for more appropriate ends are much better now.

Yet intellectual ability is only potential energy. Unless made kinetic, it is of little avail to the promising individual, and may be quite harmful. The key to effective use of talent was stated succinctly by the poet Robert Browning. Reworded rather less poetically to eliminate sex bias, it becomes "Ah, but one's reach should exceed one's grasp, or what's a heaven for?" Surely, parents and educators should make every effort to extend both the reach and the grasp of intellectually talented youths; otherwise, what's an educational system for?

The legitimate special educational demands presented by students of genuine intellectual talent are far too often confused with the drudgery or "greasy grind" engaged in by students of all abilities whose parents are overly ambitious. There needs to be some way of sorting out students of average ability who achieve high grades due to such drudgery from truly gifted students, some of whom may not appear, from their grades at least, to be exceptional. This is why talent searches use a prestigious, well-validated instrument, the Scholastic Aptitude Test (SAT), to find high-level talent. Once it has been established objectively that students have the mental ability with which to proceed faster and at a higher level in certain subjects, both parents and educators have strong justification for helping them move ahead in ways and at rates appropriate for that ability.

CURRICULAR INFLEXIBILITY

Over the years, since the days of the private tutor and the one-room schoolhouse, the ascendant philosophy of elementary and secondary education has been the age-in-grade Carnegie Unit lockstep. In most school systems this denial of individual differences has become set in concrete, in both educational theory and practice. From at least kindergarten through the sixth grade, nearly all students are required to take particular subjects in a particular grade at a particular age. From about the seventh grade onward, they are expected also to take them in standard time blocks, usually a 45- or 50-minute period per day, five days per week, over the course of a 180-day school year.

The age-in-grade lockstep is somewhat like the practice of the innkeeper Procrustes in Greek mythology, who tied travelers to an iron bed and amputated or stretched their limbs until they fitted it. This has produced a curricular structure that often provides poorly for persons at either end of the ability continuum. Some students have been more fortunate than the description indicates, because their intellectual needs cried out loudly enough to be heard. Many were helped by parents and/or teachers to break away somewhat from the age-in-grade vise.

The greatest challenge to such a system occurs during the middle school years, as educational needs of the gifted increase rapidly. Students at that stage require all the wisdom, planning, tact, and help they can get. Some will have to develop their own agenda of curricular adjustments, then plan and set up strategies for securing them. The question should not be *whether* students get the curricular flexibility and articulation they need, but *how*.

ACCELERATION AND ENRICHMENT

One of the first roadblocks encountered on the way to desired flexibility is likely to be that dread straw man, acceleration *versus* enrichment. Some inspired educational obstructer must have hit upon the glamorous word *enrichment* and contrasted it with the more prosaic one, *acceleration*. Much that is labeled enrichment is merely time-filling busywork or largely nonacademic fun and games. It might also be called "creativity training in a vacuum," that is, mostly divorced from the subject matter of the school. Even academic courses for the intellectually gifted are not likely to relate closely to the students' main interests and abilities. Usually they must take whatever educators offer in the name of education for the gifted.

The greatest obstacle is often educators' conviction that educational acceleration of virtually any kind is bad for social and emotional development. They are so firm in this belief that it is difficult for parents to view various accelerative choices objectively. It is easy not to consider fully enough the educational, social, and emotional consequences of remaining locked into the age-in-grade system, with little opportunity to forge ahead in one's special areas. The intellectual stagnation, boredom, and frustration that can result take their toll on motivation and mental alertness. When appropriate intellectual challenge finally arrives, typically as the recent high-school graduate goes off to a demanding college, zest and ability to cope academically may be inadequate. This "MIT syndrome" may result from the shock of having easily been an academic big shot in high school and then suddenly finding it difficult even to pass the college courses. Many desired professional careers have been prevented in this way. The shock, disappointment, and chagrin at that stage certainly aren't good for anyone's social and emotional development.

A thorough review of studies in the area of acceleration (Daurio, 1979) revealed no evidence of harm caused by accelerating able youngsters in a suitable fashion. The author concluded that, in order to be effective, acceleration must also be enriching. Likewise, appropriate subject-matter enrichment without acceleration now or later is almost certain to lead to boredom and frustration. The two need to be partners.

GREAT ACCELERATION IN MATHEMATICS AND SCIENCE

Some acceleration must be extreme in order to permit intellectually brilliant youths to move ahead fast and well enough. For example, during the 3-week residential precalculus summer course devised by the Study of Mathematically Precocious Youth (SMPY) at Johns Hopkins University, the typical student learns 2 years of mathematics extremely well. A few cover only first-year algebra, whereas a few demonstrate their knowledge of 2½ years of algebra, 1 year of geometry, and half a year each of trigonometry and analytic geometry. An occasional student begins calculus before the 3 weeks end. These students range in age from 9 to 14, most of them being 12 or 13 and having finished the seventh grade. The summer program students' scores on SAT-M range from 500, which is better than 49% of college-bound male 12th-graders score, to a rare 800, which is 40 points above the 99th percentile of college-bound male high-school seniors. All are at least in the upper 1% of their agemates in mathematical reasoning ability.

Rapid acceleration is feasible in the sciences as well. In one summer program, 25 students aged 11 to 15, from 12 states, learned the standard first-year high-school biology material excellently in 3 weeks (Stanley & Stanley, 1986). They ranged in SAT-M scores from above 500 into the high 700s. Thirteen students aged 12 to 15 from 6 states did exceedingly well on the College Board's high school chemistry achievement test after only 3 weeks of learning the subject. The program also offers high-school physics in 3 weeks, as well as high-school American history.[1] It is clear that the highly able young students who enroll do not need to wait their age-in-grade turn to take these

---

[1] For the history course, the qualifying score is at least 430 on the verbal part of the College Board Scholastic Aptitude Test (SAT-V) before age 13. Only 50% of college-bound twelfth-graders score that high.

subjects. Instead, they can master each of them in a short, intensive period of time and then move on in their regular schools to Advanced Placement programs, college-level aspects of each subject.

TEN SUGGESTIONS FOR GUIDING STUDENTS

Because intellectually talented students are rarely accommodated appropriately by schools without some form of advocacy on their behalf, it may be useful to share some rather pointed suggestions for program planners, parents, and students themselves to consider as they negotiate the secondary school experience.

1. *Avoid the temptation to rely on private schools, parochial or nonsectarian, as many cannot provide a simple educational solution for talented persons.* Many have small classes and some have excellent teachers, and an enjoyable social atmosphere, but even the most selective ones tend to cater mainly to students in the 120–140 IQ range whose abilities are fairly even. Only a few provide well enough for math-talented learners who are ready to move through several years of rigorous mathematics in one. Also, of course, many private schools are too small to have the needed scheduling flexibility. Many of the mathematically ablest youths identified by the Study for Mathematically Precocious Youth (SMPY) manage to work out suitable acceleration and enrichment in public schools. By going there, they save far more than enough money to take full advantage of special educational opportunities such as residential summer programs (see Stanley & Benbow, 1986).

   Parents, rather than saying, "I'll find a good private school that will take care of our intellectually talented child's special educational needs," should weigh the costs and advantages of the various educational options open to them. One avenue is to pay tuition charges at a public school not in their residential area, as was done for one boy so that he could be near a college at which he wanted to take some courses during the day. Another consideration is moving to another place in order to be eligible for better public schools. Unfortunately, such decisions aren't usually made easily, especially if religious or social values predominate.

2. *Consider carefully all available in-school and out-of-school educational supplementation.* Many schools have various academic clubs. There are annual national mathematics competitions culminating in the International Mathematics Olympiad (IMO). Students who are talented in math should get into these competitions as soon as feasible, as well as local and state mathematical or scientific competitions. Students might consider becoming

part-time college students, taking a course each term in a favorite area. Plan ahead for educational summer opportunities, perhaps including starting a savings account several years in advance. Get various relatives, close family friends, and perhaps service clubs to help.

3. *Learn to distinguish an entertaining "enrichment" activity from an academic one.* Falling into the latter category are courses in computer science, a mathematics competition, or academic summer courses. Do not think that an enrichment activity appropriately substitutes for an academic one. Sheer enjoyment may not produce much educational gain.

4. *Be aware that residential academic courses taken during summers have values far beyond the subject matter learned.* They offer stimulating chances to mingle socially, athletically, musically, and culturally with large numbers of intellectual peers and, unless students are highly talented both verbally and mathematically, also with intellectual superiors. This association with such persons, probably for the first time in their lives, should help gifted students develop a better self-concept and improve their coping skills. How nice it is to be in a place where the common denominator is being a "brain" and therefore can be forgotten for a few weeks! Furthermore, many of the instructors and teaching assistants are admirable role models.

5. *Take advantage of the excellent opportunity available in the large array of college-level examinations offered by the College Board's Advanced Placement Program each May.* Anyone may take these, regardless of preparation. They enable students to earn two semesters of college credit in about 20 subjects ranging from calculus to studio art. Nearly all selective colleges and universities in the country award credit for excellent scores on these examinations. Students should get acquainted with the AP exams and work systematically toward taking as many of them as feasible each May, beginning as early as age 12 or less and continuing until they become full-time college students. Furthermore, they should plan toward sophomore standing when they enter college, so that, for those who wish to earn a baccalaureate in three years, one-fourth the cost of an expensive college education can be saved. Credit for four or five courses will provide this standing. Graduate or professional school also can be accessed a year earlier.

If this sounds too prescriptive or visionary for students in junior high schools, consider that in 1983 from SMPY's small group at least 14 youths aged 12 to 14 who reasoned extremely well mathematically earned the highest possible grade (5 on a 5-point scale) on the AP examination for higher-level (BC) calculus. This feat, accomplished by only about 2,000 students (most often high-school seniors) in the whole country each year, is equivalent to earning the grade of A+ in a whole school year of calculus at a major university such as Northwestern, Chicago, Wisconsin, or Michigan. One of SMPY's protégés earned a 5 at age 9!

In recent years, four persons have completed Johns Hopkins University's 4-year bachelor's degree curriculum in 2 years, two of them at age 16.[2] They had come with large numbers of credits earned by taking AP exams and also by taking college courses while still in high school. Many students may not want that much acceleration or be able enough to do it well, but these extreme cases illustrate that completing undergraduate studies, perhaps including master's degrees, at age 20 or 21 is a reasonable goal for many gifted students (Stanley, 1985).

6. *Do not deter students from moving ahead in special subjects by making claims that they'll have "holes in their backgrounds."* It is easy to arrange studies so that this isn't so, especially in mathematics. It would be well for gifted students to take standardized subject tests in order to pinpoint what they do and do not yet know. Then, perhaps with the aid of a good mentor, those gaps can be filled rapidly and well.

7. *Encourage students at junior high age to take the SAT once each year, preferably in January, to see how the three abilities measured by it are growing.* If the percentile rank for the SAT-V score is greatly below the percentile rank for the SAT-M score, a student can get a paperbound copy of Funk and Lewis's *Thirty Days to a More Powerful Vocabulary* (1970) and work through it systematically. Also, they should be encouraged to take Latin and honors English, and read interesting but demanding books.

8. *Encourage students to be risk takers.* They can take three College Board high-school-level achievement tests fairly often. (Three are given for the same price as one.) One might be English composition. For the math-oriented student, Level 1 and/or 2 of the mathematics test should be revealing. Students in junior and senior high should consider trying at least six different achievement tests over the course of several years.

9. *Support the graduate-school goals of those who aspire to high academic degrees.* The intellectually talented have plenty of ability with which to obtain a Ph.D., J.D., or M.D. degree from a top-flight university, but of course not all of them will want vocations that require this level of graduate work. Their marked talents, however, can contribute toward occupational success and happiness. There is a need to encourage such students not to drop out of graduate training too soon, or avoid it entirely, because of the lure of high-paying positions. Be aware, for example, that the vocational "half-life" of the typical person with an excellent bachelor's degree in engineering is 10 years or less. Increasingly thereafter he or she must usually move into sales or management in order to get ahead. A master's degree

---

[2]They majored in biology, electrical engineering, mathematical science, and mathematics, respectively. The mathematics major, a female, was a Rhodes Scholar at age 18. For other examples of extreme precocity, see Stanley & Benbow (1983).

increases the half-life, and a superb doctorate may extend it throughout the person's career, as well as land him or her a good university position.

Computer or engineering fields will lure many of these students because of spectacular opportunities. Again, though, there is a need not to enter them only barely prepared. The bachelor's degree is not meant to be sufficient for a truly professional career.

10. *Intellectually talented students should be encouraged to pursue a fine liberal arts education during their high school and undergraduate work.* It will be their last really systematic opportunity to explore the thoughts and creations of eminent persons such as Shakespeare, Freud, B. F. Skinner, Van Gogh, Cassatt, Nightingale, Plato, Mozart, Rembrandt, Darwin, Dickinson, Charlie Chaplin, Marx, Brontë, Gauss, Noether, Adam Smith, Joan of Arc, Galois, Einstein, Buddha—some of the greatest thinkers and doers of all time. If they become too impatient to get on with technical matters, they will probably go through life a craftsperson instead of a learned person. Because individuals must live with themselves 24 hours of every day, they need to cultivate themselves in many respects in order to be worth their own company over an entire lifetime.

Most of these suggestions are serious admonitions, but of course not all of life is meant to be serious, especially not at the tender ages of these students. A good sense of humor, not taking oneself too seriously too much of the time, is a measure of emotional adjustment and maturity. Gifted students should also learn to cultivate the light touch, the kindly and generous approach to people. We want them to develop excellently academically, of course, but also to lead full lives, playing beautiful melodies on that most responsive of instruments, the self, for their own enjoyment and that of others.

REFERENCES

Daurio, S. P. (1979). Educational enrichment versus acceleration: A review of the literature. In W. C. George, S. J. Cohn, & J. C. Stanley (Eds.), *Educating the gifted: Acceleration and enrichment.* (pp. 13–63). Baltimore, MD: Johns Hopkins University Press.

Funk, W., & Lewis, N. (1970). *30 days to a more powerful vocabulary.* New York: Funk & Wagnalls.

Stanley, J. C. (1985). Young entrants to college: How did they fare? *College and University, 60,* 219–228.

Stanley, J. C., & Benbow, C. P. (1983). Extremely young college graduates: Evidence of their success. *College and University, 58,* 361–371.

Stanley, J. C., & Benbow, C. P. (1986). Youths who reason exceptionally well mathematically. In R. J. Sternberg & J. E. Davidson (Eds.), *Conception of giftedness*
(pp. 361–387). New York: Cambridge University Press.
Stanley, J. C., & Stanley, B. S. K. (1986). High-school biology, chemistry, or physics
learned well in three weeks. *Journal of Research in Science Teaching, 23,* 237–
250.

CHAPTER 13

Career Counseling for the Gifted

Linda Kreger Silverman

Career development for the gifted is a lifelong process, beginning with the values, attitudes, and training provided in the home in early childhood and continuing throughout adulthood. Career guidance is needed early in the lives of the gifted, to help them recognize their capabilities and clarify their interests, and to expose them to the range of possibilities that await them. However, the broad spectrum of career opportunities available to these children tends to increase the complexity of decision making (Milne, 1979) and many actually delay career selection.

Since the gifted are often multitalented, they have potential for success in many fields, and aptitude becomes an insufficient criterion for selecting a career. Financial security and career stability, two determining factors for their parents and grandparents, play less significant roles today in young people's career choices (Yankelovich, 1972). Questions gifted students raise are, What career would be most interesting for me to pursue? Which field would offer the most opportunity for me to develop my potential? Where do I sense the greatest need? In what area can I be of most service? These are value-laden questions, all of which can be explored in a carefully designed career development program.

An effective career counseling program provides an opportunity for students to explore their own aspirations, experiences, and interests. It exposes students to various fields, to successful adults who have made a variety of career choices, and to real-life experiences in the work world. Biographical research is included as a way of helping gifted students to identify with those who have made great contributions in spite of obstacles. An effective program enhances the aspirations of those who have not had much encouragement and deals with such questions as how to manage a career and a family. It also involves itself with others in the young people's lives who influence their career choices.

PARENT EDUCATION

Career planning is actually a family affair. Perhaps the best way of helping young gifted students in selecting careers is to educate their parents.
Parents play a critical role in shaping their children's aspirations. They are
their children's first role models, and their encouragement and discourage-
ment have lasting effects. In some families, it is expected that the child will
follow in a parent's footsteps, with all other career options foreclosed. This
has been the tradition in most parts of the world for centuries, and it is still
quite common in certain geographical regions and among some social classes
and ethnic groups.

Career counseling for the gifted ideally begins with parent education or
at least includes it as a component. Early exposure and expert instruction
provided by the family often help to shape children's future career paths.
Recent research by Bloom (1982, 1985) reveals that individuals who have
achieved worldwide acclaim in their fields before the age of 35 were groomed
for their success while still in preschool. Concert pianists, for example, came
from musically oriented families in which all members were expected to play
musical instruments and were given instruction early in life. Bloom and Sosniak (1981) found the home to be far more important than the school in
developing the talents of their subjects. In fact, in many cases, school was
found to be counterproductive to talent development. While this research
has important implications for child-rearing practices for the gifted, there is
another viewpoint to be considered.

There are two currents flowing through modern society regarding parenting practices. One position holds that parents are their children's best
teachers and that the most impressionable years of the child's life should not
be wasted. Infant education is therefore recommended, even education in the
womb. The other position advocates allowing children to have full, rich
childhoods without pressuring them to learn too much too soon. Some writers warn that the "hurried child" is a candidate for all kinds of stress-related
symptoms, from school failure to suicide (Elkind, 1981). Parents of the
gifted have a particularly difficult time sifting through these disparate views.
They recognize their children's abilities early in life (Silverman, Chitwood,
& Waters, 1986) but do not know whether to teach reading to their toddlers
or to hide all the books and slow the children down.

An important fact to remember in this regard is that there is a difference
between designing children's futures and enabling them, with parental support, to design their own futures. Parents sometimes need guidance in making this distinction, so that they do not become overbearing. Schools can
actually play an important role in helping parents learn the art of responsive

parenting. A curriculum designed to enhance the parents' role in career guidance might include the following topics:

"Creator parents" versus responsive parenting (Silverman, 1986a)
Exposure to cultural events
Family activities designed to develop interests
Critical periods in the development of special talents
How to find expert instruction
How many lessons? How much free time?
Exposing children to various types of role models
Introducing children to biographies
Holding high expectations for daughters, as well as sons
Purchasing toys, games, and books that are not sex defined
Recognizing and nurturing mathematics talent at home
Avoiding overprotectiveness, especially with daughters
Appreciating specialists and generalists
Helping children set high aspirations
"Late blooming": Delayed career selection
Reversible career decisions: Preparing children for multiple careers

The importance of avoiding sex-role stereotyping in the home cannot be overemphasized. Gifted and creative children tend to be more androgynous, exhibiting some characteristics and interests that may not seem typical for their sex (Dellas, 1969; Wolleat, 1979). Boys, for example, may display a level of sensitivity usually thought of as feminine, while girls may show levels of independence and aggressiveness associated with masculinity. Creative males tend to have unconventional career aspirations (Torrance, 1980), and gifted females who have high career aspirations are also thought of as "unconventional." Traditional feminine stereotypes are limiting to achievement in women (Kerr, 1985; Silverman, 1986b), and these attitudes are well ingrained by the time the child reaches school age (Fox & Tobin, 1978).

Children need their parents to support, guide, and nurture their talents, but they do not want to become carbon copies of their parents. They need the emotional freedom to determine their own life paths. Gifted children, in particular, are at risk for becoming what their parents want them to be, at the expense of their own needs and desires (Miller, 1981). Through parent education, educators can help release both parents and children from taking too much responsibility for one another's happiness. When young people feel in the driver's seat of their own future, instead of passengers in their parents' plans, then career education with the students can begin.

TIMING OF CAREER DECISIONS

Early Decision Makers

Timing of career decisions tends to be either earlier or later for the gifted than for their agemates (Milne, 1979). Because of their developmental advancement, gifted children begin to be concerned about vocational choice much earlier than their peers. A child who is mentally 3 years ahead of the norm for his or her age may begin setting career goals in elementary school. Willings (1986) indicates that most gifted students are thinking seriously about career choices by the age of 9 and that they find conventional career search programs designed for high school students to be "boring and trivial" (p. 95).

Some gifted children become thoroughly engrossed in their interests early in life and commit themselves to careers in those areas before they have had an opportunity to explore other options. The 6-year-old "expert" on constellations announces for all time that she is going to become an astronomer. No amount of coaxing apparently can make her change her mind. When her interest in the stars wanes, she attaches to her chemistry set and is staunchly determined to pursue chemistry for the rest of her life. These young specialists may feel a sense of security in mapping out their life goals at an early age. Sometimes these goals change as their interests change, and sometimes they remain steadfast into maturity.

Children whose parents have defined their career goals for them, and children who early in life determine their paths, seem to foreclose many options. Teachers often try in vain to broaden their aspirations. Sometimes, however, children have a better perspective on their futures than either their teachers or counselors. Willings (1986) provides the example of a 14-year-old gifted girl who wanted to be a racing driver and fashion model, despite the ridicule of her classmates. Her counselor told her she was immature, and her mother told her she'd outgrow these desires. By the age of 26, she was working as a fashion model during the week and on a racing team on weekends.

Some children develop very early an affinity for a certain life path—what might be termed a "calling" or sense of mission. Young musical prodigies who set their sights on the concert stage, or ballet dancers who aspire to greatness, show passionate dedication to their fields early in life (Feldman, 1979). They seem intuitively to realize that they must block out all distractions and forego their other potential in order to achieve their goals (Tannenbaum, 1984). There are also some gifted children who arbitrarily select a career at a very young age simply to avoid dealing with the overwhelming multitude of career options available to them. Having too many choices can be threatening.

Late Decision Makers

Although some children decide their future careers before they enter school, many gifted youth complete high school without knowing what they will be when they grow up. Most gifted students are multitalented and suffer "an embarrassment of riches" (Gowan, 1980, p. 67), making the problem of selection a very difficult one. The anxiety created by too many options more readily reaches the attention of counselors than does the problem of early foreclosure on those options. The early bloomer may even be held up as the ideal, so that students who cannot decide what they want to do with their lives feel ashamed by comparison.

Coping with multiple talents and interests is a serious problem for many gifted students (Ford & Ellis, 1979). They are generalists rather than specialists; they find all aspects of life fascinating, and they don't want to miss any of it. They need assurance that their abundance of interests is an asset rather than a liability, and reassurance that their lack of early achievement does not mark them as washouts for life.

Betsy is an example of a generalist (Silverman, 1982). As a high school senior, she had boundless enthusiasm for everything and an endless supply of energy. Her interests included psychology, creative writing, language, physics, chemistry, jewelry making, fencing, bicycling, nature, science fiction, and "people." The lead cross-country runner in her senior class, she also topped the class in college aptitude tests and the advanced placement English examination. She had a strong desire to be of service to humanity, and she wanted to master 12 languages before she turned 40.

Vocational preference tests are of little value to students like Betsy, since they cannot help them discover what they are unable to do (Hoyt, 1978). In addition, they provide only limited insight into the exact content of different fields (Anastasi, 1982). How does Betsy begin to make a career choice? Students like her experience vocational selection as an existential dilemma. They are as concerned about the road not taken as they are with finding the "right" path (Herr & Watanabe, 1979; Sanborn, 1979). Choosing to be a linguist means giving up a career as a physicist.

Giving up dreams is not easy for any child, but most children learn quite early that they must temper their dreams with the reality of their limitations. Not so for the gifted. They learn early in life that they can direct their abilities successfully in most pursuits. Any door to their future is closed only by choice, and what if they make the wrong choice? How does Betsy know she will be happy with her decision? What will her life be like if she makes another choice? Is it better to become really good in one area or to know about a lot of areas? And if she tries to hang onto all her interests, won't she become a dilettante, master of none?

Career counseling for the gifted needs to be sensitive to their multiple interests, the existential dilemmas they face in making choices, their fear of making an error, their fear of being less than their ideal or not living up to their potential, the depth of their sadness over the road not taken, and their fear that if they try to nurture all of their potentials, they will end up second-rate at everything.

Different Paths for Gifted Adults

Not all gifted individuals decide what to do with their lives in high school and college. Some do not find their calling until midlife. Very often gifted adults move from job to job within a profession or have several careers in their lives. Voltaire's (1759/1956) apt observation that anything is better than boredom is a creed for the gifted. In order for them to be happy with their work, they must be constantly learning. When they have learned all that they can in a position, it is time to move on to new challenges. This may take them to higher echelons of management within a business; more demanding research projects in science; new schools of thought in mathematics, music, and art; or perhaps to totally new careers. If high school students and their parents are informed of the possibility of late blooming and helped to understand that career decisions are not irreversible, some of the struggle around career choices can be lessened.

A former dentist, who rued the decision he had made in junior high school to study dentistry as a career, remarked, "What gives a 14-year-old the right to decide what a 40-year-old should do with the rest of his life?" In many cases, when we press adolescents to make decisions about their careers, we are recreating this dilemma. The mobility of our society may be making obsolete the ideal of a single career throughout life. Gifted students should be prepared to deal with the probability that they will make at least one major career change in their lives. Adults frequently return to school to pursue training in another field. An elementary teacher may become a college professor; a microbiologist may become a psychologist; a chemical engineer may leave that field to become a philosopher. Students can be introduced to individuals in the community who have successfully maintained multiple careers.

There are several ways in which adults maintain interests in more than one field. It is possible to have concurrent careers, as did the Russian composer, Borodin, who was also an internationally renowned chemist in his lifetime. One's career is not necessarily one's livelihood. Most musicians find that they cannot make a living with their music, and so gain skills in other fields. Music, however, remains as their major love and life's work, while their other work supplies the money for them to survive. They sometimes refer to their money-making career as their "day job" and their musical profession as their "night job." Many gifted adults put a great deal of time and energy into avocations—major interests from which they do not attempt to derive their livelihood. These can include coin collecting, playing classical guitar, painting watercolors, writing science fiction stories, and so forth.

The counselor can help students determine which of their interests would be most likely to supply them with an acceptable income, and which they might decide to pursue as avocations. When gifted students are having difficulty determining which path they wish to follow, it is wise to allow them extra time to make their career choices and to give them a broad enough educational base so that they can later move in several different directions.

CAREER GUIDANCE

Through a well-planned career counseling program, Betsy and others like her can be assisted with their dilemmas in many ways. Helpful approaches include

Preparing them for many options
Exploring with them careers in which they would have the opportunity to synthesize interests in many fields
Allowing them to delay decision making until college
Giving them real-life experiences in some of their avenues of interest through internships, mentorships, work-study, or community service
Discussing the possibility of serial or concurrent careers
Helping them determine which of their interests they could maintain as avocations
Suggesting the possibility of creating new careers
Exploring life themes as a basis for career choice

The counselor's responsibility to generalists is to guide them in planning as rich a program as possible, one that will prepare them to enter any of several careers. It is particularly important for girls to be advised to take advanced mathematics and science courses, so that they do not close those doors prematurely. It helps girls to know that there is a correlation between level of income and number of mathematics courses taken. In high school (9th through 12th grade), a good college preparatory program should include at least 4 years of English, 4 years of mathematics, 4 years of science, 3 years of a foreign language, and 3 years of social science. These are basic minimum requirements for gifted students. If it is appropriately planned, an accelerated program can be useful, with the student beginning algebra in seventh grade and taking as many Advanced Placement courses as possible before graduation.

The first 2 years of college may be well spent gaining a solid liberal arts background. College is not simply a place to gain vocational training. For the gifted, in particular, it is a time to gain an education, to open their minds to philosophy, history, literature, psychology, mathematics, art, music, and science. This rich background will serve them in any field. During this time, students can take exploratory course work and perhaps do part-time work or observations in fields of their interest.

Of course, the latter provision can only be implemented with the consent of parents, since parents are usually the ones who absorb the financial costs of their children's education. Many parents are concerned with their children's inability to decide on a career, and they may be reluctant to invest thousands of dollars on their children's higher education while they are still "floundering." Parents need to be educated about how to deal with their children's indecision. If no parent-education program is available, the counselor may need to assist the parents in understanding the student's dilemma and may even be called upon to mediate between parent and child.

Exposure to interdisciplinary course work enables students to see how several fields can be blended together in one's life's work. The counselor can expand this vision by introducing students to real-life generalists in the work world, as well as by offering them books on individuals who used knowledge in one field to further knowledge in another (e.g., Brunel's inventing the caisson for underwater construction projects after watching shipworms tunneling into a ship's timbers, and Bell's inventing the telephone after observing the membrane of the inner ear; see Gordon, 1961). Other possibilities include conducting discussions about Renaissance figures who shaped history and brainstorming sessions on ways to combine several of their interests into existing or new careers.

One of the unique aspects in counseling the gifted is that they have the potential to create their own careers (Milne, 1979). The counselor can guide them in clarifying their values and interests and in custom designing their futures (Hoyt, 1978). Insight into work that needs to be done in the world often comes from observations of discrepancies between the way things are and the way they could be (Dabrowski, 1964). Gifted children are skilled at noting these discrepancies. Many of our current careers did not exist in the past: City planners, ecologists, educators of the gifted, word-processing specialists, and video dealers are a few examples. Some analysts are predicting that 70% of the students we have today will enter careers that do not currently exist (Anderson, 1986).

Ford and Ellis (1979) recommend that career education programs designed specifically to address the needs of the gifted should be made available to teachers, counselors, and administrators. Several excellent models exist for such programs (see Feldhusen & Kolloff, 1979; Hoyt & Hebeler, 1976; Moore, Feldhusen, & Owings, 1978; VanTassel-Baska, 1981; Willings, 1986).

SPECIAL NEEDS OF GIFTED GIRLS

In addition to the existential dilemmas faced by all gifted students, gifted girls must deal with a unique set of challenges. They must overcome societal programming to the effect that the career world and femininity are somehow antithetical (Horner, 1972). They need to determine how they can juggle both a family and a career and, indeed, whether they wish to do so. They need encouragement to explore career possibilities that traditionally have been for males only. They also need assistance in risk taking and in overcoming counterproductive beliefs about their own abilities.

The gifted girl may be unaware of her potential. Many girls hide their talents so that they will fit in better with their peers, so their special abilities do not come to the attention of teachers, parents, or counselors (Silverman, 1986b). In some cases, special talents are overlooked in girls because they are not expected to be there. Fox and Tobin (1978) and Bloom (1982) have hypothesized that girls who are gifted in mathematics receive less attention and nurturing of these abilities from their families than do boys with the same talents.

Gifted girls often experience conflict around career planning. Most know that they will enter the workforce at some time in their lives, and they want to choose careers that are both rewarding to themselves and of service to others. Yet, they do not see how they can plan a career path and still raise a family. These two desires seem to be in conflict. In a career counseling program, gifted girls should be exposed to the research on different paths taken by gifted women. For example, Rodenstein and Glickauf-Hughes (1979) found that women who combined childrearing with careers derived a great deal of personal satisfaction from both.

Exposure to role models is essential (Fox, 1981). Gifted girls need role models of women who successfully combine marriage, raising children, and a career. They also need to meet women who have chosen to have marriage and a career but no children. And they need to meet successful, happy women who have made the decision not to marry or have children. Despite the double standard of the debonair bachelor and the unmarriageable spinster, the follow-up studies of Terman's population (Sears & Barbee, 1977) indicated that gifted women who were single heads of households felt more fulfilled at midlife than gifted women who had become housewives at the expense of their careers. If a girl's mother has been a full-time homemaker or held a low-paying clerical position while trying to raise her family, the girl may have little conception of what else might be possible for her. Models may be professional women who come to a career development class, to a career day on campus, or to a special course designed for gifted girls. Mentorships and internships can be arranged for girls to work directly with women in their fields of interest.

Although it is obvious to boys that they will work, it is less so for girls, so some of the focus in career planning for girls is basic education about women in the workforce. They need to know realistically that cost-of-living and divorce rates both make it necessary for most women to work while they raise their families (Verheyden-Hilliard, 1976). They also need to become aware of the differences in pay scales in different occupations. A few years ago, I asked a panel of gifted freshmen about their career choices. All 10 of the young women were preparing for some form of service occupation, while all 4 of the young men planned on executive positions. Thus, all the women were heading toward low-paying occupations, while the men were preparing for high-paying, high-status professions.

Since girls tend to be less aware than boys of the necessity of supporting themselves in adult life, career education may be even more necessary for them than for boys. Boys have more societal programming to prepare them to make career choices. They are expected to support a family; they often have parental pressures to make career choices at an early age; they have more opportunities in the society; and they have more role models. These factors make them more aware of the world of work and their place within it. Girls, on the other hand, may expect to be financially taken care of for the rest of their lives. They may have no guidance from home about career possibilities. They may feel that there is little opportunity for them in the society and may therefore lower their expectations. They also have fewer role models.

A key piece of information for the gifted girl is that financial independence is often vital for self-realization. As long as a young woman is counting on someone else to support her, she is limiting herself in many ways.

Expectations at home that are different for boys than for girls can also be limiting. An example of this occurred in a counseling group that included a brother and a sister. The boy was encouraged by his parents to do well in school and was supported in his desire to study mathematics at Yale University. His equally talented sister was told that if she did not lose 10 pounds, her parents would not pay for her education at a state college. She was fascinated by biochemistry, but they wanted her to learn a trade, such as accounting or optometry, so that she could earn a little extra money while she raised a family. She eventually won a fellowship to study biochemistry at one of the most prestigious graduate schools in the country. Even then, her parents did not approve of her career choice.

Although this story does not resolve as happily as one might hope, there is little doubt that the role of the counselor in advocating the wishes of the young woman is of great importance. For those interested in career counseling, many resources are available for use in assisting gifted girls in their planning process (see, for example, Addison, 1983; Callahan, 1979; Fleming & Hollinger, 1979; Fox, 1981; Kerr, 1985; Silverman, 1986b; Watley & Kaplan, 1971; Wolleat, 1979).

CONCLUSION

The question of combining family and career is not just an issue for gifted girls. With more women entering the workforce, with climbing divorce rates, and with men more often gaining partial or total custody of their children, males have a much greater responsibility for child care today than ever before. Career development programs must take this into account. Also, with changing values in society, many gifted young people are no longer willing to make their work the central focus of their lives (Miner, 1973). These changes mean that both sexes need to examine careers within the context of their life plans. What are their hopes, dreams, and aspirations? How will a specific career choice enhance the quality of their lives or the lives of others?

When viewed in this light, career development becomes a lifelong pursuit, with room for exploration of side roads throughout the journey. Decisions are affected by one's values and dreams, and opportunities are created, not just sought. Career counseling, then, becomes an integral part of the program for gifted students, having an important place throughout the grades and involving parent education as a part of the process.

REFERENCES

Addison, L. B. (1983). *The gifted girl: Helping her be the best she can be. Inservice resource handbook*. Bethesda, MD: The Equity Institute.

Anastasi, A. (1982). *Psychological testing* (5th ed.). New York: Macmillan.

Anderson, J. (1986, November 4). [Luncheon address]. National Association for Gifted Children Thirty-Third Annual Convention. Las Vegas, NV.

Bloom, B. S. (1982). The role of gifts and markers in the development of talent. *Exceptional Children, 48*, 510–521.

Bloom, B. S. (Ed.). (1985). *Developing talent in young people*. New York: Ballantine Books.

Bloom, B. S., & Sosniak, L. A. (1981). Talent development vs. schooling. *Educational Leadership, 39*(2), 86–94.

Callahan, C. (1979). The gifted and talented woman. In A. H. Passow (Ed.), *The gifted and talented: Their education and development* (Seventy-eighth yearbook of the National Society for the Study of Education) (pp. 401–423). Chicago: University of Chicago Press.

Dabrowski, K. (1964). *Positive disintegration.* Boston: Little, Brown.

Dellas, M. (1969). Counselor role and function in counseling the creative student. *The School Counselor, 17,* 34–39.

Elkind, D. (1981). *The hurried child: Growing up too fast too soon.* Reading, MA: Addison-Wesley.

Feldhusen, J. F., & Kolloff, M. B. (1979). An approach to career education for the gifted. *Roeper Review, 2*(2), 13–16.

Feldman, D. H. (1979). The mysterious case of extreme giftedness. In A. H. Passow (Ed.), *The gifted and talented: Their education and development* (Seventy-eighth yearbook of the National Society for the Study of Education) (pp. 335–351). Chicago: University of Chicago Press.

Fleming, E., & Hollinger, C. L. (1979). *Project CHOICE.* Newton, MA: Educational Development Center.

Ford, B. G., & Ellis, J. H. (1979). Career education: A continuing need of Illinois gifted students. *Journal for the Education of the Gifted, 2*(3), 153–156.

Fox, L. (1981). Preparing gifted girls for future leadership roles. *G/C/T Magazine,* No. 17, pp. 7–11.

Fox, L., & Tobin, D. (1978). Broadening career horizons for gifted girls. *G/C/T Magazine,* No. 4, pp. 19–22, 45.

Gordon, W. J. J. (1961). *Synectics: The development of creative capacity.* New York: Harper.

Gowan, J. C. (1980). Issues on the guidance of gifted and creative children. In J. C. Gowan, G. D. Demos, & C. J. Kokaska (Eds.), *The guidance of exceptional children: A book of readings* (2nd ed.) (pp. 66–70). New York: Longman.

Herr, E. L., & Watanabe, A. (1979). Counseling the gifted about career development. In N. Colangelo & R. T. Zaffrann (Eds.), *New voices in counseling the gifted* (pp. 251–263). Dubuque, IA: Kendall/Hunt.

Horner, M. (1972). Toward an understanding of achievement-related conflicts in women. *Journal of Social Issues, 28,* 157–175.

Hoyt, K. B. (1978). Career education for gifted and talented persons. *Roeper Review, 1*(1), 9–10.

Hoyt, K., & Hebeler, J. (1976). *Career education for gifted and talented students.* Salt Lake City, UT: Olympus.

Kerr, B. A. (1985). *Smart girls, gifted women.* Columbus, OH: Ohio Psychology Publishing.

Miller, A. (1981). *The drama of the gifted child.* New York: Basic Books.

Milne, B. G. (1979). Career education. In A. H. Passow (Ed.), *The gifted and talented: Their education and development* (Seventy-eighth yearbook of the National Society for the Study of Education) (pp. 246–254). Chicago: University of Chicago Press.

Miner, J. B. (1973). *The management process.* New York: Macmillan.

Moore, B. A., Feldhusen, J. F., & Owings, J. (1978). *The professional career exploration program for minority and/or low income gifted and talented high school students.* (Tech. Rep. No. 770103-15821). West Lafayette, IN: Purdue University, Department of Education.

Rodenstein, J. M., & Glickauf-Hughes, C. (1979). Career and lifestyle determinants of gifted women. In N. Colangelo & R. T. Zaffrann (Eds.), *New voices in counseling the gifted* (pp. 370–381). Dubuque, IA: Kendall/Hunt.

Sanborn, M. P. (1979). Career development: Problems of gifted and talented students. In N. Colangelo & R. T. Zaffrann (Eds.), *New voices in counseling the gifted* (pp. 284–300). Dubuque, IA: Kendall/Hunt.

Sears, P. S., & Barbee, A. H. (1977). Career and life satisfactions among Terman's women. In J. C. Stanley, W. C. George, & C. H. Solano (Eds.), *The gifted and the creative: A fifty-year perspective* (pp. 28–65). Baltimore: Johns Hopkins University Press.

Seelely, K. (1985). Facilitators for gifted learners. In J. Feldhusen (Ed.), *Toward excellence in gifted education* (pp. 105–133). Denver: Love.

Silverman, L. K. (1982). Giftedness. In E. L. Meyen (Ed.), *Exceptional children and youth in today's schools.* Denver: Love.

Silverman, L. K. (1986a). Parenting young gifted children. *Journal of Children in Contemporary Society, 18,* 73–87.

Silverman, L. K. (1986b). What happens to the gifted girl? In C. J. Maker (Ed.), *Critical issues in gifted education, Vol. 1: Defensible programs for the gifted* (pp. 43–89). Rockville, MD: Aspen.

Silverman, L. K., Chitwood, D. G., & Waters, J. L. (1986). Young gifted children: Can parents identify giftedness? *Topics in Early Childhood Special Education, 6*(1), 23–28.

Tannenbaum, A. J. (1984, March 1). Keynote address, Louisiana Conference on the Gifted, Baton Rouge, LA.

Torrance, E. P. (1980). Understanding creativity in talented students. In J. C. Gowan, G. D. Demos, & C. J. Kokaska, *The guidance of exceptional children: A book of readings* (2nd ed.) (pp. 70–77). New York: Longman.

VanTassel-Baska, J. (1981). A comprehensive model of career education for gifted and talented. *Journal of Career Education, 7*(4) 325–331.

Verheyden-Hilliard, M. E. (1976). *A handbook for workshops on sex equality in education.* Alexandria, VA: American Personnel and Guidance Association.

Voltaire. (1956). *Candide.* In H. M. Block (Ed.), *Candide and other writings.* New York: Modern Library. (Original work published 1759).

Watley, D., & Kaplan, R. (1971). Career or marriage? Aspirations and achievements of able young women. *Journal of Vocational Behavior, 1,* 29–43.

Willings, D. (1986). Enriched career search. *Roeper Review, 9,* 95–100.

Wolleat, P. L. (1979). Building the career development of gifted females. In N. Colangelo & R. T. Zaffrann (Eds.), *New voices in counseling the gifted* (pp. 331–345). Dubuque, IA: Kendall/Hunt.

Yankelovich, D. (1972). *The changing values on campus.* New York: Washington Square Press.

CHAPTER 14

Development of Academic Talent: The Role of Summer Programs

Paula Olszewski-Kubilius

There has been a movement in education toward viewing summer vacation months as a time to provide special educational experiences for very able learners, not just learners in need of help or remediation. Already there is a tradition of special instruction in some talent areas during the summer (e.g., Interlochen Summer Music Camp, the National High School Institute, Suzuki Camp, tennis camps), and there is currently a parental demand that "off" time be spent productively by young people.

The reports on the quality of education in our nation suggest that students in the United States need more rigorous and intense academic experiences. This is particularly true for gifted students. There is also some sentiment that schools, currently overwhelmed with issues of underachievement and minimum competency, need not—and often cannot—carry the entire burden for educating populations in need of special training, such as academically talented children. The private sector, including business and the community, is expected to play an increasing role in the talent development process.

Agencies other than public schools may provide alternative programs that can deliver experiences, services, and a curriculum that a local school cannot. Some school districts are involved in planning and running summer programs, either solely or in collaboration with other institutions, but the majority of those described in the literature are sponsored by agencies other than local school districts, predominantly institutions of higher learning.

Given the sponsorship of summer programs, several kinds of questions arise regarding their role in talent development and the relationship between educational experiences received outside of the local school and those obtained during the regular academic years.

1. What is the range of summer programs being offered to talented adolescents?

2. What program models and curriculum designs are being used for students recruited to these sites?
3. How do summer programs uniquely benefit gifted adolescents?
4. What happens to students who attend summer programs, when they return to their homes and schools again?

The Center for Talent Development (CTD) at Northwestern University facilitates the identification of exceptionally talented adolescents through its Midwest Talent Search. Nearly 20,000 young people in the seventh and eighth grades are regionally identified each year and become eligible for specialized programs during both the academic year and summer months. Since 1983, CTD has also designed and carried out a wide variety of residential and commuter programs for junior high and senior high students on the Evanston campus.

In an effort to gauge the influence of summer programs on the development of academic talent among young adolescents, the center has conducted several evaluation studies about its own programs and those serving students identified by its annual search in the Midwest.

TYPES OF SUMMER PROGRAMS

Day (1977) offers some dimensions that it is useful to note in conducting a conceptual analysis across educational programs. She suggests that programs can be compared on their underlying psychological theories (both instructional and developmental), the goals and objectives of the program (their specificity, scope, and degree of emphasis on content or process), and the major instructional strategies emphasized (the degree of reliance on directiveness and external organization and structure). Although Day applied this analysis to early childhood intervention studies, it does offer a framework for viewing summer programs for gifted students as well.

An examination of the literature on summer programs reveals that few directly espouse or are founded upon a specific developmental or instructional theory or theory of learning. A few programs (e.g., Karnes, 1981) utilize Bloom's (1956) taxonomy of learning or Guilford's (1967) Structure of the Intellect model and emphasize the development of high-level thinking skills as embodied in these models.

The goals and objectives of summer programs are broad in scope. They include attention to the psychosocial adjustment issues of gifted students, such as the need for self-knowledge, self-acceptance, acceptance by others, friendships, and a peer group (Betts, 1981; Feldhusen & Clinkenbeard, 1981; Goodrum, 1981; Sheperd, 1981). Many programs try to address the specific developmental needs of the students they serve, for example, by facilitating identity exploration or career exploration for adolescent students (Feldhusen & Clinkenbeard, 1981).

Other stated goals and objectives include the acquisition of specific skills such as those for research or self-directed study (Betts, 1981; Sheperd, 1981) or independent living (Karnes, 1981). Cognitive goals and objectives include the demonstration of proficiency in a subject area (Sawyer, 1981), increased creativity (Spicker & Southern, 1981), and high-level thinking and analytical skills (Karnes, 1981; Spicker & Southern, 1981). Some programs include goals such as exposing students to university or college life (Clark & Zimmerman, 1981; Feldhusen & Clinkenbeard, 1981; VanTassel-Baska, Landau, & Olszewski, 1984), providing interaction with experts and accomplished professionals (Betts, 1981; Feldhusen & Clinkenbeard, 1981; Goodrum, 1981; VanTassel-Baska & Kulieke, 1987), providing specific cultural experiences (Spicker & Southern, 1981), and training in leadership skills (Feldhusen & Clinkenbeard, 1981).

The instructional strategies employed by summer programs vary as to whether they primarily promote adult/child interaction, child/child interaction, or child/material interaction (Day, 1977). Some programs involve students primarily in working with other students on projects (Spicker & Southern, 1981). In other programs, students work independently, using libraries, computers, and science equipment for self-selected projects (Young, Stein, & Wedekind, 1970). Other programs are quite structured and use instructional methods that are primarily teacher directed (VanTassel-Baska et al., 1984). Several programs deliberately planned a curriculum that would give students multiple opportunities to work alone and with other students and to receive instruction from a teacher (Wright & Cunningham, 1979; Young et al., 1970).

Summer programs also vary in whether they employ a predetermined sequence of student learning experience or are predominantly student led, thus allowing students to determine the content, scope, and direction of their learning (Betts, 1981; Young et al., 1970). Of the programs that have a prespecified curriculum, some employ a *proficiency model* of instruction: Students complete course work intended for older students in a compressed time frame (Benbow & Stanley, 1983; Keating, 1976; Sawyer, 1981; VanTassel-Baska et al., 1984). Others have *enrichment* as their objective. They are also known as *nonproficiency programs*. They expose students to highly specific academic topics (archeology, probability and statistics, or computer modeling) or give them hands-on experience in a subject (archeological dig, museum program, or scientific laboratory). Still others immerse students in the arts, emphasize skill development such as problem solving in multidisciplinary areas, or focus on creative processes within academic areas (robotics, theater, or poetry writing).

The diversity of summer programs for gifted students is impressive. Instructional models, content focus, and goals and objectives vary widely. Clearly there is no single formula for developing a program, and, given the existing range, guidelines for arranging for or choosing among them might be helpful for parents and educators of gifted students.

Since summer programs are educational opportunities that occur outside the normal academic calendar, their relationship to "academic-year" school programs is an important issue. They can be designed to work in tandem with local school programs, complementing them in important ways, or they can remain relatively separate, functioning more as "academic camps"—special summer events selected by parents, sponsored by institutions or groups other than local schools, and reflecting current educational trends and developments rather than the more traditional curriculum areas and modes of study.

CASE STUDY OF MIDWESTERN PROGRAMS

One of the evaluation studies completed by the Center for Talent Development examined over 30 of a listing of 50 summer programs in the Midwest that were specifically designed for academically talented adolescents who participated in the annual talent search and had requisite qualifying scores on the Scholastic Aptitude Test. Using a detailed survey-and-interview format, the study analyzed several key factors that seemed pertinent to the organization and success of the programs:

• Sponsorship
• Program characteristics
• Student characteristics
• Type of program structure
• Success of program in matching the needs of students
• Overall program cost and distribution of cost across program components

We hoped that by examining these programs we could see how summer opportunities might better serve talented adolescents across the Midwest.

Our analysis of the collected data demonstrated wide variation among summer programs, as was anticipated from a review of the literature. The selected programs differ in intensity, level of instruction, pace, resources, and overall affordability (see Table 14.1 for a breakdown on these dimensions). In general, it appears that local school districts in the Midwest are leaving the planning of summer programs for talent search students up to the institutions of higher learning. Universities and colleges provide the majority of

Table 14.1 Frequency Distributions for Selected Summer Program Variables

Variable	Number[1]	Percent
Sponsorship (N = 31 programs)		
College/university	21	68
Local public schools/district	3	10
Private schools	2	6
Cosponsored	5	16
Student Selection Criteria (N = 29 programs)		
Student achievement only	13	45
Specific SAT scores only	15	52
Teacher recommendations	1	3
Course (N = 31 programs)		
Mathematics and computers	23	25
Science 16	18	
Foreign language	6	7
Social studies	5	5
Literature	6	7
Writing	10	11
Other	25	27
Program Description for Nonproficiency Programs (N = 17 programs)		
Content enrichment (e.g., math games)	8	17
Content acceleration (advanced work)	9	19
Special project enrichment	10	21
Thinking skill enrichment	7	15
Enrichment in the arts	1	2
Special counseling	0	0
Extra subject enrichment (e.g., paleontology)	13	27
Instructor Type (N = 24 programs)		
University professor	47	41
Second. teacher/public school	38	33
Elem. teacher/public school	10	9
University student	6	5
Professional/experts	6	5
Second. teacher/prvt. school	5	4
Elem. teacher/prvt. school	3	3
Instructional Hours (N = 29 programs)		
≤ 30	7	24
> 30 ≤ 60	6	21
> 45 ≤ 60	6	21
> 60 ≤ 75	5	17
> 75 ≤ 90	2	7
> 90	3	10
Commuter Costs per Instructional Hour (N = 23 programs)		
$\leq \$1.00$	3	13
$> \$1.00$ $\leq \$2.00$	5	22
$> \$2.00$ $\leq \$3.00$	4	17
$> \$3.00$ $\leq \$4.00$	3	13
$> \$4.00$ $\leq \$5.00$	4	17
$> \$5.00$ $\leq \$6.00$	1	4
$> \$6.00$ $\leq \$7.00$	2	9
$> \$7.00$	1	4

[1] Number refers to the absolute number of times each descriptor was checked. In some categories, many programs checked more than one descriptor.

the programs, particularly proficiency-type programs, for young adolescents. Few programs are planned in conjunction with local schools.

Institutions of higher education are well suited to providing summer programs. They have available dormitory facilities for a residential program, and they draw students from larger regions and therefore can be cost effective. Most important, they attract highly trained faculty to teach specialized topics or subjects in sophisticated ways.

Local school districts, on the other hand, have the advantages of firsthand knowledge of the special needs and characteristics of their own students, as well as familiarity with their district's curricula. They plan programs specifically for talented students so that courses offered will match well with the academic year curriculum. Programs like this can be powerful; there were several examples in our survey of urban districts that utilized the resources in their community (including local colleges) to provide summer experiences for academically talented students.

Although great diversity was noted among the small number of programs studied, we found that the great majority of summer programs for talented adolescents in the Midwest are sponsored by a college or university. Among these, typical enrollment is about 100 students, and standardized test scores are the measures most frequently used to select eligible participants. Average length of all programs is about 3 weeks, with 24% offering 30 or fewer hours of instruction and almost 60% falling into the 31-to-75-hour range. The average program tends to be enrichment oriented, focusing on special projects and topics in mathematics and science, and costs between $150 and $200 for tuition. Room and board for residential programs cost extra.

We found summer programs grouped sharply around issues of proficiency (see Table 14.2). Proficiency-based programs, like those at CTD, use

Table 14.2 Means of Selected Variables for Comparison of Proficiency and Nonproficiency Programs

Variable	Proficiency (*n* = 11)	Nonproficiency (*n* = 17)
College/university sponsorship	64%	59%
Local school sponsorship	18%	35%
Mean session length in weeks	3	3
Mean instructional hours	68	41
Used SAT scores for entrance	91%	29%
SAT-M entrance score	468	405
Sent student evaluation to school	91%	12%
Mean commuter cost/instructional hour	$3.98	$3.89
Mean residential costs/week	$243.67	$229.38

ability measures provided by the SAT in an effective way. Students are selected and placed in courses based upon proven ability. The proficiency programs in this sample essentially provide high-school-level courses or beginning college courses to students whose measured intellectual abilities are 3 to 4 years beyond their chronological age. The programs appear to focus on providing academic courses in content areas that match the ability areas used for selection (math or verbal courses). The students attending these programs are more homogeneous with respect to ability, compared to those in programs that use cutoffs on standardized, in-grade achievement tests.

The nonproficiency programs seem less focused, as evidenced by the number and variety of descriptors applied to them by coordinators and the wide variety of courses offered. They attempt to serve students who are not only academically talented but also creatively or artistically gifted. Choosing to serve both academically and creatively talented students could be done effectively if these programs employed different but relevant selection criteria for these different areas. The majority, however, use academic achievement measures, which appear to be appropriate only for the academic courses they offer.

The nonproficiency programs included fewer hours of instruction and were less intense than the proficiency programs, and appeared to be less academically rigorous. These programs might be more suitable for students scoring between 200 and 400 on an SAT subtest—students who are more likely to be served in local school programs.

Evaluation tactics also vary between these two types of programs. Over 90% of the proficiency programs send an evaluation of each student's work in the summer program (grades, course description, and standardized test scores) to the home district schools. Forty-five percent of these programs also send a recommendation for placement of the students in the fall semester. Very few of the nonproficiency programs, on the other hand, send any kind of a report to the schools after the program ends. Despite these differences, proficiency programs cost about the same as nonproficiency programs for commuting students and, on the average, are only slightly more expensive ($14 more per week) for residential students.

WHAT HAPPENS AFTER THE SUMMER?

The shape of summer programs is only one side of the coin. We have been equally concerned with educational placements that occur after these programs conclude. We wondered how students who successfully completed course work in the summer were handled by their own schools at home. Did students receive credit for their work, special advising, or advanced placement in academic-year programs? Were parents consulted or informed about actions taken by their youngsters' schools after summer work was reported?

To answer these questions, for the past several years we have carefully followed up on the eventual school program actions taken by parents and schools of the Northwestern CTD Summer Program participants. Approximately 6 months after the summer program ended, these students' parents and schools received a questionnaire from the center. The parents' survey gathered their perceptions about the effects of their children's participation in the summer program; feedback on the program itself; and information about actions taken by the school regarding credit or recognition. The survey sent to the schools inquired about actions taken regarding each student's work and the usefulness of the evaluation materials sent to them. Returned questionnaires were matched with the student to whom they referred and then analyzed.

Parents of summer program participants consistently reported that the opportunity was beneficial to their youngsters (94%), that the students had thoroughly enjoyed the program (85%), and that the faculty and staff were highly skilled (74%). More important, parents cited gains among their children in friendships (98% made new friends), in confidence (56%), and in motivation to pursue more challenging course work (36%).[1]

What is most striking about the data is the dissonance between what schools *said* they had done regarding course work completed by the student in the summer and what parents perceived had occurred. Data in the 1985 study revealed that, overall, only 8% of the "matched" surveys agreed exactly on every item; 52% somewhat disagreed with their matches, and nearly 40% totally disagreed. Typically, more agreement was found with matters concerning credit (it was often not awarded) and correct placement than there was with other special considerations (see Table 14.3). Many parents reported that their son or daughter had been given special counseling, placed in special programs, or that other provisions were made, while the schools from which these students came did not report these actions were taken for these same students.

On the other hand, we found that parents who had youngsters in a special summer program did pursue future placement decisions with their schools. Sixty-two percent[2] of the parents made contact with the school to discuss their child's participation in the summer program. Another 59% of the students also initiated a contact with the school for the same purpose.

---

[1]These figures are averaged over 1983, 1984, and 1985. See VanTassel-Baska, Landau, and Olszewski (1984) for a more comprehensive explanation of the 1983 sample findings.

[2]These are averaged over the 1984 and 1985 samples.

Table 14.3 Comparison of Parents' and Schools' Reports Regarding Schools'
Follow-up Actions for Summer Program Students for 1984 and 1985*

Follow-up Action	1985 (n = 80)				1984 (n = 61)			
	No. of "Yes" responses			% agr. for yes resp.	No. of "Yes" responses			% agr. for yes resp.
	School	Parent	Either		School	Parent	Either	
Correct placement	41	35	52	46.2	33	32	44	47.7
School credit	14	17	21	47.6	10	12	15	46.7
Special program	18	17	31	12.9	29	19	35	37.1
Independent study	4	6	7	42.9	2	4	5	20.0
Counseling	15	18	26	26.9	10	12	19	15.8
Financial support for outside work	5	1	6	0	0	0	0	0
Other	4	12	15	6.7	4	6	10	0
Special provisions not needed	7	16	21	9.5	3	5	8	0
Special provisions not made	17	14	26	19.2	10	20	24	25.0

Fifty-eight percent of the parents made at least one visit to the school to talk about their child's academic program subsequent to the summer program, and 42% made two or more visits. Thirty-eight percent of the parents were very satisfied with the schools's actions, while 34% reported that the action was inadequate and another 22% reported dissatisfaction with the school's actions.

What was most disappointing was the reluctance of local schools to award credit, despite outstanding standardized achievement scores. Even for students who did extremely well in the summer program, overall, only half were placed appropriately and/or received course credit. Of the students who achieved proficiency,[3] those in mathematics and science (72% for precalculus; 75% for chemistry; 67% for biology) appeared to have a better chance of getting credit or appropriate placement than did those in the verbal courses (25% for American studies; 40% for literary analysis; 0% for expository writing). Latin was a notable exception; 67% of the students achieving proficiency were appropriately placed or given credit.

It seems clear that cumulatively organized subjects (mathematics and foreign languages) and well-defined standard courses with little content variation from school (biology and chemistry) are followed up more easily by local schools than are courses that contain more variability across schools and teachers (writing, literature courses, or multidisciplinary courses such as American studies).

Our research seems to confirm that schools are most likely to respond to a student's summer program experience by placing the child at the appropriate content-area level or in a special program. It is rare for schools to respond with financial assistance for continued work outside the home school and with independent study opportunities. Credit is frequently not given for work done in the summer program, and students also infrequently receive special counseling. Although placement of students in special programs and at the appropriate level appear to be valid often-used actions taken by schools, in reality, they only represent a minimum level of response.

Special programs used as a follow-up can be a problem. In junior high school these programs often are enrichment-oriented, covering material at a conceptual level and rate that is below the abilities of students who can achieve proficiency in a high school honors course in a 3-week summer program. For example, students who complete algebra I in the summer and are allowed to study algebra II during the academic year do not repeat old material, but they also may not be receiving new content at a pace or level consistent with their intellectual capacities, particularly if placed in a year-long course. Thus, independent study opportunities and financial assistance for work outside the local setting are actions which, while little used at present, may be the most appropriate for many highly talented students completing summer programs.

---

[3]*Proficiency* means students obtained scores at or above the mean for high school students on the College Board Achievement Tests, used as posttests, in Latin, chemistry, biology, literary analysis and American studies. In precalculus, proficiency meant scoring at or above the 90th percentile on the Cooperative Algebra Tests, which were used as posttests.

BENEFITS OF SUMMER PROGRAMS

Well-developed summer programs for academically talented adolescents do a good job of meeting the intellectual and social needs of these students. Summer opportunities like those at Northwestern and other higher-education institutions can result in new long-term friendships, increased confidence in one's ability, and a strong desire to seek out appropriately challenging course work. The high percentage of students who achieve proficiency, make great gains in skills, and focus on suitable follow-up opportunities attests to the match of these programs with young people's intellectual needs. Some of the benefits that have been reported in the literature and that we have observed in our own programs are as follows.

Challenging Course Work. Summer programs provide an opportunity to participate in courses that are challenging and commensurate, in pace and conceptual level, with a student's abilities and intellectual level.

Self-Testing of Abilities. In summer programs students can test themselves and the limits of their abilities in demanding intellectual situations. Bloom (1985) attests to the importance of competitions and recitals in engendering self-evaluation of one's abilities, fostering growth and progress, and determining strengths and weaknesses in a talent area. Summer programs that involve students in challenging academic experiences may encourage reevaluations and subsequent goal setting that will further a student's progress in attaining excellence.

Self-Paced Programs. Many programs or courses allow students to proceed at their own learning rate—one that is comfortable yet exciting and challenging. Individual experience may help students become more aware of their own learning capabilities.

Intellectual Peer Interaction. In a setting focused upon intellectual issues, interaction with other equally able students is maximized. Classroom discussion and small-group work with intellectual peers can contribute to students' learning and encourage their active collaboration in intellectual enterprises. Summer programs often provide opportunities for engagement that other school programs cannot.

Social Peer Interaction. These programs can provide gifted students with a "true" peer group for social interaction. Such interaction helps to allay gifted students' fears of not being able to make friends or of being unusual or different from agemates.

Independent Living Skills. Residential programs afford gifted students with the opportunity to learn independent living skills ranging from personal hygiene to time management.

Athletic Activities. Programs that have regularly scheduled athletic activities or components provide gifted students with the opportunity to compete in sports and/or other competitive situations with students who may be at a similar skill level and/or who place similar (and maybe less) value on athletics.

Special Counseling. These programs are usually staffed with teachers, counselors, and administrators who are particularly attentive to and aware of gifted students' needs and often identify with such students. While other schools may need to focus on underachieving students and those with learning problems, summer programs specifically focus on the academic and psychosocial issues of academically talented students.

Environment for Greater Risk Taking. In these settings, gifted students may be more willing to take risks, both intellectual and social. Staffed with many encouraging and supportive individuals attuned to the perfectionist tendencies of gifted students, they can offer a unique opportunity for students to be more creative in their work and more confident in social interactions.

Extracurricular Activities. Activities such as debate, journalism, or filmmaking are often included, giving students a preview of the kinds of school clubs or activities that are offered on the high school level. Students can explore these as possible options to pursue more intensively in later years.

Social Networking. Summer programs can facilitate the building of social networks for students, as they get to know other gifted students from different states or even countries, as well as adults (teachers and college students) who may become lifelong friends or mentors. These individuals can serve as future resources to help students negotiate such decisions as college choice, college major, or even career choice.

College Exposure. Attending programs held on college campuses can expose students to college life, previewing not only its independent nature but also its rigor, intensity, and breadth of opportunities. Universities can be especially revealing experiences, particularly for students from small towns and/or rural areas.

226

Educational Opportunities. Student counselors and teachers can make gifted students aware of educational opportunities and options previously not considered. These include college courses, foreign study, other summer programs, early entrance into college, and double majors.

Insight into Self. Summer programs generally entail intensive efforts to meet the special psychosocial needs of gifted students. Low staff/student ratios insure many informal counseling opportunities which, along with purposefully designed social events and instructional settings, all contribute toward gifted students' gaining insight into themselves, as individuals and as members of a peer group.

CONSIDERATIONS IN SELECTING A PROGRAM

Parents and teachers who guide adolescents toward summer programs should examine several factors and consider several questions before selecting a program. Not every program for the gifted is appropriate for every gifted child. Some of the factors to consider in choosing a summer experience for a student are listed.

Students' Ages. Junior-high-age students are very different from senior-high-age students, although both groups are adolescents. A relatively focused age range is probably best, to insure that students receive attention, intervention, and services appropriate to their needs. For example, younger students may need a relatively structured setting and counseling dealing with high school and adolescence, while older students need a situation with more freedom and independence and counseling focusing on college and career.

Student Ability Levels. Some summer programs involve relatively heterogeneous groups of students, particularly when in-grade achievement tests (above 95th percentile) and grades or general intellectual measures (e.g., IQ) are used as selection instruments. Programs such as these probably garner many students who are somewhat exceptional with respect to their intellectual abilities and a few who are very exceptional. For the very exceptional child, such programs might not accomplish the goal of providing an intellectual peer group. Parents and teachers need to be particularly selective for a remarkably gifted child.

Match Between Summer Program Content and Student's Strengths. A child who is creatively gifted should be steered toward a program that focuses on creative problem solving or involves creative construction. A child who is gifted in verbal areas needs a program that emphasizes writing, literature, foreign language, or debate. A student talented in mathematics needs to pursue algebra or probability and statistics.

Instructional Model and Student Learning Style. Summer programs vary in the various instructional techniques they promote or employ, such as individual self-paced instruction, multidisciplinary courses, research and problem-solving skills, project- or product-oriented outcomes, and teacher-led instruction.

Quality of Staff. A high-powered academic experience can be provided to gifted students by individuals such as university professors or research scientists with advanced-level training in content areas. These teachers may later serve as mentors and/or important resources for students. Instructional staff should have experience with gifted students, and counseling staff should be aware of the special needs of these youngsters.

Program Length and Intensity. Some programs involve a sampling of content areas or subjects, emphasizing exposure and enrichment. In such cases, a student may take five courses and study 1 hour per day per class. Other programs are intensively focused, emphasizing proficiency and mastery. Here a student may study one subject 5 hours a day for 3 weeks. Some involve formal testing and evaluation of students, while others do so only minimally. Generally, the more rigorous and intense a program, the more selective and appropriate it will be for only those very able students who are highly motivated and possess independent study skills.

Cost. University programs that involve a residential component are generally more expensive; however, costs should be compared by taking into account the actual amount of instructional time over the duration of the program. Also, activities and extra components (e.g., an evening enrichment series or an athletic program) should be taken into consideration.

Importance of Residential Component. The opportunity to interact with other gifted students in a dormitory and under purely social circumstances may be the most important aspect of the entire program. A residential program may be particularly helpful for students who come from a small school or rural area where they are isolated from many other gifted students.

Summer Program Articulation. Students who are talented in mathematics and study algebra in a summer program will need to move on to the next level of mathematics when they return to school in the fall. Continuous progress within an area of strength will be facilitated if the summer program, either as a matter of course or upon special request, sends to the local school detailed information about the summer course and about the student's progress in it. An evaluation of the compatibility of the summer program course and the curriculum of the local school setting should be done prior to the student's participation, especially when the program is proficiency based and includes typical school courses. When the summer course is largely enrichment oriented or taken as an extra subject, a report documenting the student's participation and/or progress may still be desired by school administrators and parents.

Prior to the start of the summer program, parents should visit the school the child will be attending in the fall, to make the school aware of the nature of the program and its likely outcome for the student. Schools complain that students' schedules are set in the spring for the following academic year and that it is very difficult to alter them after a student attends a summer program. If schools are aware of the program and informed of its nature, they will be forewarned of the need to alter a student's schedule. Parents, on the other hand, will not have unrealistic expectations about what will occur after their child's participation in the summer program and will have more time to negotiate an appropriate program with the school for the coming term.

PROBLEMS WITH SUMMER PROGRAMS

While a great deal of progress has been made in offering summer programs to gifted students and in gaining local schools' acceptance of them, there are still some potential problems.

Often summer programs are one-shot events for students, bearing little relation to the academic experience occurring in school. A great deal of learning and growth can occur for students when the different spheres of their lives (home, school) work in concert, reinforcing the same goals and emphasizing similar or congruent values. Gifted students need to have their abilities developed and their psychosocial needs met, both in and outside of school.

Summer program sponsors and school administrators need to work together to insure articulation between completed summer course work and the academic-year curriculum. Students should be allowed to continue the area of study they began during the summer, even if the school does not have a specific course in that area. This would mean the development of opportunity structures, including flexible scheduling, use of junior colleges and nearby universities for courses, independent study options, and work with mentors and adult professionals.

Services for gifted students such as counseling, guidance, and attention to psychosocial issues need to be ongoing, continuous, and adjusted to their needs and rate of intellectual and psychological development. Nothing can be more devastating to a student than to be turned on to learning and self-discovery in the summer, only to return in the fall to a dull curriculum and a pervasively inattentive environment.

Summer programs that involve costs to parents and take a full year to plan and implement are proliferating at the expense, it seems, of academic-year programs for gifted students. Local schools must not allow the *primary* burden of the education of gifted students to shift to other agencies. If a 3-week summer program can have a profound impact on a student, a program that begins in elementary school and continues throughout the school year can be overwhelming in its positive influence. Collaborative models that combine the special facilities of laboratories and colleges and universities with the expertise of educational personnel in local schools need to be developed for summer programs.

There are many gifted students who cannot afford summer programs such as those described here, yet it is these students who may be most in need of those experiences. Bright students coming from economically disadvantaged backgrounds may be found in rural areas, where they may be dealing with social isolation and cultural deprivation, and in large urban areas, where schools often are focused on issues of minimum competency rather than talent development. Isolation, lack of resources or access to them, lack of role models, low motivation, and little family support may be factors that work against these students. Summer programs may be particularly helpful in providing a respite from the environmental conditions that hinder the progress of economically disadvantaged gifted students. Summer programs are not a panacea for gifted students but an important contributor to the development and fruition of academic talent.

CONCLUSION

Summer programs appear to be a growing phenomenon becoming entrenched within universities and colleges and gradually receiving more acceptance by local schools. Students can clearly benefit in several ways from these experiences. We have been impressed with how such a short-term, relatively random learning experience can cause such change and reorganization for a student. Summer programs can be "epiphanies" for some students and have a tremendous impact on a young person's life. For the first time, some students feel truly comfortable with themselves and their abilities. They learn that challenging academic experiences do exist for them, as well as comfortable social environments. They acquire knowledge that will enable them to choose such experiences and environments for themselves in the future, whether in high school, in college, or in a career. This knowledge may be the most important and long-lasting effect of participating in a summer program.

REFERENCES

Benbow, C. P., & Stanley, J. (Eds.). (1983). *Academic precocity: Aspects of its development*. Baltimore, MD: Johns Hopkins University Press.

Betts, G. T. (1981). A step forward for the gifted: A summer enrichment program. *Journal for the Education of the Gifted*, 5(3), 190–193.

Bloom, B. S. (Ed.). (1956). *Taxonomy of educational objectives: Handbook I: Cognitive domain*. New York: David McKay Co., Inc.

Bloom, B. S. (1985). (Ed.). *Developing talent in young people*. New York: Ballantine Books.

Clark, G., & Zimmerman, E. (1981). The Indiana University Summer Arts Institute. *Journal for the Education of the Gifted*, 5(3), 204–208.

Day, M. C. (1977). A comparative analysis of center-based preschool programs. In M. C. Day & R. C. Parker (Eds.), *The preschool in action: Exploring early childhood program* (pp. 461–487). Boston, MA: Allyn and Bacon, Inc.

Feldhusen, J. F., & Clinkenbeard, P. R. (1981). Summer programs for the gifted: Purdue's residential programs for high achievers. *Journal for the Education of the Gifted*, 5(3), 178–184.

Goodrum, S. (1981). Summer scholastics and arts for the gifted: A holistic approach. *Journal for the Education of the Gifted*, 5(3), 170–177.

Guilford, J. P. (1967). *The nature of human intelligence*. New York: McGraw-Hill Book Company.

Karnes, F. A. (1981). Summer residential program for the gifted: A university model. *Journal for the Education of the Gifted*, 5(3), 194–198.

Keating, D. P. (Ed.). (1976). *Intellectual talent: Research and development*. Baltimore, MD: The Johns Hopkins University Press.

Sawyer, R. N. (1981). The Duke University program to identify and educate brilliant young students. *Journal for the Education of the Gifted*, 5(3), 185–189.

Sheperd, G. (1981). Learning not to be afraid to be smart. *Journal for the Education of the Gifted*, 5(3), 199–203.

Spicker, H. H., & Southern, W. T. (1981). Indiana University's College for Gifted and Talented Youth. *Journal for the Education of the Gifted*, 5(3), 155–159.

VanTassel-Baska, J., & Kulieke, M. J. (1987). The role of community-based scientific resources in developing scientific talent: A case study. *Gifted Child Quarterly*, 31(3), 111–115.

VanTassel-Baska, J., Landau, M., & Olszewski, P. (1984). The benefits of summer programming for gifted adolescents. *Journal for the Education of the Gifted*, 8,(1), 73–82.

Wright, D., & Cunningham, C. H. (1979). A model summer program for gifted children. *Gifted Child Quarterly*, 23(3), 538–542.

Young, R. C., Stein, E. G., & Wedekind, R. R. (1970). A team teaching summer program for gifted sixth grade students. *Gifted Child Quarterly*, 14(2), 36–40.

CHAPTER 15

An Essay on Education for the Gifted

Richard Ronvik

Whether schools have a great potential to affect positively the education of gifted children, which is what most parents and communities and some educators hope to be true, or whether schools are quite limited in this regard, which is what some parents and communities and most educators feel to be true, has not been adequately tested and probably cannot be. This stems from the fact that most programs for gifted children have almost no chance of positive long-range educational effect because they are designed and implemented so naïvely as to preclude that possibility.

The reason for much of this naïveté is that many of those in the field of education for gifted children who strongly encourage and support the national development of programs for the gifted and talented, and many of the theoreticians who have designed models for the ready application to local needs, and many of the practitioners who have developed and implemented local programs for the children in this category, have a less than clear notion about why they are doing what they do.

THE TYPICAL APPROACH TO PROGRAM DEVELOPMENT
FOR THE GIFTED

A rationale for the existence of a school system's program for the gifted, is routinely required as a statement in most proposals seeking funding support. Too often, however, it is worded in lofty phrases about societal needs and benefits and lacks any pragmatic consideration of the question, Why do we need or want special programs for gifted children in our school system? Without a prior and thorough examination of this question and all of its implications, the rationale for the program becomes the mere fact that the category exists, that funding is available if applied for, that other school districts have programs for this population, and that the school system would be remiss in not identifying students to fill an officially designated category.

If the programs to be implemented for gifted children were to be the same, no matter what the overall rationale was or how it was developed, then the issue would be academic; but the reality is that this preprogram assessment will shape the overall design of the program as well as the individual types of courses that are implemented within it.

If a school system begins the construction of its programs and services for gifted and talented children merely because such a classification exists, it enters into the work at hand with a particular mind-set that will determine the course to follow. Since the program developers would be starting from scratch, so to speak, there would be little connection to anything currently existing within the schools' offerings, and the program developers would be free to develop unique and interesting programs, possibly drawing upon the theoretical models advertised in the literature. There is a plethora of theoretical cubes, triads, and circles, totemic columns, taxonomic bars, and hierarchical charts to satisfy even the most demanding practitioners in their search for innovative things to do with children identified as gifted.

Programs developed in this way tend to be creative, relatively exciting, innovative, enjoyed by participating students and teachers, and supported by parents and school administrators. They also tend to be part-time, suitable for students other than the gifted, occasionally superficial, largely separated from the standard curriculum of the school, and often resented by nonparticipating teachers and nonparticipating students and their parents. This "separate path" method of program development lends itself well to the resource room concept, the individual project approach, the once-or-twice-a-week pull-out model, and a "soft" identification and selection process.

In this style of program development, the identification and selection process can afford to be more flexible and can support a wide tolerance for error, since the part-time enrollment of gifted children in the program is not particularly crucial to their overall educational development, and the accidental or even intentional inclusion of nongifted children into the program would probably not produce any psychological trauma due to educational misplacement.

School boards and administrators are usually quite pleased with gifted programs that have taken this path of program development, since the "add-on" nature of the program is administratively simple to operate and its innovative features can be elevated to a high-visibility position for publicity purposes. In fact, the use of program activities for the gifted to show the "good things" that a school system is doing, when the activities of the program for mentally handicapped or socially maladjusted children would not be so used, is an indicator of a school system that has neither understood nor accepted the idea that program follows need and that program designs that fulfill students' needs are, regardless of the category of student, equally elegant.

COMPARISON TO OTHER AREAS OF SPECIAL EDUCATION

Once this path of program development has been opened, it becomes very difficult to retrace steps back to the point where the original rationale should have been considered more thoroughly. The other areas of special education, those dealing with handicapping conditions, seem to start from a more uniformly accepted premise. It is generally accepted that students with handicapping conditions require some modification, however modest, to the educational setting or the curriculum content or process, since the regular school program without alteration cannot meet their needs. This rationale requires an examination of the failure of the regular school program to meet the needs of a specifically defined group, and the arrangement of practical steps to create learning environments for special students that will insure success.

The field of special education for those with handicapping conditions has developed with greater concordance around central issues than the field of education for the gifted, resulting in a higher awareness of the problems involved; a greater willingness on the part of the community and school to provide the settings and tools necessary to solve the problems; a more uniform set of laws, rules, and regulations governing the ways to proceed; and a greater acceptance on the part of legislators of the need to provide the funding necessary for specialized services.

Education for the gifted, even when it is included in the general stable of special education programs, is so lacking in that concordance that it is in large part ineffective in its major goal of providing optimal educational settings for gifted children. Because it lacks focus and has, after decades of organizing and publishing, no common field theory, it in fact invites the abuse that it sometimes receives. It is difficult, for example, for program developers to answer intelligently the perennial charges of elitism when they themselves have structured their programs on models that encourage the development of interesting enrichment activities that could be enjoyed by most students but must be restricted—because of space, personnel, or funding limitations—to a few who have been designated "gifted." Moreover, if the school system's only program for the gifted is an "add-on" model or an occasional pull-out visit to a resource center, it becomes difficult to refute the charges of triviality voiced by parents who had expected a major revision of the entire curriculum to meet the needs of these children.

It is of limited help for program developers to reexamine the field literature in an effort to gain a surer footing in establishing program foundations and directions, since many of the popular proponents of gifted education endorse models designed for easy administrative accommodation. These typically follow the "add-on" concept and encourage definitions of giftedness that are so general as to compromise the credibility of the category and contribute greatly to the general trivialization of gifted education. This is to say nothing of the hundreds of circuit lecturers and entertainers, with their "fun-and-games-for-the-gifted" approach and "make-it-and-take-it" workshops, and the many vendors of program materials with their comic-book-type catalogs, all of whom have contributed to the accumulated impression that what we are about should certainly not be among the highest of educational priorities.

PROGRAM PLANNING BASED ON STUDENT NEED

If a school system were to follow a different path at the inception of its program planning—one focusing on student need and committed to restructuring the entire setting, curriculum, and process for its identified gifted children—then its offerings would be very different from those noted so far. Following this path, however, imposes exacting dues, since the initial step requires the understanding and admission that the school system's regular program has failed to meet the needs of its gifted students; and subsequent steps require major funding, staffing, training, and program restructuring to correct the deficiencies.

If the parents', teachers', and administrators' perception is that the educational needs of gifted children are generally being met in the regular classroom, then there is no point in pursuing the construction of a costly and time-consuming program to address a nonexistent need. If the general perception is that the school system is failing to educate its gifted children properly, then a process must begin to restructure the basic curriculum in every subject area in which children, because of their advanced mental capacities, are not being challenged at their level of ability. This restructuring process entails, very generally, increasing the scope of curriculum to be covered, increasing the depth of complexity of each area in the curriculum, and accelerating the instructional process by introducing topics earlier and covering material at a faster pace.

Programs built along these lines will have as their guiding framework the optimal educational setting for each gifted child in each of the subject areas included in the curriculum. While such programs may be innovative and creative, they will not have innovation or creativity as their guiding framework; they will include, in the context of the curriculum, problem-solving and thinking skills, but will not be structured around either; they will not be fixated on divergent thinking exercises or upper-level thought processes, but will include them in the larger context of the program.

Since programs designed in this way are specifically suited to the needs of gifted children, they are not appropriate for children within the normal range of abilities. The interminable requests of school administrators to increase the number of students in programs for the gifted reveals an innocent view on the meaning of program services built on needs. Such administrative requests reveal one of two naive assumptions. The first is that giftedness is a desirable quality; therefore, the more students who are enrolled in programs for the gifted, the better off we'll all be. The second is that these programs are of a higher quality than regular school programs; therefore, an effort should be made to increase the number of students in higher quality programs. Both assumptions are faulty, since the quality of a school program has nothing to do with the ability level of the enrolled students. All programs, whether for mentally handicapped, normal, or gifted students, should be of equally high quality and should be the optimal setting for the students participating. While it may be true that the gifted-students' program in a particular school system may actually be of a higher quality than the regular program, this would indicate only that the regular program was not designed or implemented properly. Programs for the gifted should never be expected to alleviate the flaws in an improperly designed program for normal students.

The ideas of decreasing the number of students in programs for the mentally handicapped and increasing the number of students in programs for the gifted would both seem to be ill advised, if the programs were indeed meeting the needs of the participating students, yet both ideas have held some popularity with school administrators. Such views not only demean good programs for mentally handicapped children by suggesting that the children would be better off out of them, but they also overestimate programs for gifted children by suggesting that children, regardless of capability, would be better off in them. The point that would seem to be missed by such views is that programs for mentally handicapped children and programs for gifted children exist solely because there is a phenomenon in the distribution of intellectual ability in humans which requires schools to make precise curricular adjustments for special students with specific needs.

IDENTIFICATION OF THE GIFTED

In setting about to find which are the special students with specific needs, we should be interested not only in administering tests to determine which students score highly, but in interviewing teachers and parents to discover the students for whom the regular school program has proved unchallenging. School systems vary in whether they carry out these screening procedures of testing and interviewing on a mandatory or optional basis. Where commitment is strong and funding is adequate to support programs for all of the gifted students who would be identified as "in need of service," a mandated, standardized screening procedure would be preferred. Where administrative commitment is weak and funding is inadequate, an optional screening procedure, implemented only when there is a specific commitment for a follow-up program, would be preferred, as there is no point in identifying gifted students if there is no possibility of providing the required program. School systems with weak commitments for gifted children's education are not likely to support in-depth, needs-based programs in any case. They would be most likely to prefer a highly visible add-on program quite separate from the basic curriculum, for which mandatory screening would be largely irrelevant.

Most of the published advice on the screening, identification, and selection of students for services for the gifted suggests using multiple criteria, since no single instrument carries the assurance that would be desirable for such educational placement decisions. This is especially true when the criterion is relatively unsophisticated, such as a single teacher recommendation or a prior class grade. To enhance the validity of the identification procedure, then, administrators drawing up rules and regulations for the governance of local programs should insist on multiple criteria and stipulate as well that the criteria be nonduplicative. To present three teacher recommendations or to endure the tedium of administering three different reading tests to satisfy a multiple-criteria requirement would only serve to circumvent the original intention of enlarging the perspective of the data to be considered.

Consideration should also be given to the appropriateness of the criteria for an intended program. One state, for example, has constructed three menu-like columns from which districts must select at least one criterion each. This forces school districts conducting specific aptitude programs in music and art to include an intelligence test or a reading test among their selection criteria for entrance into the program. Clearly, the principle of appropriateness has not been given adequate consideration.

Administrators should also insist, of course, that the identification and selection measures used match the program objectives and activities that are to follow. Students considered for involvement in programs in the performing arts should be properly screened through aptitude and audition measures and through teacher, parent, and student interviews. Whether the aptitude or the audition measure should be the most heavily weighted would depend upon whether the focus of the program was on development or performance. In cases where there is a weak link between the identification procedures and the program activities, the identification procedures, no matter how elegantly designed, are rendered irrelevant. Add-on programs, which are separated almost completely from the basic curriculum, often have weak or nonexistent links between selection criteria and program activities, and this contributes toward their development as preferential rather than differentiated services.

A differentiated program design takes into account the fact that gifted children have a greater learning capacity; hence it offers program activities that, by level, depth, rigor, and pacing, are specifically appropriate. It would be impossible to build such a program unless the connection between selection criteria and program activities were very close. However, in the case of a program whose major criterion for acceptance is the prerequisite that students score 2 or 3 years above grade level in reading, and whose activities are of a general enrichment type—including performing arts activities, field trips, and exceptional opportunities that would benefit students of any ability level—the link between identification criteria and program activities could be justly criticized and the program labeled "preferential." In short, one needs to insure that activities in programs for the gifted do not become "prizes for the smart."

In applying the multiple criteria for selection that are usually required, program administrators could consider reviewing each candidate's qualifications all at once. This would provide a composite profile, which might lead to the inclusion of some students who score low on one measure but high on others. It would be in contrast to a successive screening process in which screens of increasing difficulty are applied in order to narrow the original pool of students to a manageable size for a final and more sophisticated selection. While the latter method, with good instrumentation, can be very effective, it has the disadvantage of eliminating some candidates on an early screen who may have been successful on the screens to follow.

When selecting the actual instruments that make up the identification procedure, program administrators should consider carefully whether the selection criteria should be weighted most heavily toward aptitude or achievement measures. In programs with demanding prerequisites, such as a college-level physics course or a postcalculus mathematics course, or in programs with an immediate performance expectation, such as a competitive math team, a "quiz bowl olympics," or a citywide high school orchestra, it would seem clear that the present level achievement must play a heavy role in the selection process, and so achievement tests and auditions would be in order.

In programs with long-range developmental objectives, especially those that enroll students in the primary grades, the weighting would shift somewhat toward aptitude measures, since the aim would be to find students with a greater mental capacity and facility rather than those who have been privileged to receive coaching in reading or private music lessons.

While it is true that even aptitude tests are measuring in great degree human achievement, the foci of the two types of tests are quite different. Teachers may even be somewhat disappointed to find that children identified as gifted on aptitude measures do not always display immediate achievement skills, but these teachers can take consolation in the fact that they have important work ahead of them.

While selection criteria should be consistent within similar program types, varying standards would be in order when applied to different levels and types of services. A local school program selecting gifted students from its own school population would have more modest standards than a regional or citywide program, which in turn would have more modest standards than a state residential school. The fact that, in accepting this, there would seem to be no universal standard for defining giftedness should not bother even the purist, since the aim of selection measures always should be to remove students from unchallenging educational environments and transfer them into suitable ones. The local level is where giftedness begins to be nurtured. Regional and state programs offer even greater challenges for those who demonstrate their readiness for them.

In far too many instances the number of students in programs for the gifted is determined as much by administrative consideration as it is by student ability levels. Because of funding, space, or personnel restrictions, a preset number of seats is available. Program administrators in these situations usually screen students through the various criteria, rank them in descending score order, and assign them to the available seats. If there are more seats than students and the school system must maintain preset teacher/pupil ratios, then additional, slightly lower-scoring students are sometimes enrolled to fill the class to viable size. If there are more students than seats, then the students assigned to the program are labeled gifted and the remaining students are carried on a waiting list or are recommended for some alternate service. Obviously such a procedure is not in the best interests of all students involved, since administrative convenience is interfering with student needs, but program administrators operating within severe limitations may be confronted with the reality that less than perfect arrangements for serving gifted children may be better than no arrangements.

PROLIFERATION OF CATEGORIES OF GIFTEDNESS

The popularity of the add-on program type matches to some degree the popularity of the proliferation of categories of gifted programs. Administrators who harbored anxious feelings about providing special services for students who were already identified as gifted were openly enthusiastic about the introduction of new categories of giftedness. The modish areas of creativity, leadership, psychomotor skills seemed to many the perfect solution to making the programs for the gifted more "fair." It was felt that, if there were students who had been overlooked in the search for giftedness, then surely they could be accommodated within expanded definitions and categories. Programs focusing on the separate areas of creativity, thinking skills, problem solving, leadership, and so forth contributed to a sharp increase in the number of add-on-type programs that were quite separated from the general subject curriculum.

This proliferation of categories increased the problems threatening serious programming for the gifted, because the definitions of the categories themselves were unclear, the identification measures were not convincing, the sundering of gifted services into fashionable components encouraged the add-on approach to program development, and the standard curriculum areas—which already represented the greatest deficiencies in services for the gifted—became even more neglected.

Program practitioners should review the effectiveness of small, separate programs in these expanded categories and begin to combine them into the major curriculum strands, so that problem solving, creativity, leadership opportunities, and practice in the higher-level thought processes become natural parts of the study of science, mathematics, language, social studies, and the arts. This process of shifting an add-on-type program over to a needs-based program in a major subject area could be, for many program administrators, the first step toward building a comprehensive model of services for gifted children in their district.

BUILDING COMPREHENSIVE CURRICULA AND PROGRAMS

Once it has been determined—and agreed upon—which curriculum areas in the regular program do not meet the needs of gifted and talented children, the work on curriculum differentiation can begin. As noted already, one of the weaknesses of many programs is that the lack of differentiation in the design has produced offerings that would be suitable for students at almost any ability level. Program developers have concentrated on unique and interesting activities and on quality teaching, but they have neglected to analyze the very specifics that should make the classes differentiated for a gifted population. A program such as the International Baccalaureate would serve as an excellent foundation on which to build comprehensive program models, because the prerequisite levels necessary for student admission influence the curriculum goals as far back as the intermediate elementary grades. The International Baccalaureate program, or IB as it is commonly called, is an "across-the-board" major curriculum program at the high school level for which international examinations are offered at the 11th and 12th grades.

A second area that program administrators need to consider is the degree to which their offerings are comprehensive for the range of student ability levels that fall within the designation of gifted. While highly talented students must obviously be provided for, many programs could expand their services to include a broader base of enrollment, since student need rather than a fixed quota should govern the population served. This requires offerings that respond to the range of giftedness, serving children in their respective home schools, regional centers or citywide schools, and specialized programs and statewide residential schools, when they exist.

When the areas of curriculum scope and ability range have been pressed for expansion, a third area—range of program types—can be reviewed with an aim toward a fully comprehensive array. This may include internship and mentor programs, supplementary summer classes, college-linked arrangements, early high school involvement, local museum cooperatives, and university-based programs, in addition to the basic classes for gifted children.

A final area to be considered for comprehensiveness relates to support services. A good support system requires counselors, school psychologists, and social workers who are assigned exclusively to the program for the gifted. Special service personnel operating on a crisis basis routinely shortchange students identified or perceived as gifted, on the basis that somehow such students will "make it on their own." Also, as identification instruments become more sophisticated and test biases require more study, and as drug abuse, child abuse, and student suicide become increasingly alarming problems, program administrators need the full-time support of personnel specifically trained in these areas. All such specialized support personnel should carry full caseloads of gifted children in two categories: (1) highly gifted students who need follow-through support services in terms of special program placement, high school and college counseling, and "bureaucracy-breaking" advocacy and (2) any gifted students whose social or emotional problems are interfering with their educational progress.

When administrators of programs for gifted students can feel that they have converted their more superficial add-on programs into major curriculum strands, and that they have pushed their programs toward greater comprehensiveness in the areas of curriculum scope, range of ability level, program type, and support services, then they may wish to relax somewhat and ponder whether schools have a great or limited potential to affect positively the education of gifted children.

About the Contributors
Index

About the Contributors

THOMAS M. BUESCHER has been Associate Professor of Gifted Child Education at Wayne State University, Head of the Middle School Program at the Gibson School for the Gifted, and a Senior Researcher at the Merrill-Palmer Institute for Family and Human Development Research. He was Associate Director for Programs at the Center for Talent Development at Northwestern University and is currently a research scholar there. He holds a doctorate in special education from Wayne State University.

JAMES J. GALLAGHER is the Kenan Professor of Education at the University of North Carolina–Chapel Hill. He is a renowned author and researcher in the field of special education and the gifted.

SHARON HIGHAM was Associate Director of Programs at the Center for Talented Youth (CTY) at Johns Hopkins University. She holds a Ph.D. from Wayne State University and is currently living abroad.

MARILYN J. KULIEKE is the Director of Research and Testing for School District #214 in Mt. Prospect, Illinois, and is also a research scholar at the Center for Talent Development, Northwestern University. She holds a Ph.D. in psychology and evaluation from Northwestern.

PAULA OLSZEWSKI-KUBILIUS is the Director of the Center for Talent Development at Northwestern University and is currently a member of the faculty of the School of Education and Social Policy and the National College of Education. Prior to her appointment as director, she served as Assistant Director of Academic Programs and as Associate Director of Research for the center. She holds a Ph.D. in educational psychology from Northwestern University.

A. HARRY PASSOW is the Jacob H. Schiff Professor of Education at Teachers College, Columbia University. He has published extensively on many educational topics, including education of the gifted.

MICHAEL M. PIECHOWSKI is currently Professor of Education at Northland College. He formerly was on the faculty at Northwestern University and has published widely on issues concerning the development of gifted children. He holds a Ph.D. in counseling psychology from the University of Wisconsin.

RICHARD RONVIK is the Director of the Chicago Public Schools program for gifted students, a position he has held for 18 years. He holds a master's degree in education from Northwestern University.

LINDA KREGER SILVERMAN is founder and Executive Director of the Gifted Child Development Center in Denver, Colorado, which offers testing and educational services to gifted students and their families. She formerly was Professor of Education at the University of Denver. She received her Ph.D. from UCLA.

JULIAN C. STANLEY is Professor of Psychology at Johns Hopkins University. He is the founder of the Study of Mathematically Precocious Youth (SMPY), which spawned the nationwide talent search models currently in operation. He has conducted extensive research on highly gifted students, particularly in the area of mathematics.

JOYCE VANTASSEL-BASKA is the Jody and Layton Smith Professor of Education at the College of William and Mary in Virginia. Founder of the Center for Talent Development at Northwestern University, she served as its director for 5 years and continues to be a research scholar there. She has been a local, regional, and state director of programs for the gifted. She holds an Ed.D. from the University of Toledo.

Index